Space and the Architect

Herman Hertzberger

Space and the Architect
Lessons in Architecture 2

010 Publishers, Rotterdam 2000

To Aldo van Eyck (1918-1999)

The light consumes the chair,
absorbing its vacancy,
and will swallow itself
and release the darkness
that will fill the chair again.
I shall be gone,
You will say you are here.
Mark Strand

Preface

Space and the Architect is the sequel to *Lessons for Students in Architecture* published in 1991. The set-up of this second book is analogous to that of the first, though this time it concentrates on my work of the past ten years. Once again it is embedded in the work of others, from all over the world and from every era. Its main theme is space, which it illustrates with a collage of items that cross-reference each other freely throughout its seven chapters. The focus, then, is more that of a wide-angle lens than a telelens, with a key role set aside for designing as a process of thinking and researching.

The original Dutch edition coincided with my departure in October 1999 as professor at the TU Delft. So once again my thanks go out to the Faculty of Architecture which generously financed the book, and in particular Hans Beunderman and Frits van Voorden. Further I would like to thank Hans Oldewarris for his abiding confidence in this unruly offering and graphic designer Piet Gerards for putting it together so well. This book would definitely not have seen the light of day without the inspiring efforts of Jop Voorn, who edited and advised on both Dutch and English editions.
I also owe a debt of thanks to secretary and documentalist Pia Elia, Miriam Wuisman and Colette Sloots, as well as Sonja Spruit, Margreet van der Woude and Femke Hägen for their enthusiastic cooperation in the making of drawings and diagrams.
Finally there is and always was Johanna, the one I share every-thing with including the things I see, so this book is part of her space too.

Herman Hertzberger, September 1999/November 2000

Contents

Foreword

Who today would dare to claim that things are not going well with architecture? Has there ever been such an abundance of new examples and variants of forms and materials? Has there ever been a time when so many successive options were able to attain expression together? It is difficult not to feel overwhelmed by the sheer opulence of it all and to keep following the trail you have set out without being too wildly diverted by the new things that keep appearing.

Today, it seems, there are no more restrictions – at least in the wealthy part of the world which sets the tone in the poor part where it is imitated all too avidly. Anything goes, everything is feasible and indeed made, photographed, published and disseminated wherever new things are produced. Seemingly without limit and at a headlong pace with the call for change the one implacable restriction, this 'throwaway' production keeps on multiplying. How many buildings praised to the skies by the deluge of international magazines and other media, are still part of architecture's collective memory five years on? With a very few exceptions indeed, maybe fewer than during the era of modernism, they all melt into the background, having been sucked dry and eulogized to death, succeeded by ever new generations of buildings undoubtedly destined for the same fate.

Once everything may and can be done, then nothing is necessary. Where freedom rules, there is no place for decision-making. We slaves of freedom are condemned to unremitting change. This, then, is the paradox – that ultimately this freedom limits the architect in his scope.

What is there for an architecture student to learn when one thing and one thing alone is important to him, namely to think something up as quickly as possible and get all attention riveted on it so as to become famous, if only for a few months? After that it's back to the drawing board, or rather from the scene to the screen. Today the world of architecture resembles a football match with only star players who can do anything with a ball, but without goal posts and consequently without goals. However magnificent the action, it is unclear where the game is heading and what exactly we can expect of it. There are far more possibilities than ideas, and so our wealth is also our poverty.

If it is so that architecture in the postmodern age has been freed from narratives as truthful as those of modernism with its quest for a better future, then it must carry its meaning within itself. That the things we make are surprising and look good is not enough. They will at least have to contain something, an idea that is of some use to the world.

The architect needs to feel some responsibility, like the structural engineers and consultants who, laying claim to an ever greater slice of the cake, enter by the back door to steadily rob him of his freedom.

If the architect is a specialist anywhere, then it is in orchestrating the spatial resources and whatever these are able to accomplish. He must accept his social and cultural obligations and concentrate on the creating and shaping of space.

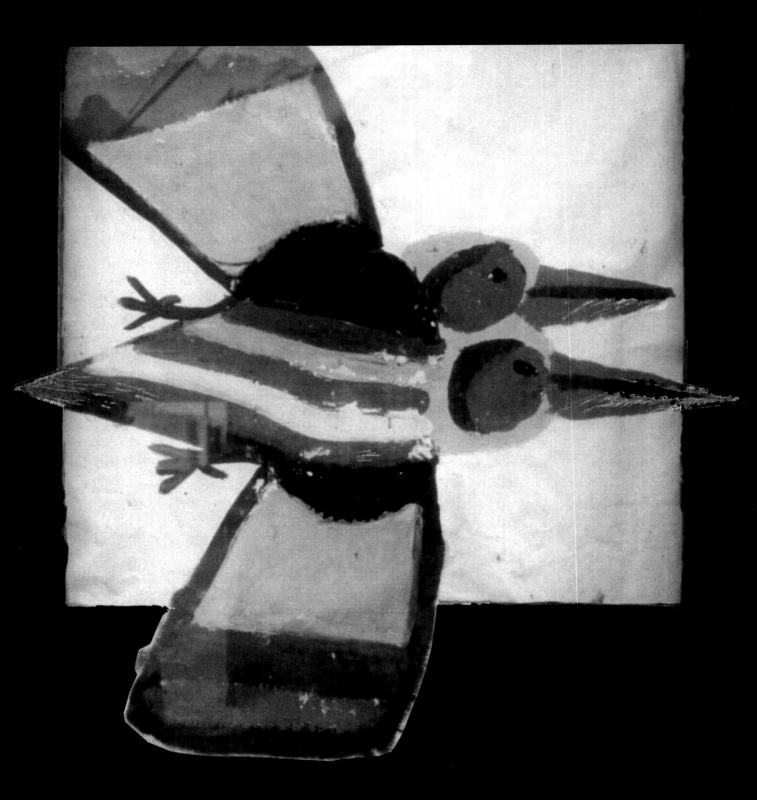

1

Space

Rietveld's space [1-4]

Rietveld wished to leave the space intact when designing his zig-zag chair. This chair cuts through the air, so to speak, without taking its place, occupying it, as any traditional tub-chair-style furniture would do. You might ask of everything you make: does it demand space or create space? Rietveld's Sonsbeek Pavilion (1954; reassembled in 1965 in the sculpture garden of the Kröller-Müller Museum at Otterlo) comprises a handful of wall and roof planes that contain without shutting in and without shutting the surroundings out; a near perfect balance between exposure and enclosure. The planes create space; they are, one might say, a localized compaction of an open system such as Mondrian had painted forty years earlier and Van Doesburg must have intended in his *Composition* of 1924. But here they have a sober, almost primitive materiality, and you really can walk between them. Perhaps more even than the Schröder house, this pavilion has everything of the furniture that Rietveld was always designing and making, be it with greater dimensions.[1] It was his furniture pieces that made the bridge so characteristic of De Stijl between the flat plane and three-dimensional space. This pavilion is an indication of space rather than an object.

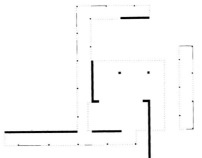

1

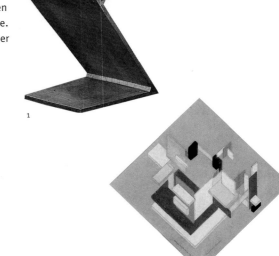

2

3 Theo van Doesburg, *Composition*, 1924

4

Garden wall of Vevey house, Switzerland [5–6]
Le Corbusier, 1924-25

The garden round this house built by Le Corbusier for his parents right on the bank of Lake Geneva, is separated by a wall not only from the road running alongside but, in the corner of the site, also from the lake itself. There the wall turning the corner combines with a tree to carve out a sheltered spot to sit with a view through a large window punched in the wall of the all-dominating Lake Geneva and the tall range of the Alps beyond. The stone table resting against the wall below the window opening as it so often does in Le Corbusier's many terraces, confirms the sense of being indoors in this external space as against the immense landscape around.

On the face of it the last thing you would think of would be to limit this grand prospect, yet you experience the openness of the lake as too unprotected and immense. By looking through the window from a

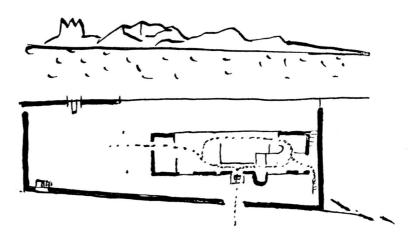

5

sheltered, relatively indoor place, you are less absorbed in the immense totality and the framed piece of landscape gains in depth because of it.

The window in the wall crops the unham-

pered vastness into a view out and, thus accommodated, or rather brought within reach emotionally, this becomes the space of a painting.

6

■ **THE IDEA OF SPACE** Space is more an idea than a delineated concept. Try to put it into words and you lose it.

The idea of space stands for everything that widens or removes existing limitations and for everything that opens up more possibilities, and is thus the opposite of hermetic, oppressing, awkward, shut up and divided up into drawers and partitions, sorted, established, predetermined and immutable, shut in, made certain.

Space and certainty are strangers. Space is the potential for the new.

Space is what you have in front of you and above you (and to a lesser degree below you), that gives you a freedom of view and a view of freedom. Where there is room for the unexpected and for the undefined. Space is place that has not been appropriated and is more than you can fill.

Space also comes from an openness to multiple meanings and interpretations; ambiguity, transparency and layeredness instead of certainty. Depth instead of flatness, a greater dimensionality in general and not exclusively and literally the third dimension.

Space, like freedom, is difficult to get hold of; indeed, when a thing can be grasped and so comprehended it has forfeited its space; you cannot define space, you can describe it at most.

■ **PHYSICAL SPACE** We call the macrocosm space, endless space. Not emptiness, because we see it to contain objects in a structured relationship and perhaps in the firm expectation that there is something for us to find there. Space travel suggests that we are doing just that and so a spatial envelope is added to our territory from where we can see the earth as an object with a outer shield of links enveloping it. There is emptiness only when there is nothing to be seen or to find. For physicists it is space to the extent that objects or phenomena exist or rather move there.[2] Outside it, outside the scope of their attention, there is emptiness. It is space insofar as we claim to recognize an order in it; whatever we are blind or deaf to, we experience as emptiness.

The microcosm, as endless as this is, evokes no sense of space, though we find more to interest us there; bacilli, particles, genes. That this 'negative' space fails to arouse in us a sense of space says much about our imaginative powers. Similarly, the mass of water below the surface of the sea is too solid to evoke a sense of space, though the deep-sea diver obviously takes a different view.

■ **SPACE AND EMPTINESS** Anything we cannot grasp we experience as emptiness. This might be a view into the distance across a sea without ships, without waves, without clouds, without birds, without a setting sun, without visually recognizable objects. The desert too stands for emptiness, despite the contours of hills and valleys and its teeming life. Here it is the absence of people and objects, the desolation, that leaves us with a feeling of emptiness. This feeling is even stronger in the deserted city, where everything revolves around people. Without people, the space of the houses, streets and squares, the space in a physical sense is emptiness, a void. Emptiness is a feeling too, one you experience the moment you know or suspect that something precious is lacking or has left, but equally so when we are the leavers.

For us the emptiest thing imaginable is the painter's blank canvas when our thoughts as observers are of paintings we know. For the painter it is space the moment he or she decides that it has to become a painting; the challenge to conquer it irrevocably robs the canvas of its virginal state.

■ **SPACE AND FREEDOM** Though space has a liberating effect, it is not freedom. Freedom is unbridled, unlimited release. Space is ordered, targeted, even if that order is emotional by nature and impossible to define. Freedom is virtual, existing only as something in the distance that is not part of you, such as a horizon that shifts when you think you have got closer to it. Or behind bars, in the minds of prisoners. Freedom is something you feel when it is not yours, you feel space when you feel free. Freedom presupposes independence, and that is a dead-end street. Space complies, seeks embedding; freedom devours, like fire, indiscriminately.[3] Freedom takes no

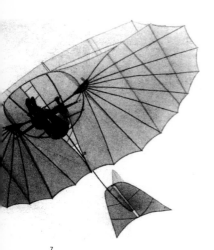

7

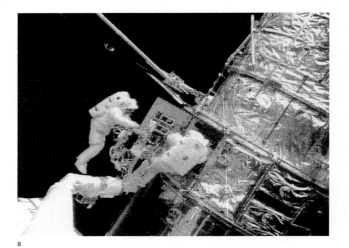

8

account of things, has no respect, is anti-social, anti-authoritarian; freedom cannot choose for with every act of choosing it reduces itself; it is a menu without end. Where everything is possible and permitted there is no need of anything. Space is a supply, that creates a demand. Space has shape, it is freedom made comprehensible.

'Freedom is amorphous.' Salvador Dali

Space arouses a sense of freedom. Comparatively speaking, the more space, the more freedom, and that which frees brings space.
Footballers or chessmen that manage to achieve freedom of movement do so within the limitations of the rules of play; that way they create space. When we talk about freedom we usually mean space. Feeling free means having the space you need.

■ THE SPACE OF ARCHITECTURE Physically, space is shaped by what it is that surrounds it and otherwise by the objects within it and perceivable by us, at least when there is light.

'Our view crosses the space and gives us an illusion of relief and distance. This is how we build up space: with an upper and a lower, a left and a right, a front and a rear, a close by and a far off.
If nothing obstructs our view, it can carry very far indeed. But if it meets nothing, it sees nothing: it sees only the thing it meets: space, that is what obstructs the view, what catches the eye: the obstacle: bricks, a corner, a vanishing point: space, that is when there is a corner, when it ceases, when you have to turn the corner that it may continue. There is nothing ectoplastic about space; space has edges, it is not simply everywhere, it does what has to be done to make the railway tracks meet long before they reach infinity.'[4]

Georges Perec

'Space is in itself, or rather it is in itself pre-eminently, its definition is being in itself. Each point of space is and is perceived to be where it is, the one here, the other there; space is the evidence of the where. Orientation, polarity, envelopment are in themselves derivative phenomena that depend on one's presence.'[5] Maurice Merleau-Ponty

When we in the architectural world speak of space in most instances we mean *a* space. The presence or absence of a mere article determines whether we are referring to infinite space, to a more or less contained space, or something in-between, neither endless nor contained.
A space is determined, meaning finite, and fixed by its periphery and/or the objects in it. A space is meant for something, offers protection to something or makes a thing accessible. It is to some degree specifically made, maybe variable as regards function, but not accidental. A space has something object-like about it, even though it may be the exact opposite of an object. We might then perceive a space as an object but in a negative sense: a negative object.
Space in architecture primarily conjures up thoughts of excessive dimensions, such as those of cathedrals by which one is willingly impressed as was the intention, yet space is a relative concept. A void in a house or any other intervention that occasionally breaks through the dictatorship of the prescribed height of 2.7 metres in Dutch housing, gives a sense of space, as does an extra-spacious balcony, terrace, landing, stair or porch. In each case it involves relatively more than one expects, more than we are used to: space is beyond.
Everybody has their own idea of an ideal space and we can all recall a number of spaces that once made a particular impression on us, yet who can describe exactly what it was that produced that sense of space?
My first thoughts are of the great hall of the Assemblée in Chandigarh designed by Le Corbusier, which we were marched through at speed after having handed in our cameras. The gigantic black ceiling with its recessed mushroom column heads – now that took guts! And the reading room of the

9

10

Bibliothèque Ste Geneviève in Paris, the tall living room of Chareau's Maison de Verre, the Mosque at Cordoba...

Even though we cannot put into words what makes a space fine or beautiful, you can say that it is always a kind of 'inside' with depth and perspective, giving a sense of widening without adversely affecting that character of inside. You might call it a sort of balance between containment and expansion that is able to affect you emotionally. This involves all kinds of factors influencing the effect of space, such as quality of light, acoustics, a particular odour, people, and last but not least your own mood.

It makes quite a difference whether you are alone in the large courtyard of the Alhambra, in the quiet of morning filled with the scent of blossoms, the only sound being the ripple of the fountains ruffling the waters in the pool so that the first rays of sunlight throw dancing reflections against the smooth marble of the surrounding colonnades; or that the entire courtyard is jam-packed with busloads of noisy tourists photographing in all directions with sweaty bodies and bare and hairy legs in clumping leisure footwear, garishly printed T-shirts and cute caps. The Galeria Vittorio Emmanuele in Milan and the Square of St Peter's in Rome, by contrast, are particularly well served by the throngs of visitors they are so able to accept. Similarly, what good is an empty stadium?

People and space depend on one another, they show each other their true colours.

There can be no-one without some memory of being affected or moved by the space of a building or city, where the visual impression aroused other feelings or at least so accentuated them that they now come the more strongly to mind.

That your own mood affects your appreciation of space is self-evident, yet not everyone can go on to describe that mood, and certainly not as suggestively as Flaubert conveys in *Madame Bovary* how your surroundings take on the colour of the frame of mind you are projecting.

'Living in town, amid the noise of the streets, the hum of the theatre crowd, the bright lights of the ballroom – the sort of life that opens the heart and the senses like flowers in bloom. Whereas for her, life was cold as an attic facing north, and the silent spider boredom wove its web in all the shadowed corners of her heart.'[6] Gustave Flaubert

'She reached the parvis of the Cathedral. Vespers were just over, and the people were pouring out through the three doors like a river beneath the arches of a bridge; in the middle, firmer than a rock, stood the beadle.
'She remembered the day when she had gone in there, tense and expectant, with that great vault rising high above her, yet overtopped by her love. ... She walked on, weeping beneath her veil, dazed, unsteady, almost fainting.'[7] Gustave Flaubert

'The nave was mirrored in the brimming fonts, with the beginnings of the arches and part of the windows. The reflection of the stained glass broke at the edge of the marble and continued on the flagstones beyond like a chequered carpet. Broad daylight shone in through the three open doors and stretched down the whole length of the Cathedral in three enormous rays. Now and then a sacristan crossed at the far end, making the oblique genuflexion of piety in a hurry. The crystal chandeliers hung motionless. In the choir a silver lamp was burning. From the side-chapels and darker corners of the church came occasionally a sound like the exhaling of a sigh, and a clanking noise, as a grating was shut, that echoed on and on beneath the vaulted roof.
'Léon walked gravely round the walls. Never had life seemed so good to him. Presently she would come, charming and animated, glancing round at the eyes that followed her; in flounced dress and dainty shoes, with her gold eye-glass and all manner of adornments new to his experience; and in all, the ineffable charm of virtue surrendering. The Cathedral was like a gigantic boudoir prepared for her. The arches leaned down into the shadows to catch her confession of love, the windows shone resplendent to light her face, and the censers would burn that she might appear as an angel in an aromatic cloud.'[8] Gustave Flaubert

11

12

■ SPACE EXPERIENCE It is often said: walk through it, film it, and the spatial image will unfold, yet the deepest impression is when even such acts fail to reveal what it was exactly that brought on that feeling of space.

The essence of spatiality does not allow itself to be defined but at most described. Hence it gives rise to an endless litany of woolly statements about architecture, at best circumscribing movements that can help us to at least get some grasp of the subject.

What makes us think of things as spatial? Spatiality is a feeling, a sensation we undergo, and particularly when the thing we see is impossible to take in at a glance and thus unspecified. Or rather, that it has such a layeredness about it that we are incapable of surveying it in its entirety. It arouses expectations.

The sense of space is sustained by the lack of an overall view of the space you are in. Even when we mean a space shut in on all sides that is surveyable in all its parts, there is, or at least so it seems, always something around the corner.

Perhaps the feeling of space arises when the expected image and the image you experience are not one and the same, in the way that sound becomes spatial when direct and reflected sound just fail to coincide at their receiver. So much for the viewpoint of the spectator.

There can be no doubt that the designer has had it all in his mind in one way or another, that is, in measurements, materials and quality of light. For him, at some stage, there were no more secrets; the architect must have had a picture in his mind of the space he was making, at least to a point, for the question remains of whether the result as realized really did agree with his idea of it beforehand.

Scale models and other three-dimensional representations help us to form a picture, but – however realistically suggested – it can only be an abstraction, deprived as it is of all those non-visual components that together shape our sense of space.

How three-dimensional is space in fact, and how far is experiencing space the preserve of the real, walk-all-over world to which architecture belongs?

To understand more of the phenomenon 'space' we should perhaps leave architecture for a moment.

Space does not by definition need to be literally three-dimensional, nor literally visual by nature. We do, though, express the space feeling in terms that refer to visual reality. That which is flat, full, narrow or limited lacks, one feels, the necessary space, and so space is more like feeling stereoscopically than seeing stereoscopically: a fuller, more complete experience.

Dancers indicate areas by exploring and enfolding them with their moving bodies, without delimiting them in a material sense. This way they create space.

Music has its own spatiality, which moreover is ambiguous by nature. Not only the acoustics, which enable you to close your eyes and hear the space you are in, but also stereophonic aids, such as CDs, can help you picture a space. Making a space audible is strengthened when the sound comes from different directions.

For the musician, the building carries the music. The composer Hector Berlioz, for example, simply could not imagine how a space could be experienced other than through the music resounding in it. Of a visit to St Peter's in Rome he wrote: 'these paintings and statues, those great pillars, all this giant architecture, are but the body of the building. Music is its soul, the supreme manifestation of its existence.'[9] Hector Berlioz

But along with these sensations in a literal space, we can also experience a sense of space in a complex and so not immediately distinguishable tapestry of voices.

'In the choir I heard many voices, each of which seemed to be singing independently of the rest; rising and falling along invisible ladders to and over each other, sometimes pairing off, sometimes crossing each others' paths like comets pulling a long tail of harmonies behind them, they kept each other floating in equilibrium, and despite the skilful embranglements all was as strong and transparent as silver scaffolding in space.'[10] Theun de Vries

A notion of space turns up in every corner of our consciousness, in language, dance, sports, psychology, sociology, economy; wherever movement is possible, and so just as easily on the flat surface.

Space as experience has to derive from an Ur-feeling, an ability to imagine a dimension that projects above basic reality, an exposure to a reality greater than we are able to conceptualize. Sense of space is a mental construct, a projection of the outside world as we experience it according to the equipment at our disposal: an idea.

13

Mountains outside, mountains inside [13]
Johan van der Keuken, 1975

'The way these mountains rise in opposition, inside and outside, as each other's mirror image – this is space as interpreted by Johan van der Keuken.
'Of course, there are few painters who have not shown us how the external space of the landscape enters the room, transforming the world for us into a more familiar image. Here, though, day and night are turned inside out, so that you see how mountains rest during the day in gigantic sleeping bags, while simultaneously, flying at night over the peaks looking in through the lit window, one mountain is already up and about.
'There is also a negative where mirror situations now seen from the other side must reside; again and again outside and night and day and inside are tucked one into the other.

'But what the photo shows more than anything else is how your experience of the world outside etches its impressions in your mind: the lithograph of your landscape of memory.
'So, in your mind, the external space is projected inside through this rectangular lens of the darkened room, into the space inside yourself; your own space.'[11]

■ **THE SPACE OF THE PAINTING** The flat plane of the painter often contains more space than the three-dimensional space of the architect. Condemned as he is to the flat surface, the painter constantly has space in mind. Giving expression to that space is indeed the perpetual concern of the painterly art, and it keeps finding new mechanisms to achieve it.

A well-painted space can be just as suggestive as reality – with this difference, that the painter chooses and fixes a moment where all the conditions – light, ambience, florescence – are so perfect that you seldom if ever come across them in the reality of 'nature'. He can compress several non-simultaneous experiences into one image. He can leave things out, arrange them, shift them, forge links between them or strengthen them – in short, he can place the image in the best possible light and so help the idea to come across better; to intensify the experience.

The painter is able to locate you in space. Using the standpoint he has chosen, he can remove much from your view to arouse and sustain a sense of expectancy.

Perspective is one of the means for reproducing reality. It is through perspective that the artist is able to achieve the most suggestive possible reading of three-dimensional space, and when you concentrate from the right position on the image of space thus constructed you can imagine yourself in that painted space.

But we must not become fixated on the effect this type of representation of literal depth has as a standard for space-experience. For all their perspective, many paintings, unable to arouse a sense of expectancy, have remained flat.

Sense of space is born of colours set side by side, that give the plane depth or set it in motion. And space can be set free in the plane, in a sideways direction, and also between two overlapping layers of paint.

Not only do painters succeed in rendering the space of our reality, the opposite is also true, that reality is a rendering of the painter's space. We also experience space as we know it from images given us by painters. Painters teach us to see and in so doing shape our image of space. By adding aspects to it that our own eyes failed to absorb, painters act as our eyes and thus shape the space of our reality. Once you are heedful of the fact that space is the painter's ultimate goal, then it is impossible to describe all the many ways in which ever new openings are found to attain it.

There the experience of space goes much further than just seeing stereoscopically. Not being clearly laid out or transparent in our perception of it, this space has more to do with layeredness and the curiosity this incites.

For painters seek nothing other than to achieve a spatiality of the flat surface, making it deeper, higher, thicker, more expansive or more transparent.

And then we have said nothing yet about the mental space that the painting offers, with its references, associations and metaphors.

The following examples from the world of painting, seen through architect's eyes, share the quality that they all appeal directly to the architect's sense of space.

'Las Meninas' [14]
Diego Velázquez, 1656

The subject of the painter depicted in Velázquez' painting evidently is in front of the canvas. It even seems to be the spectator. The foreground is made part of the action as it were, an extrapolation forwards. So the depth of the painting then lies in front of the canvas and reaches to the rear wall of the room in the painting. The complexity of the observer-observed relationship in and in front of the canvas keeps throwing up new philosophical reflections on the relativity of subject and object, seen from changing vantage points. [12]

What concerns the art historian here is whether the image in the mirror is a reflection of the painting in progress or that of the sitters. What interests us is that the real space and the space of the painted reality interpenetrate.
You can keep on maintaining that a painting gives an illusion of space, but the space 'in reality' is an illusion of another kind. Here the two illusions come within a hair's breadth of each other.

'Sketch for a Bar in the Folies Bergère' [15]
Edouard Manet, 1881

If in reality mirrors have a somewhat illusory effect in increasing the space, in paintings or photographs they reflect a mirror image in a more natural way. Not only do we see in the upper right-hand corner the man face to face with the barmaid as well as seeing the girl from the back, we can observe the entire theatrical setting behind the observer that places the girl in the widest space. Although not without perspective, this is not what gives the surface its sense of depth; or it may be the various vanishing points that lend it an undefined, fragmented spatiality. Because the mirror draws the world behind you into the painting, you the spectator are drawn into the painting yourself. [13]

15

14

16

'Interior with Harpsichordist' [16]
Emanuel de Witte, ca. 1665

An effect of depth such as that suggested in this painting is one architects would love to see in their buildings. For this, though, all the cards have to be right: the position of the two figures, and the light entering through the windows strengthening the stage-set effect of the enfilade. With sufficient knowledge of architectural and house typologies of those days it should be possible to reconstruct the entire floor plan from the painting. The actual space of the house is encapsulated in the picture.

'Louvre' [17]
Hubert Robert, 1796

This depiction of the large museum gallery suggests an effect of depth so refined that you might wonder whether observing reality through one eye would give you a greater feeling of depth. Projected on to your retina it would probably make little difference which 'illusion of space' you were looking at.

Perspective is often spoken of disparagingly, as if it were a trick, but when applied by someone who knows how to wield it, it can be more convincing than reality.

17

'Pantheon' [18]
Giovanni Paolo Pannini, 1734

The almost photographically accurate illustrations that Pannini painted of so many buildings which dominated sixteenth-century Rome make him the greatest architecture 'photographer' of the past (a shared first place with Canaletto). At first glance he keeps strictly to the perspectival reality, but here, with the interior of the Pantheon in Rome, he is in fact achieving what today's photographers accomplish with the widest of wide-angle lenses – and evidently with greater ease Pannini succeeds in avoiding altogether the distortion that becomes stronger with the increase in the angle of vision and cannot be corrected along acceptable lines in a photograph. He manages to combine in the sweep of a single static image a dynamic which the human eye is able to grasp by moving through a whole series of images.

18

Compositions [19-22]
Piet Mondrian, 1913/1917

Mondrian went to every length to shake off the effect of depth our eyes have become all too conditioned to through the customary perspectival effect in paintings. Every slanting line for him was automatically a reference to a rudiment of perspective. In Mondrian the space is exclusively in the plane itself, although in his later work the physical thickness of the painting began to play a part too. Then you see horizontal and vertical bands overlapping and continuing over the thickness of the supporting frame.

If in his 'cubist' period beginning in 1912 we still see something like contained cells, in the period centring on 1917 the composition of lines and colours become a more open and spatial system with a laterally inclined centrifugal movement keeping to the plane of the canvas.

With the object-like rectangular colour fields acting increasingly, with the passing of time, as weights in the equipoise of the constructed space, we can discern a remarkable affinity with Schönberg's *Klangfarbe* theory. Schönberg, a composer who was also a painter, sought analogous balances of units of sound whose duration, volume and timbre, depending on which instrument produced them, would evoke a new musical spatiality.

In the De Stijl group where the thinking and aspirations of architects and painters such as Rietveld, Mondrian and Van Doesburg complemented one another, the key aspect was space. Never before had painting and architecture come into such close proximity as in this period, with the possible exception of the Baroque. In the Baroque, rather than being satisfied with built space, they ultimately supplemented it with paintings that presented the illusion of additional space.

In Mondrian's studio we can see paintings hung on and in front of the walls, making a composition of the room. This composition in effect constitutes a new painting of the individual compositions from which it is assembled.

19 *Composition*, 1913

20 *Composition in Blue*, 1917

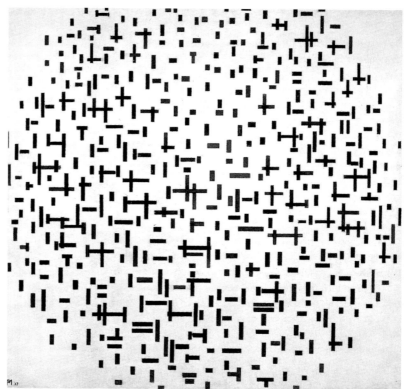

21 *Composition in Black and White*, 1917

22 Mondrian's studio in New York with *Victory Boogie Woogie*

■ SPACE IS A LONGING

Sometimes on a puff of wind,
sometimes in a storm
they fly up,
a cloud of birds
before the sun.

What dreams
give the birds flight
that they expose themselves
lightly
to so much air.

Bert Schierbeek

Our urge for space is aimed outwards, so it is centrifugal by
nature.
We wish to grasp more and make it our own; we brave the
risks of the unfamiliar, the unexpected, to increase our circle,
our experience, our awareness. Space is expectation; and
ultimately a desire to arrive somewhere.

'The undefined remains / indefinably enticing'

Judith Herzberg

As soon as a new area of space becomes emotionally and physically accessible, its anonymity crumbles. Each step is a new
designation, a new signifié, so that step by step it becomes
appropriated as part of our familiar world.
As a region becomes more and more familiar, no matter what
kind of region, the indefinableness, the unexpected, seeps
away, and with it its spatiality until finally it is appropriated
and absorbed; a region for our homecoming.
If space-accessing desire has centrifugal directionality, once
that space is colonized our attention turns to ever more drastically opening it up and exploiting it in our minds. More and
more associations take hold and, with these incorporated in
our familiar world, our focus in time becomes increasingly

inward-looking, concentrated on the mentally and emotionally
newly accessible area. This is how our centrifugal desire makes
the switch to centripetal attraction; space, appropriated and
familiar, becomes place.
Desire with its tension and risk of the unknown, undefinable
and unexpected tends to dissolve in a need for consolidation,
safety, attachment, protection and delimitation.

■ SPACE AND PLACE The distinction between space and place
is clearer than one might suppose from the way these two
words are used. For they are all too often confused. Place
makes us think primarily of restricted dimensions, a play
area, balcony, study niche, parts of the house or house-like
parts, born of articulation, large enough to contain several
persons and small enough to provide the necessary 'cover'.
Place implies a centre of attention such as is exemplified to
perfection by a table.
Places can also be very large, as long as they are suited to
whatever is to be enacted in them.[14] Place is where you recognize yourself, something familiar and safe, specially for you.
When a large number of people have the same feeling and
derive from it the sense of being linked together, it is a collective place, such as where Liberation Day is celebrated or
where the dead are remembered, or a centre of religious com-
munion. The sense of place can equally be of a temporary
nature such as when the national football team wins.
Place implies a special value added to a space. It has a particular meaning for a number of people who feel attached to
one another or derive from it a feeling of solidarity.
Space, whatever its purpose, can come to mean place, whether
for individuals or for small or larger groups. Place is then a
special added signifier, or rather, signifié of that space. What
you as an architect can design are the conditions that make
space fit to be read as place; that is, by supplying just those
dimensions or rather the articulation and 'cover' that in a certain situation bring about the right sense of appropriateness
and recognition.[15]
The thing that turns space into place is the infill given it by

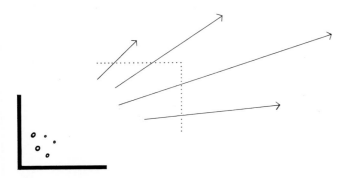

23

its occupants/users. A location then becomes a 'particular' place coloured by occurrences past and present which lend it associations. When we say we are making a place, we in fact mean making the space in such a way that the conditions for its infill endow it with the quality of place.

If place is an ultimate emotional appropriation of a space that originally was unsignified but is potentially signifiable, we can then say: space is a quality that contains the new, that can be filled in to make a place, so that space and place can relate as 'competence' and 'performance'. Space and place are interdependent in that each brings the other to awareness, enables the other to exist as a phenomenon.

Birds searching for food need to carry their nest in their minds when passing outside their territory; there can be no adventure without a home-base to return to. You have to travel in search of space, to confirm the place you call your own; you must return home to recharge for a new journey.[16]

'The need to get away? The desire to arrive?'[17]
Mark Strand

Space is longing, an expectation of possibilities, outside, on a journey, dynamic and open, away.

Place is pause, inside, redemption, home, at rest.

Making space and leaving space are inseparably bound, there must always be that openness to new interpretations. The dilemma here is that the more suitable and right you make something, the stronger one particular significance will clamp to it. This significance then leads a stubborn life of its own. The more riveted space is to significance, the less space there remains for other significations and experiences.

Space and place cannot exist without each other – each summons up the other. If place is heat, fire, then space is fuel.

We need both as basic elements of architecture: views to the front and cover behind.

24

2

Mental Space and the Architect

■ DESIGNING IS A THOUGHT PROCESS Too often we find the creative process of the architect depicted as a succession of flashes of inspiration that the privileged evidently receive as a gift and others vainly keep waiting for, as though ideas are some kind of thunderbolt from on high. When you see architects continually out to trump one another with new ideas, you end up wondering at times just where the hell they get them all from.

That architects have to think primarily in forms is rooted in a misunderstanding. In the first place, they must have an idea of the situations as these affect people and organizations, and how situations work. From there concepts emerge: that is, ideas regarding these situations take shape. Only then does the architect envisage forms in which all the above might be cast. Surprising architectural responses are invariably the ultimate formulation of the results of a thought process. They did not appear out of thin air, as gifts from the gods for the particularly talented.

Architects, including the seriously gifted, construct their ideas, even if these are keys to utterly new insights, out of raw material that in one way or another had to be already present in their minds. Nothing, after all, can be born of nothing.

Designing is a complex thought process of potentials and restrictions out of which ideas are born along fairly systematic lines.

New responses issue from combinations and quantities other than those we already knew. We do things with what we have in our minds, and more cannot come out of them than went in. All neuropsychological explanations notwithstanding, it works the same as it does for the cook who can only use what he has in his kitchen when putting his meals together. Ignoring the fact that a good cook can do much more with his ingredients than a less gifted colleague, in both cases the point is to fill the pantry with as many ingredients as possible so as to have richer combinations and thus a wider range of possibilities at their disposal.

The ingredients the architect can draw from are the experiences he has had throughout the years, and which he can directly or indirectly relate to his profession. Considering that the range of his discipline is infinitely broad and is literally about everything, that means a multitude of experiences. So it is important for the architect that he has seen and heard a lot in his life, and anything that he did not experience first-hand he has a pretty good idea of; that is, he must empathize with every situation he has come across.

25

26 Air shafts of a wine cellar, Ischia, Italy

28 Le Corbusier, sketches of Villa Hadrianus, 1911

27

Notre Dame du Haut, Ronchamp, France [25-28]
Le Corbusier, 1950-55

The chapel of Notre Dame du Haute in Ronchamp marks a new period in Le Corbusier's work and thinking. It was already noticeable in the Unité in Marseilles, and also in the 'Manufactures' in St Dié, that he had closed the chapter of the dematerialized 'heroic' period. Seen in retrospect there had been signs as early as the beginning of the thirties of a more grounded, sculptural development. If the Unité in Marseilles can still be regarded as a beton brut variant upon earlier ideas – in principle still executed in planes with a number of strongly plastic additions such as the pilotis and the roofscape, while the colours in refined patterns of soft hues become more primary – the Ronchamp chapel is architecture of quite another kind. It has much of a hollowed-out sculpture that resolutely confounds, it would seem, the entire evolution of twentieth-century architecture.

Whether or not you find it beautiful, you may wonder if that is the way to crown the top of a hill, like a untamed species of Parthenon. You can advocate or vilify it but it is impossible to ignore it; the influence it has exerted on architectural history is prodigious and still astoundingly relevant today.

Our main interest in the chapel is how and when an architect like Le Corbusier managed to conjure up this wholly new formal idiom.

The first sketches for this building see Le Corbusier harking back to travel sketches made many years before, in which he noted down things that evidently affected him and that he wished to keep hold of, supposedly without knowing at the time what possible good could come of them later. At issue on this early occasion was a particular way of bringing in light reflected down through a curved shaft, much like air through a ventilation shaft such as those found on old sea vessels (which fascinated me as a child too). The literal way these found forms were ultimately adopted is astonishing, embarrassing almost, if only because one could not believe or rather refused to believe it could be done so simply. But every bit as astonishing is that these forms (because forms and not just ideas have been adopted here) take on an entirely new guise in the new light in which Le Corbusier sets them. They were placed in a new context, and so transformed utterly. It is hard to comprehend today that they had been around earlier than that and were merely unearthed. It seems as though new forms are less invented than rediscovered, interpreted differently and used differently too. We are able to understand where they came from, but not what is so fascinating about them and even less why they are still successful today.

■ **INGENUITY, CREATIVITY** A culture where conditions and values shift all too easily requires an unremittingly critical attitude towards outmoded concepts (and naturally towards new potentials too). In literally every situation you have to keep asking yourself whether the familiar path is still the most effective, adequate and/or advisable choice or that we are threatening to become victims of the daily routine and the straitjacket of existing clichés. Each design decision it seems, each choice we make, needs sounding out every time against changing criteria, but all too often inevitably calling for new concepts. This is why we need ingenuity and what we usually term creativity.

Put briefly, the beginning of the design process could boil down to the following: First there is a task, clearly couched or making a first vague appearance. You are after an idea that will give you a concept you can use to further elaborate the design. Looking around you and drawing from your memory where the ideas you once thought interesting are stored, you head off in search of analogies that might well yield an idea. Though identifiable as missing pieces of your jigsaw puzzle, these links are all too often transformed – disguised, in other words. The art then is of course to see through those disguises. We can assume that each new idea and new concept must be a transformation or interpretation, respectively, of something else,developed further and brought up to date.

There is no way of finding out how the idea came to you; was it there already, was it generated by old images or only strengthened, confirmed? This is a complex interaction of suspecting, seeking and recognizing, in the way that question and answer vie for primacy.

■ **ERASING AND DEMOLISHING OLD CLICHES** To find new concepts as an answer to new challenges you first have to unmask the existing clichés. This means stripping the mainsprings of the programme underlying the architecture of the routine that has seeped into them by breaking open the programme and opening it up to new arguments. Whenever a programme is judged critically it transpires each time that it has lost much of its validity. This is why we must shift emphases and shake off ingrained habits. This is easier said than done. The issue is to demolish existing clichés.

A great deal has been written about creativity and how it might be acquired, invariably pointing out the importance of forging links with other things entirely. However, it is stressed far too infrequently that the difficulty of finding the new is mainly that of shaking off the old. Room for new ideas has to be conquered by erasing old ideas engraved in our minds. If only one could keep beginning with a clean slate, approaching each task as an unknown quantity, a new question that has yet to be answered. Unfortunately this is not the way our brains work. Associations well up immediately, whether you want them to or not, major and minor skills nurtured by experience and developed by professional expertise, tried and trusted recipes that stand there in the way of genuinely new ideas. Ingenuity in finding new concepts is all too often seen as something exclusive, reserved for the few who are gifted in

that respect. When the prime concern is indeed the ability to shake off existing clichés and each time face the task as an unknown quantity, then the problem is mainly a psychological barrier that is going to need some demolishing.

If the old, well-known part belongs to our familiar world, the new is basically a threat. Whether it can become absorbed and therefore accepted depends on the associations it evokes and whether these are regarded as positive, or at least not as negative.

A child, then, may see a flash of lightning, whose dangers we know and to which we feel a certain ingrained fear, as a kind of firework with all the feelings of gaiety that brings. 'All I have done throughout my life is to try to be just as open-minded as I was in my youth – though then I didn't have to try.' This is a remark Picasso must have made in later life.

When plans emerged to keep the Eiffel Tower after all – it was originally to have been a temporary structure – a storm of protest blew up, most of all among intellectuals who saw the city disfigured with a monster culled from the hated world of industry. And that when in the very latest generation there was almost no-one to be found who was not inspired by it as a presage of a new world.

Whether you like a thing or not depends on the affection you feel for it. This is not only something you have or acquire later, you must have had it to begin with to have liked the thing in the first place; affection is as much a condition as a consequence.

29 Robert Delaunay, *The Eiffel Tower*, probably 1913

Eames House, Los Angeles [30-32]
Charles and Ray Eames, 1946

The story goes that in 1946, when Charles and Ray Eames decided to build themselves a house and studio, they were forced to restrict themselves to steel beams and columns standardized for assembly plants and obtainable from a firm of structural engineers, as material was scarce so soon after the war. And if this were indeed true, you might wonder if they really felt restricted by the thus imposed reduction of their house to a pair of box-shaped factory sheds, which they placed on the highest part of their eucalyptus-strewn site in a line along the property boundary.

These industrial designers, constantly alert as they were to everything that was new and potentially reproducible in series, sounding them out and absorbing them into their world, clearly saw this as a challenge. Typically, rather than feeling limited by having only those means at their disposal that industry allowed at the time, they were inspired by the possibilities this situation brought.

And so it was that the factory shed was transformed into a house with a form unknown before then. The point is that they saw the opportunity to look beyond the factory-building forms such as the prominent open-web steel joists and suppress those associations with others closer to the domestic ambience. Charles and Ray Eames succeeded in erasing the factory element by means of simple yet marvellous elevations, likewise composed of standard

31

32

30

elements, with areas of colour and, on the inside, sliding light-absorbent panels, the effect being as much Japanese as Mondrianesque. Again, the tiled paths and planting right up against the elevations betray the sort of care that regrettably one only expects to find in dwelling-houses.

The basic, even bare, container aspect of the building is equalled only by the opulence of its infill and contents. This consists of an endless and varied collection of objects and artefacts from all over the world, brought back by the Eameses from their travels – fascinated as they were by everything made by human hand the world over in a never-ending diversity. And what better accommodation for all

these items collected by those irrepressible souls than these prefabricated containers. These lent themselves perfectly to being coloured in and indeed to becoming part of the collection.

When Ray Eames laid the table for her guests, it was not with the obligatory tea or dinner service of so many pieces and accessories to match, but according to quite another principle. She went through the abundant collection of plates and cups-and-saucers, finding for each guest a set deriving from differing services but combined to meet other criteria – a beautifully conceived combination of pieces chosen to match their user.

The familiar image of a table laid homogeneously yielded to a gay miscellany of colours and shapes, like a miniature 'musée imaginaire', of a new homogeneity, be it more complex and full of surprises.

Two arrangements, two paradigms, both with their attendant associations.

The so-many-piece table service stands for comfortable circumstances and ancient descent, for such services get passed down from generation to generation and only in the hands of an old and established, culturally developed family do they survive through the years unchipped and generally unscathed. Combinations of table services that are brought together from here, there and everywhere rather than comprising a set, are the province of the less well-to-do who can afford less and cannot boast an illustrious past. The infinitely varied collection of Ray and Charles Eames represents the cultural elite of the small group that expresses its passion for exploring the world with its great diversity of cultures and customs, in a collection as precious in its heterogeneity as the family table service is in its homogeneity. Once the question of what you can or cannot afford has been dispensed with, respect for the past acquires another value and another form. This example shows that old values, however interesting historically, are all too easily clung to against one's better judgement; and that suppressing and replacing such preconceptions creates new space, new room to move.

Nemausus housing, Nîmes, France
[33-38]
Jean Nouvel and Jean-Marc Ibos, 1987

These two all-metal blocks, set at right angles to a provincial feeder road to the city like some means of conveyance – more bus or train than ship – amidst a development that is more rural than urban, sit surprisingly well in their context. This is because we have become oblivious to the metal boxes of every imaginable shape and size setting the scene in increasing numbers throughout our cities and landscapes. But it is certainly also because of the magnificent way these two lock in from either side of a strip of gravelled parkway flanked by plane trees as if they had always been there. The allée of slender planes continues to dominate the picture, visible from all sides as the housing blocks 'hover' on posts that are more slender still. Here Le Corbusier's pilotis principle is applied so convincingly après la lettre that one cannot help but be converted.

Other than in the Unité whose heavy columns all but blocking the view generated an inhospitable no man's land, these buildings stand on stilts in scooped-out, and therefore sunken, parking strips so

33

that the parked cars do nothing to obstruct the view through.

Apart from the eye-level transparency on the ground plane this response is also a brilliant natural solution for the problem of parking which, although not new in itself, is here as open as it is objective through the minimal and simple response without balustrading or concealing walls to block the view.

34

35

36

37

38

This project also stands out in that everything is done to provide a maximum of space. Its access galleries are as broad as station platforms from which you enter your home with as little fuss as possible, much like entering a subway train, efficiently but anonymously. Only the doormats identify the entrances as front doors and these ultimately are more image-defining even than the loud-and-clear graphics consistently derived from the world of transportation that are also used to number the apartments.

The balconies have perforated forward-tilting sheet-steel spandrel panels which give the building its unmistakable elegant appearance, but behind which an utterly different and more varied character emerges through personal use. Each component has a certain over-measure seldom encountered in housing, which may be why it gives off such a strong sense of space. The inhabitants respond with an almost un-French eagerness with additions of their own. Perhaps it was the restrictions imposed out of considerations of architectural purity – such as the architect's ban on adding to the crude concrete walls worked by an artist, and the metal grid landings between bedroom and bathroom – that in a presumably unintentional paradox were the very reason why tenants responded with all kinds of modifications of their own. These additions are nowhere to be found in articles about the building, yet it is these that best illustrate the space opened up by the construction.

Maison de Verre, Paris [39-42]
Pierre Chareau, Bernard Bijvoet and Louis Dalbet, 1932

When it proved impossible to acquire the upper apartment in the courtyard in the Rue Saint-Guillaume, it was decided to remove the entire lower three floors and slip a new house into the existing building. Then a problem arose: the steel columns that were to shore up the remaining portion suspended like a stone bridge in the sky, could not be brought into the building in their complete state. As a result, shorter lengths consisting of sundry steel sections were combined and assembled on site using tie plates and rivets. So ultimately the solution was all-technical in the spirit of the bridge constructions of those days, which for us at least, used as we are to welded joints, have a nostalgic air about them.

Was it originally the intention to clad these columns, thrusting up resolutely through the tall space, so as to mask at least something of their explicitly technical look? We shall never know. What is certain is that the columns as rendered in the well-known perspective drawing contain nothing of this turn of events, germane as such developments are to the practice of building, though generally unexpected.

There must have been a moment when the architects, reviewing the whole in the light

39

of the overall formal world they had generated for the house, decided that it was complete at this stage. And not just that, they had it painted in two colours in such a way that the technical build-up in parts would be more prominent still.

Chareau must have been taken with these columns, unexpected images as they proved to be, fully regaled and free-standing in the space. For aside from the black and red-lead colouring he clad the flanges at places with slate panels. This is something only an artist would think of, one with his roots in Art Deco as evidenced by the innovative use of materials and joints at so many places in this house. So we see Chareau uniting the redolence of disparate worlds into an amalgam with its own individual aesthetic. Add

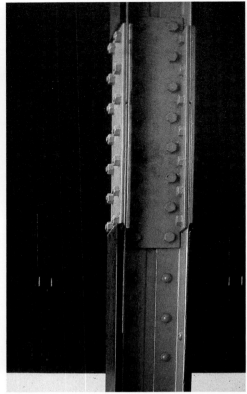

40

the furniture which together with the steel structure presents a kind of biotopic unit, and it then becomes clear that our acceptance of this aesthetic is grounded not in some law or precept that guarantees beauty, but entirely in the positive associations that each of the components present here evokes in us.

Clearly then, forms and colours (and of course words) change when lifted from their original context and placed in another setting. Extricated from their earlier system of meanings they are now free to take on a new role.

Place things in another setting and we see them in a new light. Their meaning changes and with it their value, and it is this process of transformation as enacted in our minds that gives architects the key to creativity.

41

42

Doll's house, *AD* competition [43-44]
Jean Nouvel, 1983

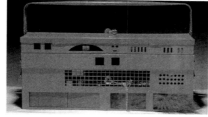
43

44

In the competition held in 1983 by the magazine *AD* to design a doll's house (of all things), the submitted plans gave the expected broad spectrum of reductions of contemporary dwelling forms, in the way that doll's houses through the ages were for practical reasons invariably cutaway models of usually well-to-do houses from particular style periods.

Jean Nouvel (of all people) submitted a design and won. And although by no means the greatest of his designs it is certainly one of the most remarkable. Who would have thought of a toolbox as a space for accommodating your childhood memories? Dolls instead of steel implements, one could scarcely imagine a greater contrast. But the oblong terrace-like collapsible drawers unfold their contents so that at least everything is there at hand, a lot more clearly organized than most traditional doll's houses. Although not directly a model of a house that we know, you could well imagine it as such. And although not a reflection of an existing type, it does give an illusion, an idea of a house.

Do children really feel the need for a reduction of a literal house, where you always have too many corners that are inaccessible, and with the frustration that you cannot really get inside it and always feel shut out as a result? Here in this toolbox your things are always safely stashed away and it is made to carry around.

Come to that, you can imagine Nouvel returning to this idea sooner or later (just think of the 'pull-out' stands of his super-revolutionary competition design for the St. Denis stadium).

This concept breaks dramatically with the customary doll's house cliché. Not just in terms of the outward appearance and how it fits together, it also shows a revamping of ideas about what it is that children might want from a doll's house, taking note of the fact that they have less need of something representing a literal reality. With their capacity to think conceptionally, they are content with merely the idea of a house.

■ Looking at the task before you in another light is the same as looking at another task, and for that you need other eyes. The problem is that everyone is constantly searching for recognizable patterns that are interpreted as rapidly as possible, in other words, that gain a place in our familiar world. And the more familiar our world, the way we have built it piece by piece, the more trusted insights we have at our disposal and the more difficult it is to avoid them. Inventiveness is in inverse proportion to knowledge and experience. Knowledge and experience keep forcing us back into the old grooves of the old record of meanings, the way a knife keeps returning to the original striations in a sheet of cardboard. Finding new concepts would not be difficult if only it were easier to shake off the old ones.

The first of Marcel Duchamp's ready-mades, dating from 1913, showed that presenting an 'everyday' object as a work of art could turn it into something new. He placed them in an utterly different context where something else was expected of them, so to speak, without him having changed or added anything (save for the customary signature of the artist). *'That Mr. Mutt (Duchamp's pseudonym in that circumstance) made the Fountain with his own hands or not, is not important. He CHOSE it. He took a common object, placed it so that its functional significance disappeared under the new title and the new point of view – he created for this object a new idea.'*[1] A bicycle wheel or urinal it seems can lose its original purpose and meaning and take on another. This process of transformation evidently enacted in our minds is nowhere more clearly revealed than in the art of the twentieth century. By being able to perceive a thing differently, our view of things changes and the world changes with it.

A mental clear-out, making space in our minds by ridding them of so much ballast that once meant something to us. And if anyone was familiar with disassembling and clearing out associations, meanings and values, it was Picasso.

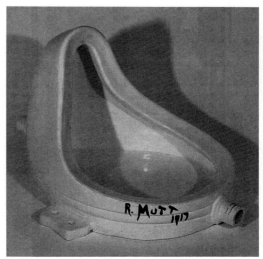
45 Marcel Duchamp, *Fountain*, 1917

Picasso's eyes [46-50]

Picasso's 1942 combination of a bicycle's handlebars and saddle as a bull's head is, after Duchamp's ready-mades, one of the most miraculous and meaningful art works of the twentieth century.

While a 'normal' collage draws a new narrative from disparate components each with its own story, here two parts of the same mechanism combine into a single new (and different) mechanism that inevitably and inescapably calls to mind the head of a bull. Indeed, so strong is this association that it is difficult to continue seeing anything of a bicycle in it.

The bike is forced into the background by the bull. Theoretically at least there must be a transition point where the components are so caught up in each other's new sphere of influence that, in a sort of magnetic impacting of meanings, the bull all at once appears or disappears to be replaced by the bicycle, or a notion of bicycle. It may resemble the conjuror's disappearing trick, but there is a touch of magic here too! Picasso himself considered this work complete only if someone, the thing having been thrown out on the street, were to convert it back into a bike.

Yet the artist must have originally seen the animal parts in the cycle parts; he evidently saw them less strongly anchored in their original context. This then is the lesson we can learn from it: new mechanisms can ensue from another assemblage of parts freed from their original context by taking them up in a new chain of associations. That Picasso was persistently able to see forms in their 'autonomous' – unsignified – state, loosed so to speak from the relationship they formed part of when he came across them, is clear from his studies of eyes that seemingly change into fish and then into birds without effort.

Forms for him – and materials too! – were clearly free and stayed that way until engaged, temporarily, in a particular chain of meanings, or rather, 'system of significations'.

On further consideration we can well imagine that for Picasso it was but a small step for a plate to very literally signify a *corrida*. The fact is, he was obsessed with bullfighting and it was one of the themes that haunted him the way another might see the arena as a well-filled dish.

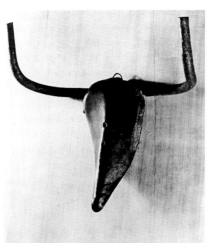

46 Pablo Picasso, *Tête de Taureau*, 1942

47 Both bicycle and bull, here during preparations and practice for the actual fight

48

49 Pablo Picasso, *Plates*, 1953-54

50

Dining table, Paris [51-52]
Le Corbusier, 1933

51

Le Corbusier's table, consisting of a thick cantilevered marble top on two steel legs, found many times in his work and used by him in his own house in the Rue Nungesser et Colli as a dining table, can be regarded as a new 'mechanism'.

While not all tables were wooden and had four legs, this had been pretty much the norm, and it was simply accepted that at times the legs would get in the way even when located at the corners (such as when tables are combined to accommodate a larger gathering).

The steel central legs of Le Corbusier's table with their weighted feet allowed a reasonably stable top to cantilever on all sides, giving free leg room all round. A drawback of this solution (one that has to be put up with) is that the enormous weight establishes a place-bound quality. So there are disadvantages as well as advantages. It all depends on circumstances, but it is certainly a novel idea, which makes it interesting to find out how it was arrived at.

On visiting a hospital one day Le Corbusier saw a dissecting table, being used for anatomical purposes, according to Maurice Besset, making the purely functional advantages mentioned above all the more logical.

To see the thing as a dining table was a particularly blunt transformation, one that obviously didn't bother Le Corbusier, nei-

52

ther when he was designing it, nor when it was used daily by himself and his wife. Evidently he could banish the visions of cadavers from his mind and even the channel meant for running off blood is by no means an unpractical consideration for a dining table.

Bizarre though this example may seem, it once again shows that forms are able to change their meaning. But it also shows that Le Corbusier was able to see this particular form distinct from the chain of associations originally linked with it and slip it into a new chain. The form was freed, so to speak, of its meanings and the framework once containing them, to be given a new infill, 'signified', with other meanings in another context which it was now at liberty to accept.

■ Forms shift as it were from the one meaning to the other, depending on the meaning that presents itself in a particular situation through the associations aroused by and thus linked to the form. So we can say: form + association (1, 2, 3) → meaning (1, 2, 3).[2]
It has to be so that associations attendant on a form are dependent on what you are doing, what is occupying or maybe preoccupying you; and whatever it was that impressed you earlier and therefore *signifies something to you* is forever being projected on to one or other form, suppressing that form's previous meaning in the process.
Thus we see the emphasis shift from the certainties of an established order entrenched in forms as fixed meanings, to the perpetual dependence of each form on the context in which it figures.

Twentieth-century painters saw the opportunity to free forms and materials from their chains of meanings enabling them to take on other meanings and thus new concepts.
Creativity in that respect is the capacity to see 'things' differently by lifting them from their present context so that they lose their original meaning and, seen in a new context, evoke another and so become something else.
So here in fact we have one thing that has been transformed into another through what amounts to an instinct on our part to read it differently. This is the opportunity seized upon by artists like Duchamp and Picasso, and Le Corbusier for one succeeded in doing the same for architecture.

■ Forms and things can apparently adjust to a new situation and be primed to accommodate a new and opportune purpose. Looked at this way, creativity is seen to originate in an extreme capacity to adapt, in the sense that not only are you adapting to the potentials of things but at the same time those things are adapting to suit you.

'Regarding the form of the granito washbasins we wanted to build-in at various places in both Centraal Beheer and De Drie Hoven, I got no further than a list of conditions that this form had to satisfy, such as filling watering cans and washing hands. The dimensions were in fact already fixed seeing that they needed building-in to the brickwork, and they had to be cast in concrete. But what on earth was the form going to be? I tried to impress my thoughts on the others and demonstrated the movement you make when washing your hands by describing circles in the air. Everyone knew that there was only enough money for something very simple and square at the most. It was clear that this rectangular form was completely at odds with the flowing movement I had outlined and would be impossible to keep clean besides. Until, all at once, a polyester hard hat appeared before us on the table. Someone's straying eye had seen it lying in the cupboard. The perfect oval form, exactly the right size, ideal as a mould, simple to install and obtainable for free from the contractor.' (1986)

The theory is as follows: new organizations/mechanisms/concepts are found by stepping outside your task and relating it – i.e. by association – to other known tasks and applying them to your case. The difficulty here is the usually limpet-like adherence of these known tasks to their 'original' meanings, something like a chemical compound with a strong affinity, making it difficult for us to conceive of them as freed and interpretable. The space for creativity lies in managing to forget, in demolishing foregoing prejudices and above all in an ability to un-learn. A matter of learning to unlearn, then. The age-old question which inevitably looms up here as else-where is this: Is creativity something you can acquire or is it entirely a question of aptitude? And although without aptitude you will obviously make little headway you could still say that the easier it is to pull apart forms and meanings, the greater the potentials for creativity; this means seeing forms more as self-sufficient phenomena, open to more and ever new meanings. Which brings us back to Picasso's ability to see the handlebars of a bicycle as form distinct from its meaning. The question now is whether you could cultivate this potential, and if so, how.

The precondition for creativity is that only the smallest amount is fixed for you, meaning that the largest amount is open-ended. The more doubt you have about the fixed meanings and established truths imprisoning you, the easier it is to put these in perspective and the more curious you need to become about other possibilities, other aspects.

Creativity depends on the ability to open your eyes so as to see things in other contexts and in particular beyond the restrictions of the arguments in the closed circle of the 'architectural world'.

It is more a question of mentality than of insight and teachers should perhaps do something about this by no longer scaring students with all that discipline-bound information and instead using the time to challenge them to enlarge the circle of their interest, to see more, to bring in other aspects; to arouse their enthusiasm, receptivity and curiosity, that they ask more questions than they expect answers to, that they experience more of the world, that they widen their frame of reference. Education, and this includes education of architecture students, should before anything else unfold mental space so as to explore the unknown, the new, the other and put it within their reach instead of filling the space in their heads with what we know already.

Make them hungry instead of nourishing them with information.

■ PERCEIVING Perceiving is the ability to extricate certain aspects from within their context so as to be able to place

53 Wash basin, De Drie Hoven and Centraal Beheer, 1970

them in a new context. You see things differently, or you see different things, depending on your intentions in perceiving. Each new idea begins with seeing things differently. New signals bombard you, persuading you that things are not the way you thought, making inevitable the need or demand for a new response. To observe and so understand your situation, your surroundings, the world, differently, you have to be capable of seeing things in another light, seeing those same things differently. For that you need another sensibility, resulting from a different perspective on things, your surroundings, the world.

The architect's most important attributes are not the traditional emblems of professional skill, the ruler and pair of compasses, but his eyes and ears.

At a certain moment in the nineteenth century, painters began painting the patches of light in the shadow of trees, where sunlight falling between the leaves perforated so to speak the areas of shadow. You could say that those patches of light must have always been there, and they undoubtedly were as long as there were people to look at them, yet those painters saw them for the first time. At least they only then became consciously aware of them as an essential aspect of the configuration we call tree. Their attention focused on the exceptional quality of trees as providers of shade and shelter, and on the fact that people tend to linger there rather than elsewhere. Searching for other things, with the shift in attention that brings, they became conscious of aspects they had in fact always seen without being aware of it.

Often it takes painters and their interpretations to make you aware of how things hang together. For instance we see the landscape of Provence influenced by the way Cézanne experienced it; we are in fact looking through the painter's eyes. You become aware of what you are actually seeing only when that perception occurs in the right context at the right time. Prehistoric caves with paintings on the walls, now regarded as pinnacles of artistic endeavour, were discovered at a second viewing, long after they had been closed up because no-one had then seen anything in them.

People began perceiving things that until then had simply had no part in the general frame of reference. There was no interest in them because the focus was on other aspects that were more relevant to them then. So other glasses were needed, so to speak, 'to see what had not been seen to be seen'.

The same tree observed by an ecologist, a biologist, a forest ranger, a painter and a transportation planner is seen by each through different eyes and therefore regarded and valued quite differently.

Whereas the biologist probably assesses its health above all, the forest ranger calculates roughly how many cubic metres of timber it would give him, and the painter appreciates its colour, form and maybe the shape its shadow throws. For the transportation planner it is bound to be in the wrong place. All look at things through their own glasses and consequently assess things quite differently, each within their specific context.

We can regard such specific contexts of assessment as a system of significations, and this system is accessible to the focused eye of the practised observer. Eyes that are experienced in a particular area see the smallest difference that would be missed by those skilled in other areas and remain hidden to them. So, for instance, it seems that Eskimos can see from the type of snowflake whether it comes from the mountains, the sea or from any other direction, something that is of vital importance to them to be able to find their bearings in an endless expanse of snow that otherwise has nothing recognizable to offer.[3] Indians are able to distinguish the presence of hundreds of plant species, and from several hundred metres away too. If this is inexplicable to us, it is equally inexplicable to them how, for example, we can distinguish and identify so many kinds of red lights and other signals on the roads at night, lights that cause us to slow down hundreds of metres away because they tell us that something may be wrong farther along the road.[4]

Everyone has an eye for a particular system of meanings because it is of special and relevant importance to them. They hardly see the other things if at all, such as the jungle-dweller

54 Max Liebermann, *Restaurant 'De Oude Vink' in Leiden*, 1905

who left his native forest for the first time and paid a visit to Manhattan. When asked what struck him the most he replied that the bananas were bigger than those back home. Thus throughout the history of painting, and in that of architecture, we see different aspects coming to light that, each as a coherent system of meanings, made claims on the attention, evidently because at a certain time they were important or simply regarded as particularly attractive. Focusing on certain related aspects infinitely increases your powers of discernment vis-à-vis that relationship, yet it seems as though you can only focus on one area of it at a time.

Fixated on that one area, you are blind to everything else which, though potentially perceivable, fails to get through to you. It is as though you need all your attention for that one aspect on which you are concentrating and to which you are clearly receptive.

When holidaying as a family in France, our children were dragged from one cathedral to the other without their interest being aroused in the slightest. They only had eyes for coffee-makers, scooters and most of all a new phenomenon in those days: parking meters. Until one day in Auxerre they suddenly made a beeline for the cathedral. Had we finally managed to kindle their enthusiasm for the richness of this form-world that occupied and inspired us so? It took us only a short time before we succeeded, having scrupulously scanned the surroundings, in isolating from its exuberant backdrop a type of parking meter they evidently had not seen before.

Travelling through a remote desert area in India en route for Rajasthan, in all the stations you are served tea in fragile earthenware bowls that most resemble off-yellow flower pots without the hole at the bottom. Once empty they are thrown out of the train window where, with a dull plop, they smash to smithereens on the pebbles between the rails. The reverse of this phenomenon is that of our throw-away plastic cups; considered worthless in the West, there they are so exceptional that anyone succeeding in acquiring an intact example places it as a source of admiration among the other treasures set in a special place in the house. Isolated as a unique examplar in a culture of mainly handcrafted artefacts it can only be regarded as a creation of unattainable refinement. It is only with the greatest care that we managed to bring back undamaged to our industrialized world one or two of those supremely fragile bowls as an elementary example of primitive production, where they occupy a special place in our home as relics of a world lost to us long ago.

We only perceive what we more or less expect to find, confirming our suspicions as it were, in other words there is an element of recognition. Thus discoveries are in fact always rediscoveries and, invariably, the missing pieces from an already conceived totality.

The researcher can do little with phenomena he encounters that are impossible to fit into his research, based as it is on a known theory. Should he not wish to ignore those new phe-

nomena, all he can do is accommodate them in a new theory using inductive reasoning. It is not merely that we can only see things as part of a context (system of significations, field, paradigm), for a thing only has meaning and value when placed in the context of the relationship in which it performs, the situation, the environment it occupies. To be able to perceive something it has to hold your interest, you have to have been searching for it to some extent, even if unconsciously. It seems as though certain fascinations, perhaps borne with us since our childhood, persist in guiding or at all events influencing our preferences and decisions as well as our powers of discernment. You could call this secret force intuition.

Schliemann, the man who discovered Troy, was apparently able without prior knowledge to point out the right hill to start digging which indeed was to reveal the city, covered by nature as it had been and quite invisible. It cannot have been anything other than coincidence, but why did he decide to start digging there as opposed to anywhere else? Psycho-analysts explain the accuracy of his actions through the resemblance of the Trojan landscape to that of Schliemann's childhood in the Rhineland.[5] His intuition – what else can you call it? – arguably was guided by an unconscious experience that had stayed with him from his childhood.

There has to be an impulse to excite the interest; curiosity comes before perception.

When Le Corbusier came across that marble table on two solid legs in the dissecting room of that hospital he must have recognized the form as an answer to one of the questions that had been haunting him: the dining table he had still to design that would not be the usual four-legged affair. Or had he long borne it in mind as an 'interesting solution' for possible use at a later date?

Le Corbusier's sketchbooks [55-72]

'Le Corbusier, in collaboration with many others, particularly Pierre Jeanneret, was altogether responsible for the following:
152 architectural projects, 72 of which were executed
24 urban plans
419 paintings
43 sculptures
48 writings and books
gobelin tapestries, wall paintings, graphic work, and of course furniture.[6]'
The significance of this dazzling display of labour lies not only in the quantity as such but also in the sheer wealth of ideas it contains.

In the explosion of ideas that his investigations gave the twentieth century Le Corbusier is comparable only with Picasso: Le Corbusier the architect is the Picasso of architecture. No other architect has taken the possibilities of the twentieth century and so comprehensively exploited and indeed generated them.

It is generally known that Le Corbusier always carried a sketchbook around in which he noted down everything that made an impression on him.
Thinking in terms of what is customary among architects you might compare this activity with the making of travel sketches – in which case Le Corbusier has to have been the eternal traveller. It seems that even in the most impossible situations he would be eagerly gathering material he needed or thought he might need some day.

It is only by looking at the thousands of sketches in the Fondation Le Corbusier, often hastily done but quite as often meticulously detailed, that one really gets an idea of all the things he saw, of his enthusiasm for just about every aspect of life, forever scanning his surroundings. Often more written than drawn and intertwined with their captions, the speed and the compact form they were set down in suggest a kind of personal shorthand.

And Le Corbusier saw everything – particularly the things painters notice and architects tend to overlook: ships, trees, plants, shells, bottles, glasses, rocks, forks, hands, cats, donkeys, birds; and women, sitting, standing, lying, their hands, their feet, their breasts. Lots of furniture, all manner of objects for everyday use and everywhere the human figure in every imaginable situation.

Evidently it was subjects from his immediate environment that comprised his world, a world that made no distinction between official or formal architecture such as that of palaces, cathedrals and the like, and an informal architecture of peasant huts, where temporary and transient things loom as large as solid, massive edifices 'built for eternity'. Interestingly, there is no hierarchy among the images Le Corbusier collected. To him the difference between things were bricks of equal value with which he built his new world, a world of new relationships. If there was one architect who saw his way to giving exceptional shape to the demands ordinarily informing the everyday environment and so reconciling them with the sweep of form that has invariably accompanied great architecture, then Le Corbusier was that architect. In every period of his work, he considered everyday use and everyday experience of the whole and of each of its parts to be quite as spectacular as the form viewed in isolation. The attitude towards his surroundings evidenced by his sketchbooks is the same as that permeating everything he ever built, namely an unremitting capacity to get into the minds of the people who were to use his buildings, what their

55

56

57

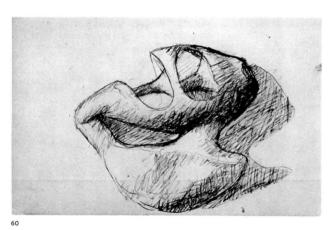

58

59

60

61

62

63

actions, their experiences would be. It is this ability to empathize that colours all his work as his and his alone. A Corbusian building is already inhabited at the design drawing stage, a quality that does not dim with the built result.

It is just this thought-provoking line – from jottings of observations by way of design sketches through to the building as built – that makes Le Corbusier's work ideal for study and consideration. You can see from his work the ins and outs of the design process and how an idea is born.

The pioneering responses of a typical twentieth-century architect like Le Corbusier ensue from the fact that the images absorbed everywhere and from every age are not applied lock, stock and barrel but transformed by being confronted with each other, and so stripped of their original meaning that they are free to accept new ones. And it is the incomparably rich 'library' at his disposal that is felt in every corner of his work as a positive charge, rather than seen in the literal sense.

Thus the wealth of ideas in Le Corbusier's œuvre issues from the rich library of images he had accumulated for himself. It would of course be folly to conclude that having this wealth of experience is the key to being a good designer, but it is one of the conditions – no more, but no less either! Although all designers obviously have their own way of working there is, broadly speaking, a certain analogy in the thought process involved. You might imagine it going something like this:

All the images you absorb and record together constitute a collection stored in your memory; a library of images, if you like, that you can draw on when confronting a problem. Often these images, memories of things seen earlier, are immediately 'applicable' in the sense that they inspire you. Moreover, there is always the tendency to inadvertently relate everything you see to what it is that is occupying you at the time. You are continually scanning your surroundings for things that might give you an idea of how to solve your problem of the moment. (Thus we see Le Corbusier often accompanying his sketches with explicit references to ongoing work.) Usually, though, the images get stored in your 'library', and have an indirect impact when consulted to help you develop an idea. This takes place through association, necessarily with some degree of analogy. Associations, as it happens, are seldom useful in a literal sense but bring you closer to ideas or solutions so that these open your eyes to other possibilities, other paradigms, modes of organization, mechanisms, and thus widen your horizon. Just as experiencing an unfamiliar cuisine stimulates you to new ways of preparing food without actually knowing the recipes, so associations too can encourage you to abandon well-trodden paths, suggesting to you that the answer to your problem might lie in another direction altogether. The increase here is not in the number of recipes but in your capacity to arrive at new things, new mechanisms.

The more you have been through, seen and absorbed and the richer the experience stored in your 'library', the larger your arsenal of potential indications from which to pick a direction to head in. In short, your frame of reference has widened. (This is why you can tell immediately from the designs done by first-year students – regardless of their ability to organize, say, a floor plan – whether they had a experientially rich or poor upbringing simply by looking at the forms they use.)

Being able to solve a problem along fundamentally different lines, in other words to create another mechanism, depends on the richness of one's experience, much like an

37

64

65

66

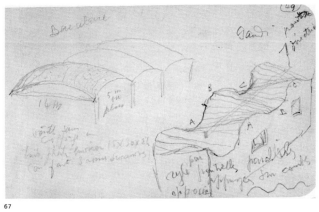

67

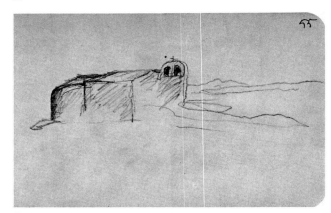

68

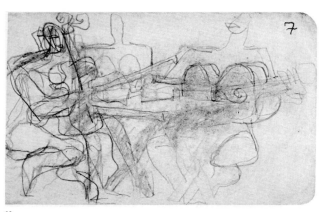

69

70

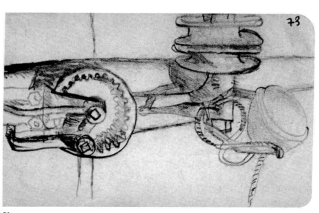

71

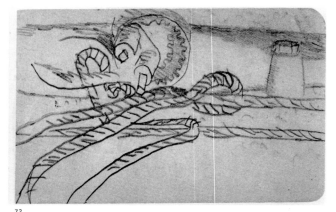

72

individual's linguistic powers of expression can extend no further than his vocabulary allows. Nor should we forget that the one person can get more out of a given material than the other.

The forms we have stored in our memory consciously or unconsciously thrust themselves upon us as we design. In fact it is very much the question whether there is anything at all you can think of that does not derive from the accumulation of images in your mind. Could your output possibly be more than what you take in? Knowing many recipes does not make you a cook, although you would certainly have to be familiar with them, deviate from them, so as to arrive at culinary creations of your own.

A new idea can only be born out of dismantling a previous one.

Designing, despite all ideas, methods, processes, techniques and theories, is like watching aircraft take off: however attentive you are and however probing your analysis, to actually take off yourself is another matter entirely.

And should it be so that your design faculties indeed sharpen as your collection of images increases, and that your abilities are indirectly determined by the wealth of experiences you have managed to harvest – then what matters above all else is to use your eyes and ears and at least be receptive in every situation and ask yourself if that situation might not have something in it for you.

In principle your material is everywhere, on the street, in the room, at all times. Being an architect is more than a profession, it is, before anything else, an attitude towards your surroundings!

It is crucially important, then, that you really are affected by what you see and hear.

Being receptive to influences is something you can learn up to a point. Whether or not something truly makes an impression on you is contingent on earlier experiences, the circumstances in which you had them and the associations for you. (Travelling through Morocco the music you heard everywhere had not the slightest effect on you; much later, at home, when the radio suddenly played the same type of music, then it did make an impression and all the imagery of that particular journey flooded back. Clearly the music struck home because it brought back positive memories.) So although we have no control over when we will be moved, and by what, we can at least exercise our eyes by acquiring the habit of recording things on paper. Each of us should be capable of evolving a personal way of formulating things, so as to be able to retain 'for personal use only' all those snatches of what we hear and see, and of what goes through our minds during conversations and reflections.

While on the subject, it seems clear that of all the means of recording besides writing, drawing ultimately is the most appropriate and, for our purpose at least, infinitely more effective than, say, taking photographs which we all do at times.

In many instances photos are undeniably a more appropriate means to convince others, in that the presented situation appears to be more 'objective' and therefore more plausible. With drawings, there is always the danger that the inevitable artistic pretensions will overshadow the information that is to be conveyed. However, the benefits for yourself of drawing are that by looking at things with greater precision, and above all by becoming more selective in what you consider important, your acuity in recording will increase.

Drawing etches the images into your memory.[7]

■ Even today Le Corbusier is still the greatest purveyor of ideas, concepts and images which, stored in his schemes, are still being adopted by the latest generations of architects, whether consciously or unconsciously. So what he himself accumulated from the past gets imperceptibly passed on as inspiration and converted into fuel for modernity.

A great many, mainly young architects see little in the past with its forms, materials and working methods which they regard as no longer applicable because these belong to another brief, with other labour relations and for other social contexts. Might knowledge of past forms guided by nostalgia not encourage an eclecticism of old stylistic traits?

Yet the occasions when Le Corbusier adopted historical forms almost literally, as in the Ronchamp chapel – call them direct influences – are few and far between. Come to that, everything he borrowed, or stole if you prefer, became profoundly modern through his intervention, such as the use of coloured glass, admired by all and sundry in Chartres Cathedral without it occurring to them that it could be applied in a modern setting.

Influencing is in the main an indirect and usually unconscious process of transformation, but you can also perceive in such a way that, looking through the expression of the form, as it were, you can single out what of it may be of use to you. You are then interpreting what you see in a new role that is apposite and applicable to you. This is how characteristics come to be selected with a more universal value than their original stylistic manifestations.

Unlike historians, who tend to foreground traits that adhere typewise to a particular period, architects are more keen on those elements that do not. Because these have not lost their validity they could well be of use to us. And we visually extract what we can use, indifferent to what the original intentions may have been, and label it timeless. It is the timeless that we seek.

And these days timeless means of all time. Elements unhitched from a particular time frame are those with a more general significance and ever present in different guises, evidently because they can be traced back to basic human values which persist, if with varying emphasis, in the way that different languages share an underlying generative grammar. You need history not just to see what happened when and where and how different or unique it was and if there are breaks in the thinking, but also to establish what it is that is unchanging, to recognize the underlying structure of similarities that we can merely piece together, like a pot unearthed shard by shard.

History keeps unearthing different aspects of an unchanging structure under changing conditions.

'The only available escape from the fundamental limitations of our imaginative faculty lies in directing our attention more to the experiences we all have in common, the collective memory, some of it innate (!) some of it transmitted and acquired, which in one way or another must be at the base of our common experiential world. ... [W]e assume an underlying "objective" structure of forms – which we will call arch-forms – a derivative of which is what we get to see in a given situation.

'The whole "musée imaginaire" of forms in situations whatever their time and place can be conceived of as an infinite variety out of which people help themselves, in constantly changing variety, to forms which in the end refer back to the fundamentally unchangeable and underlying reservoir of arch-forms. ... By referring each one back to its fundamentally unchangeable ingredients, we then try to discover what the images have in common, and find thus the "cross section of the collection", the unchangeable, underlying element of all the examples, which in its plurality can be an evocative form-starting-point.

'The richer our collection of images, the more precise we can be in indicating the most plural and most evocative solution, and the more objective our solution becomes, in the sense that it will hold a meaning for, and be given a meaning by, a greater variety of people.

'We cannot make anything new, but only reevaluate already existing images, in order to make them more suitable for our circumstances. What we need to draw on is the great "Musée Imaginaire" of images wherein the process of change of signification is displayed as an effort of human imagination, always finding a way to break through the established order, so as to find a more appropriate solution for [the] situation.

'It is only when we view things from the perspective of the enormous collage, that, with the aid of analogies, we can resolve the unknown and, by a process of extrapolation arrive at solutions which can improve the circumstances.

'Design cannot do other than convert the underlying and the idea of ever being able to start off with a clean slate is absurd, and moreover, disastrous when, under the pretext of its being necessary to start completely from the beginning, what already exists is destroyed so that the naked space can be filled up with impracticable and sterile constructions. ... The various significations of everything that has taken place, and is still taking place now, are like old layers of paint lying one on top of another, and they form for us, in their entirety, the undercoat on which a new layer can be placed; a new signification which will slightly alter the whole thing.

'This transformation process, whereby the outmoded significations fade into the background, and new ones are added, must be ever-present in our working methods. Only by such a dialectical process, will there be a continual thread between past and future, and the maintenance of historical continuity.'[8]

In the above quote dating from 1973 the emphasis is mainly on forms, conceived as time-dependent interpretations of more universal 'arch-forms'. What we are concerned with in this book is the kind of space those forms generate and for this we must expand the idea of a 'Musée Imaginaire' of images to include the space forms that they result in. Whereas forms always more or less bear the stamp of their time or place, space – even if their counterform – steps outside that time and place, conceptually at least, and is therefore less time-bound.

When considering architecture of other times or places, we need to turn our eyes from the things to the space these give shape to, and look beyond what is too specifically formed to distil the essence of that space, thus shifting the emphasis from the architecture to what it is that it manages to generate in the way of views and protection and what can happen as a result.

The more you have seen or the more impressions you have experienced in whatever other way, the bigger your frame of reference. We cannot be greedy enough in our cravings as 'receiver' of images wherever, whenever, whatever.

Everything can produce useful associations: butterfly wings, feathers and fighter planes, pebbles and rock formations, images that enlarge the space at the architect's disposal.

And then there are all the imaginable situations people can find themselves in; you have to recognize and identify these to bring those people to the centre of attention.

Your ability to generate ideas that lead to new concepts is contingent on the wealth of your frame of reference. And the wider the horizon of your interests, the sooner you can break free of the snare of architectural inbreeding of forms that are doomed to keep reproducing while their substance diminishes; and the greater your chances of avoiding the backwash of tricks and trends everywhere about. It is precisely by not thinking of architecture that you come to see analogies with other situations that incite new ideas (by seeing it more as X you discover its potential fitness for Y).

Your frame of reference, as it happens, also works in reverse: in the design process, it is by establishing which potential possibilities are unsuitable as a response to a particular task, the negative selection if you like, that you become aware of the direction you must then follow. Not only do you become more aware while working of what you are in fact looking for, criteria of quality also suggest themselves. These set themselves up as touchstones that inform you whether you have 'arrived' or need to keep on searching: designing is rejecting. More important than being sure of what you want is knowing at least what you don't want, and so to design is most of all to keep looking and not be too easily satisfied with what you find.

The richer and more universal the influences you concede, the more mental elbow room you create for yourself. It is a question of exploring everything there is, everywhere and of all time to discover how old mechanisms can be transformed into new ones by eradicating the old meanings and rebuilding them for new ends. It is, then, a question of making your frame of reference as wide as possible.

■ EXPERIMENT-EXPERIENCE The more experience you acquire, the clearer the bigger picture becomes, but regrettably it is also the case that the closer your experiments bring you to knowing what works, what is fit and what is not, the more your open-mindedness disappears and experience slowly but surely strikes home.

This process shows a certain analogy with the way space seems predestined to make the transformation to place.

Accumulated practical acquaintance leads eventually to experience, habituation and finally routine, as a result of repeating formulas that have proved to be successful.

In spite of yourself, you measure every new experience against the quality of all foregoing experiences of a like nature, so that your chances of finding something new that is better than what you already know keep diminishing, and so for most people the need to continue searching will diminish too.

So we see everyone doomed by a natural process of selection, so to speak, due to the tendency to follow self-made paths, thus with a minimum of risk.

When this preference for previously trod paths goes hand in hand with a decrease in curiosity, it means that we are adapting more and more as time goes by to the possibilities, instead of seizing and exploiting these possibilities by adapting them to us.

The more you experience, the more experience you gain. All garnered experience remains in place and works with you in establishing values, and so influences your thinking and irrevocably restricts your freedom. Experience is what you know of the world and because of it you adapt to the world, whether you want to or not.

'Our brains persistently urge us to change our surroundings in such a way that we fit there, but when the limit is reached the reverse happens: our expectations and needs are modified until they fit the surroundings. The first happens in childhood, the second after that. Only artists manage to persist in the first stage.'[9]

First we make the world, later the world makes us. The architect's thinking, which guides his creative process and production, is controlled by the tendency to deepen and perfect his earlier discoveries on the one hand and to keep doing it differently with the hope of making new discoveries on the other. That's how we move constantly between experiment and experience.

That is to say, risks and danger (periculum) obtain when we embark upon experiment, whereas experience safeguards us against them.[10]

The more experience takes over, the more earlier weaknesses will be eliminated and in time what we experience as quality will gain strength.

Experience finds its own way and every teacher helps it in this by being naturally inclined to want to administer knowledge. Experience rests on knowledge and insight, whereas experiment by contrast is out for discovery, finding the unknown. Experience assumes that the aims are clear. This is not the case with experiment. Yet all too often we see ideas launched like unguided missiles with an excess of energy and enthusiasm, yet the targets are vague or simply not there. It would be fine if experience and experiment were to act as complementary categories, but unfortunately they oppose one another instead and that is the dilemma of the creative process.

If only we could escape our experience.

3

Spatial Discoveries

■ What we call spatial discoveries are mechanisms and concepts that initiate essentially different conditions, with architecture the medium par excellence to achieve them. Architecture being eminently capable of expressing (and therefore 'formulating') itself with spatial means. This is the field of activity that the architect should concentrate on categorically, certainly if he wishes to lay claim to a specific cultural task and if he wishes to produce something that changes the way people perceive, so that they see themselves and their surroundings in another light. Spatial discoveries open doors with which existing systems can be disrupted and new paradigms followed or perhaps even opened up in the case of a new spatial concept.

Instead of limiting itself almost exclusively to the outward appearance of buildings and how they change over time, the history of architecture should concern itself more with changes in thinking and the changing possibilities and circumstances influenced by those changes, and that directly or indirectly formed both the need and the inducement for ever different methods of building, forms, techniques and thus repeatedly provided the impetus for spatial discoveries. History is marked by moments of revolutionary breakthroughs. We then say that the time was ripe to do things differently, with other constructions, forms, spaces. Sometimes this happens unexpectedly, but often it is announced long before and amounts to a final stage that in retrospect makes sense as the logical conclusion of a route embarked upon earlier.

Take, for instance, Gerrit Rietveld's celebrated red-blue chair of 1918. If in 1903 or thereabouts we can observe the back becoming an autonomous element in chairs by Mackintosh and also Frank Lloyd Wright, Rietveld's teacher, P.J.C. Klaarhamer, continued this deconstruction throughout the entire chair. Although clearly influenced by Berlage, Klaarhamer's design is definitely more forthright and deliberate.[1]

Rietveld, obviously aware of the work of his predecessors, rounded off the story in resolute and spectacular fashion. He had also come into contact with the painters of the De Stijl group, in which Mondrian and more particularly Bart van der Leck were working with discrete planes. Rietveld lifted these out of the two-dimensional surface and placed them as volumes in space. This was a move, as much deliberate as revolutionary, away from having the elements of a structure interlock and thus negatively influencing one another, instead treating them as pure volumes. El Lissitzky would later return Rietveld's chair structures to the flat canvas.

One of Rietveld's motives presumably was that, armed with the possibility of industrialized production, he strove to construct all the elements of his chair from a single plank, with as little material waste as possible and enabling simple assembly of the parts thus acquired.

Whenever new spatial concepts emerge in response to new challenges these are often turning points. After that they become common property and then, ultimately, outmoded. Customary solutions that were once questioned as to the possibility of improvement, can be thoroughly unsettled merely by a shift in emphasis. This opens the door to new ideas. These in turn lead to a new mode of organization and then inevitably to new concepts of space.

Take the library: we all know the changes it has been through. Beginning as the place where manuscripts were kept, it later became a place where single imprints could be studied, only accessible to a select group of initiated sleuths, where intellectual as well as material property needed expressing above everything else. These days it is a 'public' institution, where in principle everyone is welcome to read or borrow books. So the idea of a library evolved from preserving texts to disseminating knowledge. As culture and scholarship became more open, both the space of the library and its organization changed accordingly.

And so a lending library, rather than being an institution where you are obliged to know beforehand why you are visiting it, can be conceived of as a place that invites browsing or searching so as to stimulate unexpected discoveries. The resemblance to a large bookstore is then so great that it is but a small step to reorganize it as such. Then, in a chain reaction, come the consequences (the consistent rules of conjugation,

73

74

75

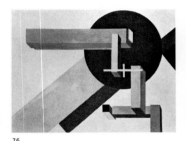

76

so to speak) leading to a new concept for this new paradigm. So we see that this new organization with its particular spatial demands and potentials causes the spatial concept to change.

With the search function taken over by digitized systems, such as the Internet which is there for everyone, the concept will evolve further – who know? – perhaps to a return to exclusiveness, so that reading rooms, those traditional meeting places, might conceivably have a new future ahead of them.

A new paradigm always means that the paradigm it has come to replace is forced into the background: this automatically initiates the need for a new architectural idiom. Once this is in place, everyone goes along with it and it is impossible to imagine that things were ever seen differently.

Throughout our history there have been shifts of attention accompanied by shifts in terminology and values. Using analyses of our attitude towards categories of people that depart from the norm such as the insane and the incarcerated, Michel Foucault showed that there have been times when there were deviant epistemes – that is, coherent 'frameworks of discourse' of general validity which define the conditions governing actions and judgement during a certain period of history.[2]

Systems of collective value judgements, repeatedly exposed as prejudices during time cycles of every conceivable form, are suppressed by new ones that act as the social programme and breeding ground for changes in architecture.

That architecture is also subjected to change and erosion of value judgements transpires from the most obvious examples in practice.

Measures that we take for granted such as the moral and legally underpinned obligation towards invalids, simply did not exist twenty-five years ago; at that time no-one gave it a thought although the phenomenon itself has not changed.

The same applies to our present-day concern for the environment and energy, when all at once the fear of relative scarcity took hold generally.

In the Netherlands these days there is the desire to give up land – little though we have – that once yielded a profit but has now become a millstone due to the necessary upkeep. Give it up, that is, to the water. The very land that took centuries to wrest from the sea is now being returned to nature under certain conditions, a state of affairs that makes living along or on the water only too relevant.

Again, we are being made dizzy with new inventions, new advances, computers. Other ideas, in whatever field, keep giving fresh cause to abandon what we were busy doing for something else. We should seriously wonder whether it is possible at all for there to be fundamental changes in architecture that are not bound in some way to social changes – changes in our thinking about human relations, that is.

It can also be that a change in society, even a small one, is due in part to spatial discoveries; these are the spatial discoveries that we architects dream of.

Yet the entire world-view does not have to change for there to be innovation in architecture. It goes without saying that there is repeated cause for change, particularly on the smaller scale, to constituent parts of that world-view. In the designer's day-to-day practice these present an undercurrent of impulses to come up with new ideas from one project to the next, ideas that lead in turn to other concepts.

New paradigms need not always lead to other goals; frequently these are achieved by other means, often making more efficient use of new possibilities. We see things differently and those same goals then appear in a new light.

A culture develops because we, influencing and inspiring each other, continue to build step by step on what has come before and theoretically it means an ever greater degree of perfection. But the greater the perfection of a system or principle, the less need there is for change and the more hermetic things get. Until all at once it transpires that we have been hammering away at something that is long out of date. We need external impulses all the time to upset the balance, so as not to get bogged down in prejudices. And to keep all the options open on space.

Prune a tree or bush at the right moment and it gives it a renewed vitality that you previously did not think possible.

77 Boullée, interior of a public library

78 British Museum, London. Reading room

So it seems that innovation not only generates renewal but itself has a renewing impact, if only because of the panache it gives off in the process.

Changes, small ones as well as big, are the sparks that feed fresh impulses to the motor of architecture and keep it ticking over. They enable things to happen that were not originally within the frame of attention and therefore not among the options.

Whereas the panache of the Heroic Period of architecture was unthinkable without the underlying social optimism, and the physical space produced was more or less equal to the psychological space that accompanied it, these days it is mainly the capacity of production that unleashes the optimism and generates panache, it is true, but a good deal less space. This is the very reason why it is all the more important for us to pick out and explore less naively and more levelheadedly what it is that has changed in the world-view within which we operate. New generations continue to draw motivation and enthusiasm from the conviction that they can contribute to new formulations and new images.

Just as our economy seems unable to function without growth, so too architecture cannot survive without change and it looks as though the process of aging and replacement, not only of buildings but equally of values and ideas, is rapidly gathering momentum. We seem to get even more quickly bored with what was new yesterday, and these certainly are golden years for young architects who, with a repeatedly new view of things, are falling over each other to take the helm with new ideas and to create new challenges that in turn require new responses.

With change and the perpetual challenge of regeneration as parameters of architecture, every young architect is obliged to hurl himself into this maelstrom. He has the opportunity to shine and he has to grasp that opportunity if he is not to fall by the wayside. We must remember that his clients are in the same boat, they too must stand out if they are to get work. We are in fact all condemned to change. Whereas change and renewal meant improvement by the old standards, if these are not specifically aimed at the future there is no progress, merely change for change's sake; in which case it is about the excitement of the new, the unexpected, the previously unimagined, without the question of quality being foregrounded. New is necessary, while the predecessors were rather hoping that progress would be made on the strength of their discoveries. Not only is each generation out to prove itself and can only do that by declaring what their forebears thought and did to be invalid and useless and therefore out of date, but it is quick to lose interest and keeps needing new things all the time. Which is why each new generation of architects seizes on new needs, demands and challenges; this gives them a welcome alibi for their craving for change and stimulates inventiveness.

Exaggeration is inevitable. It could hardly be otherwise with new aspects being continually moved into the foreground, forcing old aspects into the background. A good many theories get concocted not because they are better but simply because old ones have lost their appeal: 'That's that out of the way.' The upshot is that so much that is worthwhile 'disappears' into history, although there is admittedly plenty to take its place. Luckily, besides the inevitability of the new, there is still the persistent feeling of 'there's always room for improvement'! And when ambition proceeds in concert with critical acuity new discoveries ensue. It is here that we must seek real, i.e. genuine, renewal and the only standard in architecture against which we can measure that renewal is the space that is freed by it. Everything that architects make can be judged according to this standard. I would like to demonstrate that here using a number of examples of the incomparably large quantity of space yielded by twentieth-century modernism (a name with staying power, it seems), despite the scepticism often voiced on the matter.

It is only where architecture generates other space, creates other experiences and satisfies other conditions which cause sensibilities to change, that it signifies anything of value. Architecture is more than just a free-ranging, narcissistic phenomenon.

79 Bibliothèque Ste Geneviève, Paris. Reading room

80 Strahov monastery library, Czechia

It is such moments as these that we look forward to, when spatial themes, inspired by ideas from beyond architecture, come into being. Ideas that are brought to expression and if possible reinforced by the medium of architecture, recognizable steps in an advancing civilization. Architecture not merely in spite of itself but, moreover, as the moving force behind shifts in thinking, however slight these shifts may be. In rare instances, then, architectural space can act as a model for social change.

Nobody, I hasten to point out, claims that architecture can change the world, but the two do change each other, step by step, one grain of sand at a time.

You have to step outside the context of your profession and be in a position to draw your ideas from a wider context than that of architecture which although itself revolving keeps taking its arguments from other arguments within its own system. Ideas relating to form or space can never derive from architecture alone. This raises the crucial discussion of whether there is any real point to such ideas. What are the things you can and cannot say with architectural means, and do they lead anywhere?

As an architect you must be attuned to what goes on around you; open yourself to the shifts of attention in thinking that bring certain values into view and exclude others. The extent to which you allow yourself to be influenced by these shifts is a question of vitality. That architecture changes is not just a hedonistic, narcissistic, unconditional hankering, as in fashion, for the spectacularly original in the design of the exterior, but over and above that its ability to capitalize on what it is that shifts in society and in the thinking on society, and the new concepts that are discovered as a result.

Architects must react to the world, not to each other.

81 Hans Scharoun, Staatsbibliothek, Berlin

'Scholastic information' [82]
Robert Doisneau, 1956

The image of the classroom as a hollow stone space, shut off from the outside world, where the children are forced to concentrate on the teacher and his blackboard, is as persistent as the idea that what children need at school before anything else is knowledge.

The school building's organization, but also its outward appearance, helps in every respect to lend weight to this principle of education. The work of the architect represents in concrete form this education paradigm, which seems nineteenth-century to us though it is still found today all over the world. The windows are set high enough to limit the view out to freedom as much as possible. They serve merely to let in sufficient light and only as much air as is barely necessary.

For whatever it is that the three main protagonists in the photograph below are thinking, the building merely provides a backdrop. As close and unyielding as their environment is, it fails to prevent them from facing up to their situation as best they can, and even turning it to their own advantage.

Open air school in the dunes
[83-84]

The wave of social engagement that gave education a new perspective at the beginning of the twentieth century also forced a rethink on the principles of school architecture. Now that the focus was on the less able and neglected children of the disadvantaged urban proletariat, the first proviso and obvious task of a school was to work on redressing their poor physical condition. Noble though these motives undoubtedly were, the persistent myth of a healthy mind in a healthy body was certainly there in the background. And however doubtful this may be in medical terms, spatially this was translated into openness and open air. The more air the better, and that meant nothing less than getting rid of those walls. Thus the concept of the open air school was born, and with it the dissolution of the great weight that had come to be expected of the buildings. The school building's dominant presence in the nineteenth-century notion of education was equalled only by its demonstrative rejection now, as the most extreme consequence of the new spirit. Yet save for this promise of fresh air there is little else we can discern in the two photographs that is new. With the classes still arranged in the traditional fashion, with the teacher and blackboard as twin foci, they seem hemmed in by phantom walls, and the space of the surroundings with all its potential for adventure is, for the present at least, distinctly out of bounds.

83

82

84

Open Air School, Suresnes, Paris [85-93]
Baudoin & Lods, 1935

Built six years after Duiker's open air school in Amsterdam of 1930, the school in Suresnes likewise grew from the idea that learning and working should really take place in the open air, but took this principle a stage further.[3]

The school was regarded as an institute, in this case set up by a progressive-minded local councillor, that besides imparting knowledge was also and more importantly to bring the physical condition of particularly the weaker pupils up to scratch. Thus the school gained an aspect of welfare. This new paradigm was of course an imposed condition and even a necessity for creating a wholly new conception of schools in which emphasis came to lie on collective facilities such as washrooms, dining rooms and restrooms. Each class was conceived as a physically distinct free-standing pavilion.

Not just the design but the construction and the materials are other than usual, for in this new concept there is literally no trace left of anything even reminiscent of the hitherto customary mechanism of classrooms off corridors with a stair at each end. This response to a new set of questions has landed us, so to speak, in an utterly new world.

Today schools fulfil yet another, wholly different role in society and, given the emphasis these days on social training, we would no longer know how to handle classrooms configured as autonomous, separate units, without a main assembly hall and without countless non-class-related ancillary spaces for groups of children.

But what still moves us today about the open air schools is the radical and fundamental way their architects responded to

the new paradigm. Nothing illustrates the idea of that optimistic period better than the canonical photograph showing the children at their studies – with a roof over their tall space yet out of doors too owing to the generously opened-out external walls. This is abidingly different from the chill classrooms with windows placed high to preclude children from being distracted from the teacher and the blackboard by goings-on outside, a set-up that is still today by far the most prevalent universally. Interestingly, the children in the photograph are sitting with their backs to the world outside, presumably in the interests of concentration, so that it is the teacher who benefits most from the space afforded by the view out.

There are now plans in the pipeline to restore this unique school, but the chances

85

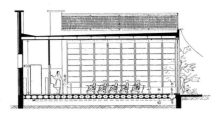

86

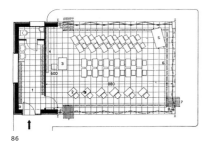

87

88

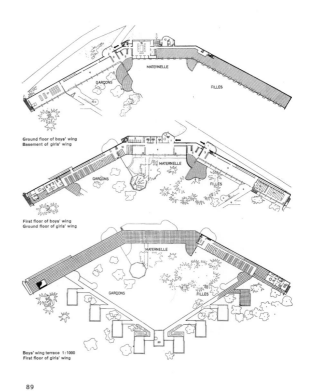

Ground floor of boys' wing
Basement of girls' wing

First floor of boys' wing
Ground floor of girls' wing

Boys' wing terrace 1:1000
First floor of girls' wing

89

that the large glass folding walls that smoothly slid back to turn inside into outside, will then be able to open are slim indeed in view of the enormous weight of the double glazing used nowadays, which would necessitate an unduly heavy construction to support it.

Today's demands for insulation have meant a change in the way buildings are constructed. This shift in priorities has clearly left its mark on the spatial aspect. We certainly should not expect that the way space is used in the future will keep alive even a reflection of how things were. The concerns of future users is so far removed from the aims this perfect machine of a building was designed to meet, that only the broad organizational lines can hope to survive, if that.

With its classrooms scattered across the site as free-standing pavilions, the school is a collection of fragments. Only the elongated block of general facilities terminating the north side of the site gives the whole some impression of being a large-scale institute.

The pavilions are linked by footbridge-like canopies which more or less keep you dry en route and can themselves be walked upon. The cohesion suggested by this continuous system of aerial walkways, which is felt the strongest when walking through the foliage of what are by now extremely large trees, has more of a landscape than of architecture and buildings. This is strengthened by the explicitly functional layout of the grounds, with places for working out of

doors, for play and games, and for resting in the open air. The main impression one gets of the entire complex, then, is of a built landscape.

90

91

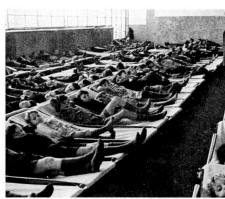

92

93

■ After the fortress-like school buildings where children had
no business to be out of doors except in the fifteen-minute
break, followed in the twenties and thirties by the concept of
the open air school, it was the new ideas on teaching of the
sixties that most of all inspired an educational paradigm that
placed the school in another social context entirely. Where
the open air school was mainly a response to a principle of
health that did nothing to disturb the organization of classrooms into autonomous units, the social 'paradigm' that is
increasingly determining how schools are organized is encouraging a new spatial concept which places greater emphasis on
the area outside the classrooms where children can gather
either spontaneously or in an organized way. Steadily the
classrooms are being relieved of their sanctity. At the same
time the corridors are becoming more than just circulation
space and getting more closely related to the classrooms than
just by way of a small window in the door which only the
teacher can look through.

In the Montessori School in Delft[4] and later in the Apollo
Schools in Amsterdam[5] the classrooms are grouped round
a hall where at least as many activities take place as in the
classrooms themselves; it serves the school community
the way a main square serves a small town.

In today's school social skills are coming to be just as important as the traditional subject matter, skills such as working
together, living together, learning how to get along with each

other. This requires another concept of space that is less oriented outwards but is all the more present on the interior and
marked by a greater spatial openness among what were originally separate rooms.

In this respect the concept of the following school designed
by Takis Zenetos was notably radical, though the scheme as
built shows that the architect had to pull back on many points
vis-à-vis his original design.

If the spatial concept in the next few examples follows
developments in society, these developments are certainly
spurred on in turn by the spatial potential offered by these
schools.

School, Athens [94-99]
Takis Zenetos, 1969

The school in Aghios Dimitrios in Athens, designed by Takis Zenetos, stands like an abandoned ship in the clearing in this modest residential area. But though dilapidated, the clarity of form is still present, revealing at a glance the exceptional way this school is organized.

In a departure from other schools, particularly the larger ones, where classrooms are accommodated in wings like carriages in a train as are the auxiliary spaces, this one groups them in a three-storey semicircle round a central open courtyard which is continually crossed by pupils and teachers between classes.

The open galleries along the uppermost classrooms give a view, over their full length, of the almost circular inner court to which they are linked by strategically placed staircases. This results in a smooth-running if emphatically present circulation, with the mass movement between classes an expression of community. The staircases further link the basement level with the world above. Though this area is inhospitable and unattractive, one look at the design drawing shows that it was precisely here that the idea underlying the design of this school could have been most perfectly expressed.

It was Zenetos's intention, the drawings tell us, that below the inner court there was to be a large auditorium for performances, assemblies and other activities involving the whole school. This formed a second, equally large courtyard set below the first and suitable for better concentration and for the more deliberate and specifically directed exchanging of ideas.

The classrooms lying along the semicircular periphery show a significant variety of space organization models clearly allied to the ideas on education and educational theory that had taken root in the Sixties.[6] This placed emphasis primarily on the assumed inbuilt motivation of children who are curious and enthusiastic by nature rather than needing to be incited – like an engine that can be started without a spark. If today this seems like an overly optimistic outlook, the important thing is that the architect picked up on socially innovative ideas and has shown that one could stimulate effectuation of these ideas with spatial means. Here the architect is not following a trend, but creating the space that invites and incites innovation, space that is thus itself a model for other society-related forms.

To adopt such an up-front position is risky and obviously entails the danger of failure. In this case we are right in suspecting that the present local education, which is not exactly known for being progressive, saw no chance of making even partial use of the possibilities on offer.

What has been left, then, is an inspiring example of an educational model that can still be read from the building as it is today; the formulating of a social ideal. The organization of the space involves not only the grouping of classrooms and other rooms

94

95

96

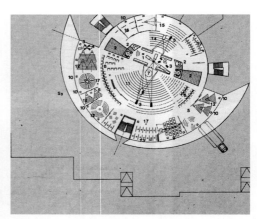

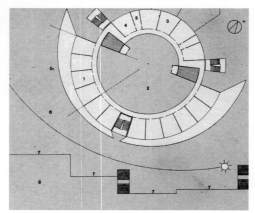

97

98

99

but also the construction. This is dominated by solid concrete beams with improbably large cantilevers characteristic of Zenetos's work and which from a distance unmistakably call Duiker to mind, also because of the comparably explicit presence of the unifying construction.[7]

The cantilevers stress both the openness and the unity of the whole where partition walls between rooms, and between them and the shared areas and circulation zones, seem relatively minor and temporary additions.

The most spectacular outward-facing element is undeniably the system of sunbreaks consisting of concrete blades. Making use of the jutting cantilevers of the main beams, they impact as imposing and expressive 'canopies'. The lower the calculated position of the sun in the sky, the further they extend into space. Hence these image-defining canopies express formwise the course of the sun throughout the school day – much like a giant sundial. At no point does this inbuilt solar protection screen off the view, and seen from inside it is taken-for-granted and unobtrusive in equal measure, as is to be expected in a country where the sun is a major influence on life.

The influence of the climate on the form of the construction is another recurring theme in the work of this scandalously underrated architect, who translated into the Greek context the fruits of the modernist 'French-tech' tradition of, amongst others, his teacher Jean Prouvé – a tradition that would later spawn Jean Nouvel.

De Polygoon, primary school, Almere (1990-92) [100-115]

In this school the classes are ranged along an elongated streetlike space, not, like all preceding schools designed by us, grouped round a main hall. Flanked by the series of classrooms on either side, this all-pervasive space owes its spatial impact to the curved roof resolutely drawing together all its components. The open full-length strip in the middle comprises supplementary facilities laid out like a string of islands. This strip of smaller open and enclosed spaces is interrupted by open plaza-like islands for group activities serving four classes. These can be more or less screened off using sliding panels. There is room for specialized activities such as handicraft, a library and a computer park as well as spaces that can

be closed off for remedial teaching or other more individual educational activities. But there is room too for a number of extra workplaces without prescribed functions and suited to the variety of educational situations that can arise in a modern school. The classrooms all have bay window-like zones that open almost their entire length to the central 'street', like shops with large display windows. Naturally they can be temporarily closed off if need be by curtains or screens; had they been designed in closed-off mode the reverse would not have been possible. Besides enabling you to look in as you walk past (the classroom opened to the 'street'), the street encourages working outside your classroom while still

belonging to the class. Added to that, the entire length of the street is flooded with daylight through continuous strips of rooflights. These are so placed above the zone of 'bays' that together with the glass in the tops of the bays, they mark out this threshold area as an activity zone. For the most attractive workplaces are found where there is a concentration of daylight. Together, bay and daylight zone are largely instrumental in shifting as much as possible of the activity – traditionally occurring along the outward-facing windows – inwards, to the internal street space. This means that the classrooms make a claim on the collective interior space and, in effect, on expanding their useful floor area. Thus we see a com-

100

paratively greater emphasis placed on making active use of the central street space. Although inviting a more informal use educationally speaking than inside the strict confines of the classroom, this high-street-like zone can still be described as a 'learning street'.

At the official hand-over of this school building, the various sponsors from the building world were given the opportunity to display their products each in a different classroom for the visitors who came in droves. All at once the school resembled a

103 shopping mall. Here the concepts of school and shopping centre are a lot closer than one might otherwise have suspected, with the open elevation principle informing high street and learning street alike.

A seemingly inconsequential detail, though decisive in practice, is the presence of cloakroom recesses, so that all the walls are not hung solid with coats. Indeed the walls are regularly a point of application for activities and 'places'. The traditional school building type with its inhospitable corridors a mile long for circulation pur-

108 poses only and bristling with hooks for hanging coats, is still with us and even the most celebrated architects are setting a bad example in this respect.

101

102 Usine de Dégrossissage d'Or, Geneva

103

104

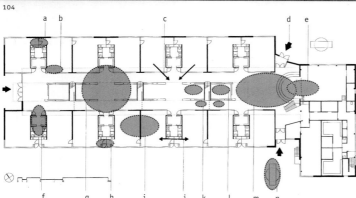

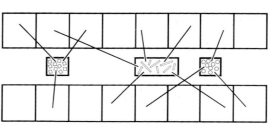

106

105 a Kitchen unit in all classrooms b Bays like display windows leading to collective area (as if it were a high street) c Visual contact between classrooms and learning-street d Three entrances of equal importance. Flexibility in use; separate entrances for primary and secondary schools e Play area and central hall can be combined f Cloakroom recess serving two classrooms. Walls in collective area kept free of coat pegs g Shared area ('square') for four classrooms h Direct access to outdoors from primary school classrooms i Sliding partitions or doors enable two classrooms to become a single large one j Short cuts between classrooms k Sliding door creates study area in corridor l Work areas; from entirely closed off to open using sliding partitions m Assembly space for entire school n Shelters at entrances instead of canopies. Places to wait and play or shelter from sun and rain.

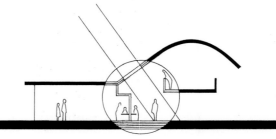

107

108 Corridor in a traditional school, dominated by coat pegs

The cloakroom recesses, the display-window openness of the classrooms, the provision of daylight in the learning street – all these are determining, decisive conditions without which, however brilliant your school design is otherwise, the rest means nothing.

No matter how the ongoing discourse on education develops, the traditional autonomy and dominance of the classroom is bound to keep on diminishing. The consequences for the school building is that emphasis will shift further from the classrooms to the space beyond. An increasing need is emerging for a multiplicity of places where ever new groups of children can concentrate on ever new subjects. This requires new concepts and these have to come from somewhere, though not necessarily from school-building. Often another situation you are occupied with points you in the right direction. In the present case it was fitting out a factory shed for an international seminar for architecture students

102 (**INDESEM**). Making use of the internal subdivisions suggested by the columns in the space, we partitioned off group spaces at each side, leaving a toplit central volume in-between. A stage and a bar, the main meeting point, were installed at the extremities (no school of architecture without a bar as its centre!). All discussion during that seminar took place in the central space

109

110

111

where everyone was regularly to be found. This basic configuration, perfect for the equally basic situation it was constructed for, served as the initial inducement that ultimately brought me to the 'learning street' model for a primary school. Time and again it comes down to recognizing situations outside the field of vision of your drawing table or computer screen as having a bearing on the task you are working on, and then managing to transform these situations to fit your own.

112

SHELTERS As an alternative for canopies and other facilities at the front door and dictated by the fear harboured by the authorities that local kids would keep hanging around there with less honourable intentions, we designed free-standing shelters which offer the children the opportunity to wait for or seek out each other at the front door.[8] These shelters, consisting of a concrete slab as a seat topped off with a steel roof, are a fundamental attribute. They are popular when it rains but most of all when it is very sunny. They are used before and after school but also during the infants' playtime as an oasis of certainty in the vast expanse of playground.

113

114

115

Petersschule, Basle, Switzerland [116-119]
Hannes Meyer and Hans Jakob Wittwer, 1926

This competition design for an eleven-class girls' school in the old centre of Basle close by St Peter's Church is one of the icons of Modern Architecture, most importantly through the legendary perspective drawing (drawn by Paul Klee, the story has it).

Of course it is the terrace cantilevering an astonishing distance into space that dominates the otherwise fairly low-pitched block, its blatantly exhibitionistic construction presenting a brazen contrast with the lethargic rural surroundings in which it has been placed.

What first appears to be a spectacular if fairly redundant canopy was intended, according to the design report, as addi-tional outdoor territory above a ground plane without recreation space. It was to be a hanging terrace where children could play, leaving the ground-level space free as public space. Although this seemingly free-floating cantilever roof would unquestion-ably have produced an incomparable spatial sensation, that could not have been the principal intention. All in all it seems that Hannes Meyer, unhindered by a none too great capacity for architectural expression, was mainly concerned with what were then regarded as the basic conditions for better education and the role of the school build-ing in this endeavour. His was a strictly orthodox stance, more severe even than his Dutch colleague and friend Mart Stam. The issues that preoccupied him were the more down-to-earth ones like good lighting in the classrooms, and he may perhaps have been the first to call for a more scientific approach and objectivity in school architec-ture. It is interesting, then, how this show of unquestioning faith in the potential of modern technology should so spectacularly, and for us inexplicably, overshoot the mark in economic terms.

Hannes Meyer is the last person you would expect to find indulging in such a light-hearted exercise. But even if a few square metres of outdoor space were merely a pre-text and inducement for this constructivist

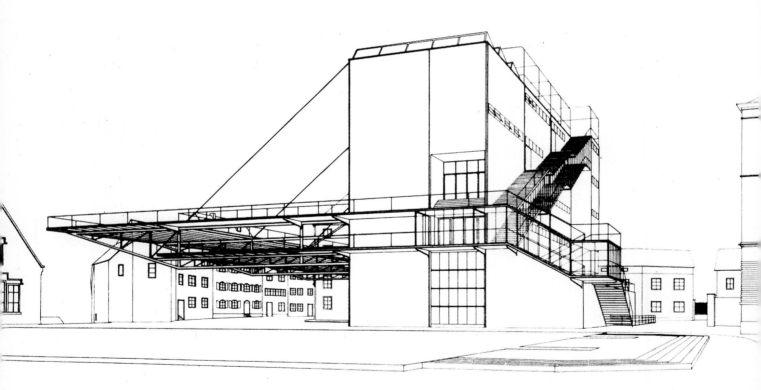

116

117

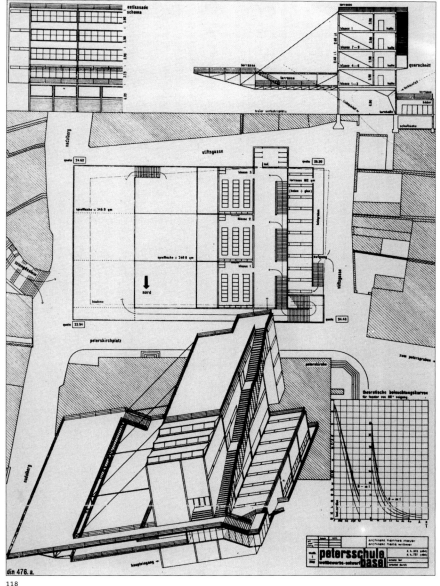

118

show of strength, it still means more than just the desire to impress. The first-hand influence of the Russian Constructivists is unmistakable, witness Ladovsky's restaurant (1922) suspended from the rock face and Lissitzky's Wolkenbügel ('cloud-hanger') project of 1924 and their gravity-defying cantilevers that sought to escape the earth-bound state that symbolized the established, traditional world.

Having said that, for all their utopian efforts to achieve primal conditions, these were monumental projects, be it more of an inverted monumentality.

The brash vitality and enthusiasm projected by the audacious and challenging construction of this school design evokes the image of a new world where the education is better, where there is more concern for child development, even though here it only gets as far as expressing more physical freedom. It was hardly to be expected that this design, so outspokenly critical of the traditional environment, would win the competition. Its message had too much of a threat about it.

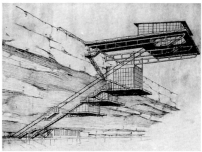

119

La Maison Suspendue/The Suspended House [120-123]
Paul Nelson, 1936-38

Nelson regarded this design for a 'house of the future' as a study into how you might combine industrial means into a *machine à vivre* in the footsteps of many at that time including Le Corbusier, Buckminster Fuller, Eileen Gray, Pierre Chareau and Jean Prouvé. The idea was that 'prefabricated functional space units, independent and changeable, were suspended within an interior space formed by a fixed external envelope, creating their own interior volumes and ever varying spaces'.[9]

The message was that autonomous, industrially fabricated units, each with its own particular form and accessible along ramps thrusting through space, really could be replaced.

The various components of the house hang as more or less free-floating objects in the space of the box/container defined by the outer walls, leaving the space of the house virtually intact. This keeps the ground floor entirely free, with no columns or other 'obstacles'.

This design presents a new notion of space, a *plan libre* enacted not between fixed floors but in a box where complete freedom prevails, not just in the length and breadth but heightwise too.

Within the periphery of this box the greatest possible spatial freedom obtains. Yet this is determined unequivocally by that periphery. It is a world of its own, so to speak, bounded and inward-looking, unrelated to what is outside it. Gravity seems to have been suspended in this internal world, and the hovering structures of El Lissitzky have to all intents and purposes become reality. Here tectonics are irrelevant, unless we call it a negative tectonics. This extraterrestrial fairytale has its own laws – and that is exactly where the container's limitations lie. When all is said and done, it is, when seen from the outside, simply an object into which you can retreat from the world in *a space* masquerading as *space*.

Inside, you are unaware that gravity is being taken care of by the large joists which, invisible from inside the container, convey the weight of the suspended units to earth. It seems as though Nelson took Chareau's Maison de Verre as the model for this project. That house too consists basically of one extremely tall space with movable elements

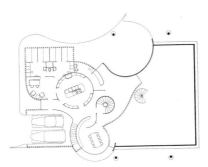

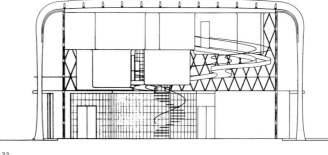

122

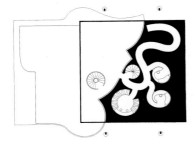

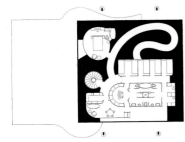

121

of a 'technical' resonance. Incidentally, there the constructivist columns are generally speaking not in the way. It too is an inward-looking internal world scarcely penetrated by the world outside.

All we know of the Maison Suspendue is the intriguing model (in the MoMA in New York) made, as it happens, by the same Dalbet without whom Chareau and Bijvoet's dream would never have become reality. Today, the notion of autonomous components, set freely in a kind of aquarium like fish fixed in place (and the negative of a scooped-out mass), linked by walkways freely cutting through space, is as topical as ever and keeps reappearing in designs in countless variants.

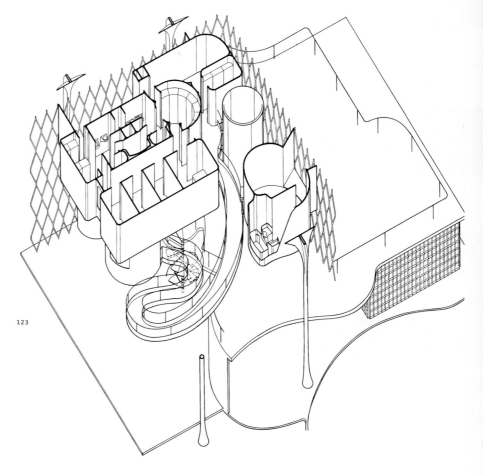

123

University centre, Malmö, Sweden [124-134]

The competition brief for restructuring the university in Malmö called for a clearly legible centre sited at a distinctive spot in the city, on the water. This prompted us to design a roofed city plaza that would be used as evidently by the university community as by the city. The two have something to offer each other when it comes to social life. As a sheltered plaza it is the ideal place for university celebrations and parties and, as a public place, every bit as perfect for non-university purposes.

The form of the double-folded plane spells out the idea in no uncertain terms, though it can be elaborated in widely diverse ways. This main shape may be construed as an outline sketch, an intelligible and evocative rendering of the basic idea, a frame for possible interpretations. The folded shape expresses the intentions and potentials as an ideogram, without endowing these with a fixed form.

Everything inside the enclosed space belongs to the university, though the built

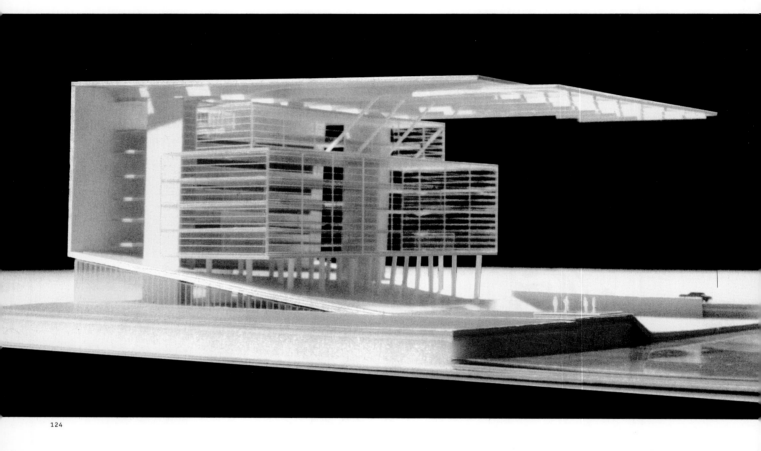

124

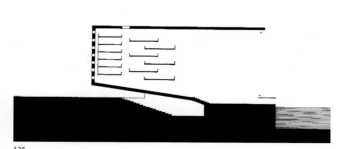

125

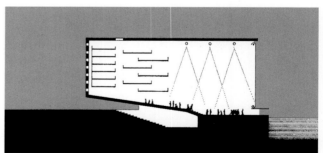

126

space is as yet free, qualitatively and quantitatively. Equally open to interpretation is the eventual look of the sloping plane mediating between the 'building' and the plaza; whether it will have stairs as in a monumental entrance, like tiers of seats, or be terraced or raked.

Beneath this sloping plane there is leftover space facing outwards because of the form, that is, resolutely averted from the plaza. A form that shuts in, inevitably shuts out also. This space faces onto the street, automatically precluding it from belonging to the university – an urbanistic certainty that just this form can deliver.

Here the concept determines not just a spatial envelope and a zoning into territories but dictates the urbanistic capabilities of the place: i.e. its competence.

The pre-eminent example for such a plaza because of its unsurpassed attractions under differing circumstances is the Rockefeller Plaza in New York. There the spatial

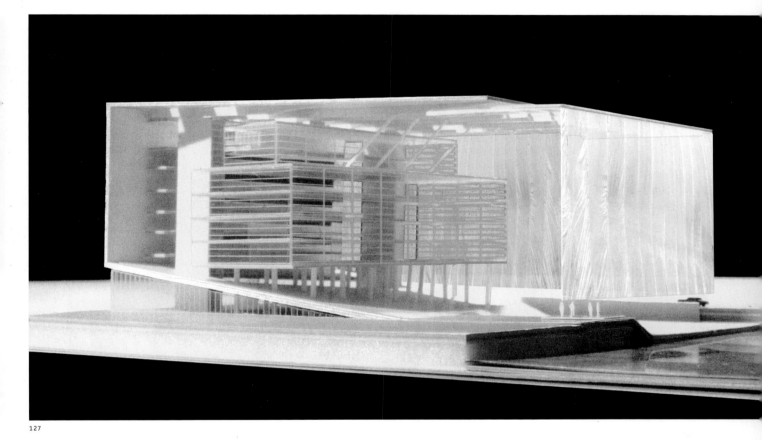

127

128 Rockefeller Plaza, New York

129 Columbia University, New York. Library steps

conditions are the main reason for its intensive use, particularly in the winter.[10]

The great roof juts far out over the plaza to protect it like a giant umbrella. Its accommodation is both practical and symbolic, bringing light to the inhospitable climate up north with its chilly, early darkness and lacking everything that draws life outside in the Mediterranean zone. There are cables to erect canvas walls from the sides of the roof so as to transmute the plaza into a 'room' of urban dimensions screened off from wind and weather. Looking like a giant circus tent or a miniature roofed stadium, this urban room can, in its role of theatre or sports hall, do duty as an occasional city centre.

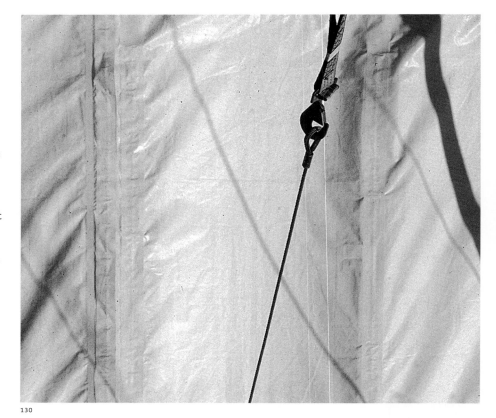

130

131

132

133

134

Guggenheim Museum, New York [135-137]
Frank Lloyd Wright, 1943-59

The form of this late work by the master
has often been criticized, mostly for its
exterior resembling a giant kitchen appli-
ance. There has been negative criticism,
too, of the almost naive and simplistic
manner of conveying the spectators by
means of a spiral past the collection, so
that the surface under your feet is always
sloping. Yet in one respect at least, this
concept is unsurpassed, namely in the way
the circling ramp winds as an open gallery
through the full-height void giving a constantly changing view of both the artworks
and the people across from you. This gives
you a foretaste of what is to come as well
as an unbroken view of the other visitors.
It is hard to imagine a space form that
offers those in it a better overall view of
everyone else.

It is this gradual change in level, and the
absence of separate floors as distinct units,
that transforms the ground plane into an
unbroken expanse, its spiral shape going
on to generate minimum visual distances
and maximum visual angles.

If the intention of the *promenade architecturale* is lacking here in the sense that by
being continuous the space does not essentially change, it lays all the more emphasis
on the succession of paintings and people.

135

136

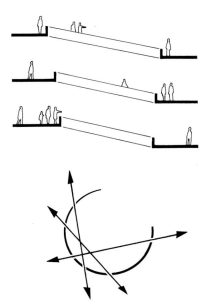

137

Hong Kong and Shanghai Bank, Hong Kong [138-146]
Norman Foster, 1981-86

Norman Foster's Hong Kong Bank is most celebrated for its perfect finish. This 'most expensive building of the past century' was more instrumental than any other in setting the tone for the new smooth-tech detailing that would conquer the world. Just as interesting, however, is the public throughfare beneath the building which ensures that it does not simply take up space but that the major part of the ground floor is traversable and thus still part of the public domain and a link in the pedestrian route through the city.

Obstinate and aloof though the building may be as regards the details, the internal organization broadly speaking is dictated by the public underpass, urbanistically in other words. The construction is fully attuned to the fact that the ground floor could remain columnless and assume the scale of an urban plaza. This was expressed visually in the constructivist configuration of trusses that gives the building its distinctive appearance.

Follow the underpass through the building and you can look up through its immense belly of billowing glass skin into the cathedral-like atrium space above, bounded by open galleries of offices. Originally it seems the idea was to leave this space entirely unglazed and open on the underside, that is, to the outside world. Then the interior would have literally been made part of the city, but even the most state-of-the-art fire brigade would be adamant about such flamboyant gestures. Likewise the public entrance, which in most such buildings grabs the attention in no uncertain fashion and demands positioning up front, ended up confined to an escalator which – the height of informality this – casually gets under way in the public realm on the ground floor. This takes up almost no room and contributes to keeping the plaza beneath the building free and open. On entering the building, you reach a reception area on a central platform at the end of the atrium. The traditional Chinese practice of Feng Shui stipulated the seemingly random angle at which this escalator stabs through the glass skin indiscriminately and apparently unaware of the impact it is making.

138

The gently sloping underpass with its spectacular view upwards and the entrance deprived of every sliver of monumentality combine in a eye-popping spatial sensation. This adds an explicitly accessible, urban dimension to the building's aspect of unassailable exclusiveness. And all that, when to draw up the bridge to this fortress of finance and power merely requires closing off a single escalator.

139

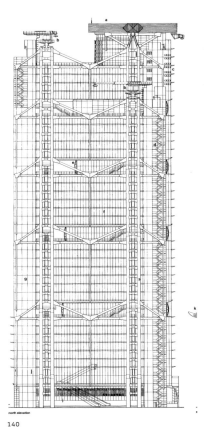

140
north elevation

141

142

143

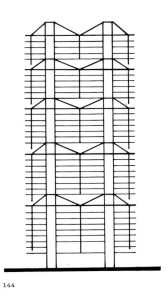

144

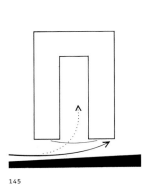

145

146

Bari Stadium, Italy [147-150]
Renzo Piano, 1994

Stadiums have remained essentially the same formwise since the days of the Roman amphitheatres. The content and substance of the games may have changed greatly, but their aim is still to gather in the greatest number of people in the closest proximity to each other and to what is being enacted. Sight lines and maximum distances are the key limiting conditions to achieve this aim, which usually results in practically the same form and roughly the same dimensions each time.

Basically speaking, the deeper a particular form is engraved in our 'tradition' the less reason there seems to be to change it, or rather the more difficult it is to see reasons for doing so.

In general, modernizing stadiums is a question of secondary changes, meaning that these will have little effect on the main shape. (With the technical advances at our disposal we can expect the trend to roof off the entire structure to continue, certainly where the chance of rain stopping play might put business interests at risk.)

The Bari Stadium, built for the 1994 World Cup, stands in the open, ancient landscape like a spaceship recently landed from another planet.

Seen from the inside, it consists of an enormous dish horizontally articulated in two portions leaving a large slit enabling visual contact with the outside world and, in

147

148

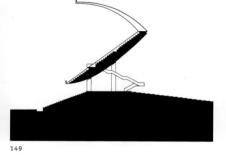

149

150

principle, views from outside of the activities in the stadium.

Thus, inside and outside worlds remain in touch, generating a degree of visual contact without parallel on such a vast scale. Another extraordinary feature one never comes across in stadiums is the way this large-scale horizontal articulation divides the structure, as it were, into a section dug into the ground and, held clear of this, a supplementary rising composition of stands.

By applying the principle of articulation not only horizontally but vertically, the public, which in stadiums takes on almost terrifyingly massive proportions, is split up among separate petal-shaped galleries. This reduces, practically as well as psychologically, what would otherwise be a perpetually uncontrollable number to more manageable units.

This articulation principle is understand-

ably carried through to the system of entrances and exits. It is when crowds of spectators are on the move that their sheer mass most effectively suppresses individual movements. So a system of decentralized exits, with all of its parts clearly in view, is the ideal solution for alleviating the intensity at such times.

Escalator in Musée Georges Pompidou, Paris [151-152]
Renzo Piano and Richard Rogers, 1977

151

This building was conceived as a gigantic container where all facilities normally found inside are shifted to the exterior, the few obstacles left inside not being enough to hamper exhibitions of any kind. The recent internal remodelling, as it happens, has regrettably impaired this pellucid concept. The building is entered by way of a hanging system of escalators in a tube whose course takes in the full length of the building. This mode of entry, as if on a conveyor belt and thus compelled by one's fellow passengers to stand still as if in a lift, takes place alongside the building, on its exterior, in a glass pipe serving every floor and each of whose branches is in effect an individual entrance to the building.

In the tube there is no sense of being outside, nor indeed of being inside. It is to all intents and purposes a single elongated entry zone of urban scale that conveys you through the city. Should your more or less enforced stay in the tube – unlike in, say, a train – give rise to feelings of claustrophobia, then this feeling is more than made up for by the magnificent view. Transcending the street space as you rise ever higher, a panoramic prospect of the city unfolds before you in a spatial experience that has few equals.

152

Roof of Unité d'Habitation, Marseilles, France [153-162]
Le Corbusier, 1946-52

The idea behind the Unités, which Le Corbusier first designed for Marseilles and later for Nantes, Berlin, Friminy and Brey en Forêt, is that they are in a sense self-supporting, like a residential district but stacked. This aspect is best expressed by incorporating a shopping street (which incidentally has only recently begun functioning properly) and by the active use of the roof. It is these elements that give the Unité the aspect of a ship and make all other blocks of flats seem emasculated, aimless structures.

The roof of the Unité in Marseilles is like a ship's deck with a difference; a recreation area for the entire community and perhaps the occasional architecture tourist.

On this roof, far away from the clamour of the city now closely hugging the building, a tranquil, almost Elysian atmosphere prevails, where the residents and particularly the children are drawn to the small paddling pool to sunbathe as if on some faraway arcadian beach.

It is astonishing how this all-concrete landscape – coloured only at odd places with glass mosaic, such as in and around the pool, a great grey sculpture without plants or other palliative additions – can exude such a mild and generous air.[11]

This roofscape is quite unlike anything else except perhaps certain other superb roof gardens of Le Corbusier's mostly designed as part of a private house, the first being at Maison La Roche in 1923. There are habitable roofs to be found wherever the climate permits but these are always part of the private domain. Here, then, is a new type of communal space with something of the grandeur mostly found in privately kept and managed gardens and courtyards but now for the full use of all residents.

The architect's efforts to make each component at once sculptural and useful can be read at every scale: the broad, flat, rounded edges of the paddling pool, just right for children; the exceedingly deep seats in which you can safely snuggle, the curving free-standing walls for dressing and undressing behind, the sloping surface

153

154 Udaipur, India

155 Oil sheiks, United Arab Emirates

156

157

158

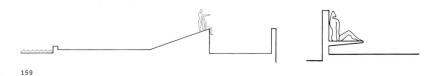

159

160

with its additional height giving an unhampered view on all sides over the extremely tall parapet surrounding the roof.

All these facilities and the form they are given attest to an abiding attention to the inviting nature of the form which for Le Corbusier always automatically takes pride of place before its sculptural expression. Hanging above his workbench was a large illustration: the legendary idyllic photograph of this concrete landscape that must 162 have constantly served him as a criterion: a naive expression of hope and utterly opposed to today's almost cynical lack of faith in what architecture can mean to people.

Buildings like the Unité configured as vertical housing estates have already become an architectural and urbanistic phenomenon that claims the attention of each new generation of architects, the overriding concern being whether it really is possible to organize a single building into a urban fragment. Yet a truly revolutionary discovery is the idea of a roof acting as an alternative ground floor and communal garden, and the way this roof/ground is unmistakably fitted out with buildings of its own that fully extinguish the sense of being on top of another, larger building.

Though the Unité is a building whose autonomous form and colossal dimensions irrevocably sets it apart from its surroundings, the downplayed ground floor activating the shopping street halfway up and more particularly the roof endows it with qualities of landscape. Were it to be incorporated as a megaform in the landscape 568-569 like the Roman aqueducts or Alfonso Reidy's 571, 573 residential megastructure its objectness would disappear. It may be too big as we know it, but it might equally well be too small.

161

162

'White City', Tel Aviv, Israel [163-170]
Patrick Geddes, 1925

The expansive residential area in the centre of Tel Aviv known as the White City is marked by an unimaginable number of rectangular houses, miniature urban villas of three to five storeys in blocks six metres apart in a supremely homogeneous development.

This homogeneity is further enhanced by the incomparable unity of their modern architecture, born in the early Thirties of a rare like-mindedness among architects such as Arieh Sharon, Ze'ev Rechter and Dov Carmi, educated at the Bauhaus before emigrating to what was then Palestine. Although no individual masterworks spring to mind, together they managed to generate a remarkable quality. This is largely owing to the strongly sculptural effect, the harmony of the many windows, balconies and flat roofs sporting roof gardens, and the reduced ground floor levels where freestanding columns predominate.

The coherent architectural effect among so much substance strengthens the urbanistic idea whose quality is at least as outstanding. Patrick Geddes had already spent many years in India working on various urban design schemes, for New Delhi among others, when he was approached by the British authorities to draw up a plan for Tel Aviv, rapidly swelling as a result of the by then steady flow of immigrants. Completed in 1925, the scheme attests to an exceptional urbanistic vision that has in no way lost its power over the years. Even the overwhelming

163

increase in motorized traffic, which laid low all other schemes of that period, was absorbed here with a minimum of effort. Geddes with his garden-city background

164

165

166

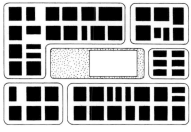

167

must have envisaged more for the gardens now receding for the traffic, as well as for the 'free' ground floor now stuffed with cars parked between the columns. Yet although the gardens have since been sacrificed in part, there are trees in abundance and it is these that define the unity of built development and architecture as well as that of the urban design.

Geddes' plan divides up the area with main thoroughfares set more or less at right angles to each other in what amounts to a gridiron. Rather than ceasing abruptly, the pattern locks pliantly into the surroundings, its lack of severity presumably intended to generate the greatest difference

between quadrants. In a deliberate move, its streets are less east-west oriented and square to the coastline than parallel to it, giving rise to oblong quadrants running north-south. This meant that many more houses could be east-west aligned to maximum advantage. Though this in itself illustrates Geddes' sound insight, he went on to dimension the quadrants so as to allow for an inner ring of housing back to back with the outer, and enfolding an open area for community purposes. The dimensioning of unit depth, front and back gardens and street channels was done with great sensitivity and a fine focus. Every centimetre of ground was used to the full and clearly assigned as either private or public. Private gardens round the houses were not regarded as additions but as essential components, and Geddes must have had great expectations of the paradise the residents would make of it. For one thing, he explicitly prohibited the use of fences between the gardens. Access from the inner ring and the central clearing is gained by way of a staggered system of secondary roads so

168

169

170

attached to the primary street pattern as to prevent them being used for taking short cuts. Unlike the 'mainways' these 'home-ways' were made as narrow as possible so as to preserve the enclosure of the 'home blocks'.

Although this entire part of the city consists almost exclusively of free-standing single- and multi-family blocks, the whole has an unmistakably urbane character. There is nothing to recall a villa park and despite the abundance of green space between buildings the sense of city blocks persists. This is undoubtedly the consequence of strictly maintained building lines and the relatively small space between the

blocks. The result is an urbanistic response as surprising as it is unique, whose impact is enhanced by the supreme homogeneity of its architecture. But the plan's quality is first and foremost owing to Geddes' idealism. He managed to implement his utopian mentality, seemingly without undue compromise, pairing a moralistic patriarchal British colonialism with an undiscerning ardour for this new idealistic state where arguably anything was possible. And the fact that the result is still functioning well after seventy-five years only proves that this is urban design of real distinction.

Maisons à Gradins [171-179]
Henri Sauvage, ca. 1908

If the formal idiom wielded by Henri Sauvage (1873-1932) is nineteenth-century
through and through, his urbanistic enthusiasm for the 'stepped house' (*maison à
gradins*) makes him a bona fide twentieth-
century urbanist. Even before 1908, the
time of Tony Garnier's Cité Industrielle, and
long before the revolutionary proposals to
reorganize cities by Le Corbusier and others,
Sauvage had been preoccupied with the
idea of stacking dwelling units in a stepwise
configuration so that all would possess a
full-width terrace.

Unlike Le Corbusier and all the others who
claimed to open up the city by abolishing
the traditional street pattern, Sauvage's
residential pyramids respect the perimeter
block as the basic premiss while the stepped

171

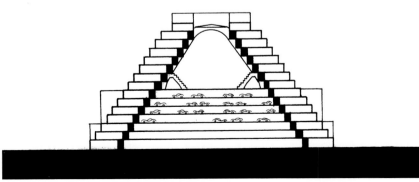

172

front facades give the streets more space
for air and light.

This shift backwards is made at the expense
of the space inside the blocks, including
the private gardens, transforming it into a
hollow cavity, the belly or rather 'interior'
of the block, beneath the slopes of housing.
This is the price paid for the openness
gained on the outside. At first Sauvage was
at a loss as to what to do with these cav-
ernous interiors, and could only suggest a
swimming pool, as evidenced by his second
project built to this principle in the rue de
Amireaux (Paris, 1922). Time would have
proved him right given the explosive growth
in the number of cars requiring ever more
parking space; this interior would have been
ideal for the purpose. Though he only lived
to see the very beginning of this development, he had proposed as early as 1928 that
his residential pyramids be filled with parking structures, in those days a truly vision-
ary solution undoubtedly fuelled by his
irrepressible urge to convince the world
that his ideas made sense.

That aspect that has changed in the block
as a whole can be found to inform the
apartments individually too. The tiers of
balconies over the full width of each apartment endow it with a villa-like quality, and
even with a building height far outreaching
the seven floors customary for Paris there
will be no undue sense of great mass.

173

Likewise, what was gained on the outside at the expense of the inside applies equally to the apartments. Their rear side is entirely blankwalled, so that they are oriented in one direction only, with no possibility of being compensated by sunlighting at the rear as in a traditional block.

Sauvage's concept lays emphasis on the spacious 'outdoor rooms' for all apartments built as more or less autonomous units onto a kind of mountain slope. This way he avoids the plight of many apartment blocks built later which all too often have the horrifying aspect of storage systems. Moreover the street profiles widen as they ascend, without the disadvantage of the aloofness typifying the tombstone cities built since.

The two built projects in the rue Vavin (1912) and rue des Amireaux (1922), however interesting they are as a sample, fail to evoke the radical image of the city that 177-178 Sauvage had in mind. In that respect, 'les gratte ciel', a much larger project built in 174-176 1932 to a design by Morice Leroux, is inter-179 esting in its closeness to Sauvage's dream. Sited in Villeurbanne near Lyons, it allows one to experience the stepped street profile in reality, making all the more clear the quality of the public realm that Sauvage must have envisaged. Here it is only the private terraces on the upper floors that are really worthwhile, and even then most of these are not what they might have been. Yet it proves that the concept is clearly capable of generating a first-rate street. In a complementary sense it shows the achievement of Sauvage's concept for the public realm.

174

175

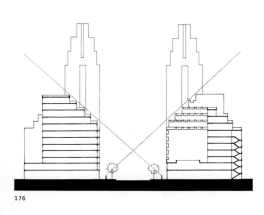
176

177

178

179

Centraal Beheer (a workplace for 1000 people), Apeldoorn (1968-72)
[180-187]

At the end of the Sixties it was bound to happen that something of the emancipatory waves then cleansing Dutch society of the conventions that had been bogging it down, would rub off on something as formal as an office building. The row upon row of neat little rooms to either side of endless corridors no longer fitted the bill, if only because of the emergent more open collaborative networks as were being etched in ever sharper profile in the then new forms of organization. We called it 'a workplace for a thousand people'; away with those corridors and rabbit hutches!

It became one great horizontal expanse, where everyone has their place in a 'settlement' of tower-like units – more a city than a building.

Instead of rooms, groups of up to four users share open balcony-like working platforms that overlook one another across a common void extending throughout the complex. The square 'towers' assemble like buildings in a city ordered by a gridiron with views through and thus to all sides. This 'building', an entity subdivided into smaller buildings, is no unambiguous volume but an open structure, a three-dimensional grid where the internal/external relationship is fundamentally confused: you are in fact neither inside nor outside but in a permanent state of transition.

180

181

If this complex impacts on the world outside as a collection of towers standing in serried ranks, inside it comes across as a honeycomb of spaces. These towers are strung together by the basic structure, the spatial skeleton that holds it all in place, all the while acting as the periphery of the internal spaces, the 'negatives' of the towers, so to speak, but then shifted half a phase horizontally in respect to the basic structure.

Just as the towers and cruciform spaces are each other's negative, so the glazed 'streets' holding the towers clear of one another and pouring light into the internal spaces are the negative of the basic structure. Outward appearance and inward spatiality are a transformation of each other, illustrating a metamorphosis from volume to space and vice versa. This circumstance of spatial equality does much to stimulate anti-hierarchic use. So the directors, instead of having their own contained rooms, merely have slightly more chic furniture and more surface area at their disposal. The upshot is that ranks and positions in the company are scarcely if ever expressed in spatial terms. As a visual experience the openness of the system has something almost exhibitionistic about it. It demonstrates how spatiality is the pre-eminent means for expressing a sense of solidarity. Since 1972 the company has undergone great changes both socially and organizationally with appropriate modifications within the building – both the clothing of the personnel and the materials of the upholstery have been spruced up considerably in those thirty years. Miraculously, though, the built structure has in fact remained unchanged. The tree has merely

183

182

183

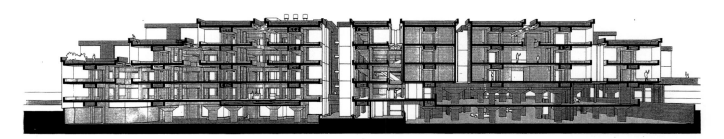

184

185

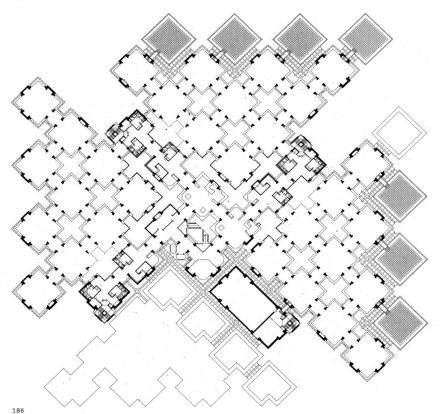

186

exchanged its foliage, and not for the last time either.

THE BASIC PREMISS[12]

We have to build a workplace. This workplace is to accommodate a thousand people for five days a week, eight hours a day. This means that for five days a week they are spending half their waking life in the workplace; they are, on average, longer at the office than at home. This means that the 'builders' are obliged to make a place of work where a thousand people can feel at home. They must have the sensation of being part of a working community without the feeling of sheer numbers taking over.

VARIABLE AND EXPANDIBLE

In a company like Centraal Beheer modifications are the order of the day. Some departments get bigger, others decrease and there is always the possibility of having to expand the complex as a whole. The building should be capable of taking up all such internal forces while continuing to function on all fronts.

This is not so when the building is a fixed organism with a predetermined form. This

187

is why we sought to achieve a 'building order' that is in a perpetual state of emergence and yet always complete.

This means that change can be experienced as a permanent situation. Because the building as a system remains in a balanced state, i.e. keeps functioning, every component should be able to fulfil another role in each new circumstance. Each component, theoretically, should be able to take on the role of every other.

The building, designed as ordered expansion, consists of:
1 a basic structure that impacts throughout as an immutable zone, and, complementing it,
2 a variable, interpretable zone.

Office landscape or large articulated space?
Two main types clearly present themselves as examples among designed or existing office buildings:
a the traditional rabbit-hutch system with displaceable partitions
b the extremely large office space (*Bürogroßraum, Bürolandschaft*) enabling desks and cabinets to be arranged in complete freedom.

The advantages of the latter over the traditional system should be obvious.
1 *Flexibility*: the arrangement can be adapted to suit every conceivable reorganization without recourse to hammers or even screwdrivers.
2 *Better contact*: communication is made easier because everything stays in one space. No psychological thresholds to cross, and greater flexibility in conveying information.
3 *The sense of togetherness*: a division into compartments as in the traditional system only tends to separate office workers. Being together in a single space rules out the feeling of being cut off from everyone else. It is even not unthinkable that in a communal workspace a sense of togetherness will emerge.
4 *Anti-hierarchy*: in the traditional system a hierarchy obtains around what it means to have one's own room, the number of bays that room occcupies, whether it has a rug, and so forth. In point of fact all that these artificial differences do is CREATE DISTANCE.

In a communal workplace this can be replaced by a classification better suited to a modern company.

CREATING DISTANCE IS
ANTI-COMMUNICATION
Thresholds between those giving orders and those taking them can be frustrating, as much for the work as for the people. Looked at this way, extremely large office spaces prove to have advantages that also appeal greatly to Centraal Beheer, judging from the discussions had with all categories and members of staff. At least, when the considerable technical difficulties brought by large workspaces can be resolved.

These problems are:
1 *preventing noise nuisance*: One discussion should not disrupt another. It should be as impossible to overhear others as it is to be overheard yourself.
2 *making an acceptable artificial lighting system*: As daylight is only able to enter extremely large spaces at the periphery such a space is entirely dependent on artificial lighting. This will have a considerable bearing on the ambience in the space.
3 *sufficient views out*: What holds for interior daylighting is equally true of views out. The general preference for a place at the window in a traditional type of office seems largely ascribable to the need for views out (contact with the outside world) so as not to feel shut away.
4 *environmental control*: Ventilating extremely large workspaces is still only possible with the aid of some or other form of air-conditioning, the main problem being that of the thermal load that complete dependence on artificial lighting brings.

Even assuming that these problems can be solved, extremely large office spaces still have certain not inconsiderable disadvantages attached that need to be acknowledged, disadvantages that cannot be solved by technical means.

1 *the massification effect*: Though the idea of 'massification' is difficult to define and is often splashed about regardless, we all have some idea of what is meant by it. Everyone can be observed by everyone else: 'You're never alone for a second'. For most people it is difficult to be themselves in an

environment which continually calls for adopting an attitude. The greater freedom of action inherent in a greater flexibility mainly concerns the organization, in other words the work. Whether this greater freedom has anything to offer the people who have to do the work is doubtful. They may have more freedom in choosing where they sit and the position of their desk, but there is no question of a genuine choice: the bill of fare has not changed essentially and will still taste the same! The problem we have touched upon here is – now that the social aspect clearly has the upper hand – that of our individuality coming under fire. The work is under threat too, for those who now have trouble concentrating are going to find themselves experiencing even greater difficulties in that respect.

2 *the sardines-in-a-tin syndrome*: There is absolutely nothing stopping us from keeping those desks and cabinets coming until the workplace is jammed solid, with suffocation a real option. We may well roundly condemn this as the wrong way to proceed, yet when it comes to the crunch there is nothing more natural than to keep putting off that long overdue extension.

THE LARGE ARTICULATED SPACE
At Centraal Beheer our aim was to achieve a large space, in principle without dividing walls but also lacking the drawbacks listed above.
We began from the assumption that to attain complete flexibility means paying the price in other respects. Besides, only limited use will be made of that flexibility in the long run. However you organize it, the users will simply keep on working in groups which in terms of size are going to remain within certain limits.

The building coordinator of Centraal Beheer, W.M. Jansen, took this work hypothesis as a basis for a study he made of the company that provided us with stepping-off points of relevance to our brief.
Proceeding from three concepts – *work situation, social group, functional group* – it became clear that the great number, seemingly amorphous and elusive by being activated at every reorganization, is in fact quite clearly composed of groups which in reality will change little whatever that reorganization may be.

This departure-point we then translated into floor units. The primary unit is 3 × 3m, corresponding with a group of 1, 2, 3 and 4 persons plus the equipment they need for the job. Four such units provided with circulation space and supplementary facilities constitute an 'island'. This can in principle accommodate four basic groups (maximum: 16 persons) as follows:

4	4
4	4

On average an island will contain 12 persons, for example:

3	3	4	3	4	1
3	3	3	2	3	4

The designed office spaces consist of many such islands, each with a surface area of 9 × 9m, set side by side and joined by 'bridges'. The areas between the islands are either open – meaning open contact with the level below – or a continuation of the floor surface. In other words these islands may be free-standing or 'frozen together'.
The open areas (voids) between the free-standing islands have the following consequences:
1 They give a strong feeling of alliance with those working on higher or lower storeys. In fact it adds a dimension to the *Bürogroßraum* concept; the *sense* of working together in a single large workplace becomes *reality*.
2 Lacking the possibility of being crowded out with desks, thereby ruling out the sardines-in-a-tin scenario, these voids possess a margin that ensures an element of breathing space. In principle it is structurally possible to fill in these floors later. This would, however, bring back the danger of reaching saturation point. The fact that this always requires alterations usually means in practice that such steps are only taken after the most careful consideration – also, one must assume, of the obvious drawbacks involved. So potentially, then, this margin can be transformed into useful floor area, but not as a consequence of uncontrolled growth.
3 The space will be strongly articulated in part through the system of columns. Besides, this articulation, based as we have seen upon a structure of functional and social groups, coincides with the 'articulation' of its users.

The more floors there are that continue uninterrupted (or were filled in later), the closer the space becomes to the aforementioned type of the extremely large space. And yet there remains an essential difference, namely the presence of the built structure, particularly the relatively many columns – of hefty dimensions too – which continue to define the primary surface units and have a catalysing effect on how the seating is grouped.
Other than one would expect, the presence of many columns increases rather than diminishes the choice of possible groupings.

Villa VPRO, Hilversum [188-196]
MVRDV, 1993-97

At last a breakthrough on the office-building front which, too long entrenched in its position of supposed efficiency and representation, continued to perfect materials and constructions but spatially remained bogged down in a paradigm of the most favourable ratio of net to gross floor surface area.

The new building for the VPRO broadcasting organization is a villa in the sense that no two square metres are the same. Every single cliché in office architecture and organization has been knocked away except one, the system of columns. This has remained as an unnoticed, almost rudimentary relic from a distant past, and it really is the only traditional system that keeps some control over this unruly design. There is no orderly stacking of floors, much less anything resembling repetitive units within the concrete frame. This building is like an element of untamed nature evolving before your very eyes as an unbroken space extending throughout the entire volume of the building. Views through and vistas yield one surprise after another. Countless thrill-giving moments, such as crossing a gorge over a mock-rickety bridge or ascending and descending the hilly landscape of floors, lead one a merry dance during this spatial voyage of discovery.

The order of this building is almost systematic in its diversity; anything is possible, and there are indeed plenty of surprises in store. That each of the various technical 'layers' satisfies its own intrinsic rationality can be read off from the drawn analysis which charts each system individually. In their built form, however, they manifest themselves as a complex superimposition that reveals nothing of the order prevailing over the various components. (It is the reverse of a score of a musical work in many parts whose individual voices only make sense when sounded together.)

Leaving aside the withdrawn boardrooms, the usable space of the building unfolds as a hilly, uneven variant upon the type of office landscape conceived in the late Fifties (though it can be seen to a limited degree as far back as Frank Lloyd Wright's Larkin Building and Johnson Wax Administration

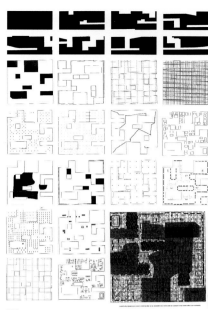

188

Building). In the Villa VPRO the operative words are snugness, conviviality, tumult and communication. This single flowing workspace is unbridled and exuberant, with a kasbah-like feel to it and seeming to lack order. It takes to heart the modernist credo that anything not only can but also should be done.

189

190

191

192

193

It must be said that the 'landscape' or (better still) 'nature' metaphor is only applicable within the confines of the orthogonally cropped block whose section reveals the innards in its periphery, the way blocks of stone hewn from a rock face reveal their layers at the cut surface. There is nothing here to suggest that the building mixes into its surroundings; it is more like a slice of landscape in the sense of a demonstration model or sample. This is also the case with OMA's Educatorium in Utrecht whose entire anatomy is best seen from the street.

Here in Hilversum the exterior is quite literally a haphazard slice through the curved, folded, perforated interior. What we see from the outside is no more than a 'random' aspect. Defined by its internal space and not by its outward appearance, it is a building where a sense of freedom and views out prevail. In this respect it is perpetuating a typical Dutch tradition.

578-580

A PLACE FOR THE VPRO [13]

Part one of the preliminary study named a parkland setting (Deelplan IV) as the best site for the Villa. Set in the grounds of the European Broadcast Facility Centre (NOB), it is an idyllic spot on a gentle slope in magnificent natural surroundings.

The zoning plan obtaining at the time provided the maximum permitted building line as well as a maximum height of 18 metres so as not to obscure from view the crest of a local hill (Hilversumse Heuvel).

This upper limit was defining for the roof of the new building. The area of natural landscape taken up by the Villa has been replaced by designing the roof as a field of heather: the ultimate garden of a house looking out over the landscape, the peatlands and the distant television tower. Beneath this roof are six 'layers', ramps and plateaus like a geological formation. A suc-

cession of routes winds through the building linking the roof with the park.

194

195

196

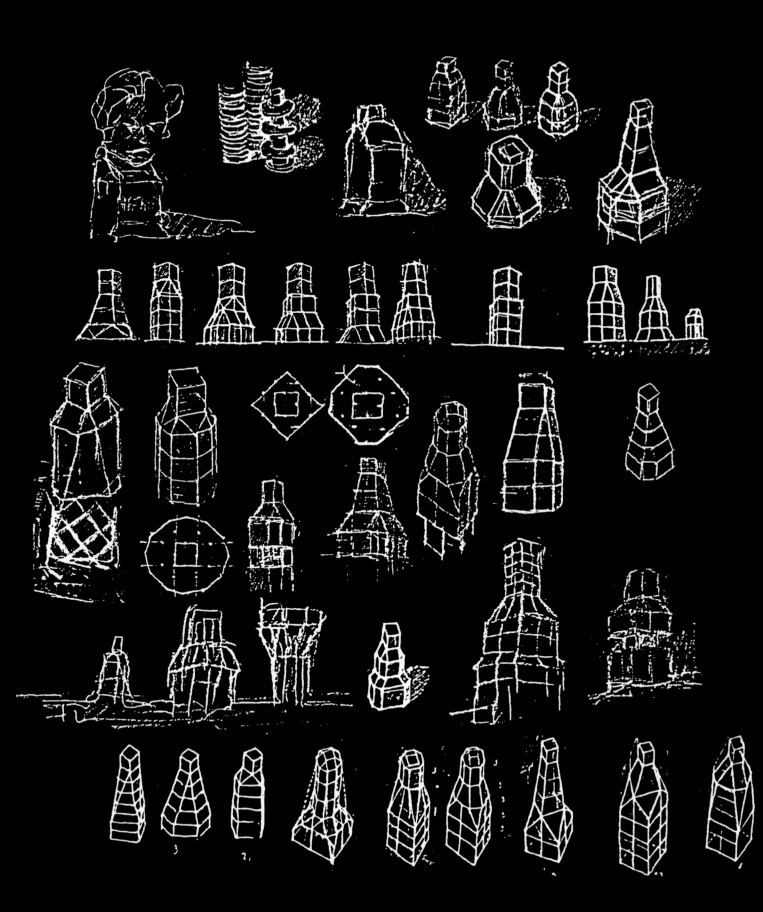

4

Space and Idea

■ THE GUIDING CONCEPT Architecture must be about some-thing other than just architecture. Just as the painter needs a subject, so too the architect needs to have something to say that rises above the obscure jargon that architects share with one another. But it must also rise above obediently following and implementing some brief. Many of our colleagues are happy when they manage to cram everything in, within the budget and within the site boundaries. Though this may be an achievement in itself, you cannot call it architecture yet. Moreover it is debatable whether anyone stands to benefit from it at this stage.

Often it seems to be something new but is in fact an age-old formula that appears new when looked at differently; the proverbial old wine in new bottles.

Actually every new design should by rights bring new spatial discoveries: exhilarating spatial ideas not encountered in that form before, in response to newly diagnosed conditions. You should be asking yourself each time what it is you really want, what idea – limited or expansive – you are trying to express. If this is a formal fabrication only, however interest-ing theoretically, is it of any good to anyone, and if so, in what way? Again, though, what is to be given up, sacrificed, what is to be gained and what lost and for whom? Inevitably, these questions imply what it is you in fact expect of archi-tecture, except perhaps instant fame.

On completing each design, you should once again ask your-self whether the result, despite all its efforts to look inter-esting, is indeed more than merely built output expressible in so many square (or cubic) metres of building; while there is nothing wrong with that, neither is it a reason to call it architecture, let alone art. This makes the self-satisfaction of architects about the import of their offerings more than a little disconcerting.

Every new step in architecture is premised on disarming and outspoken ideas that engender spatial discoveries: call them spatial concepts. A spatial concept is the way of articulating an idea in three-dimensional terms. It is only as clear as the idea that produced it. The more explicitly it is expressed, the more convincingly the architect's overall vision comes across. A concept can be defined as the more enduring structure for a more changeable 'infill'. It encapsulates all the essential features for conveying the idea, arranged in layers as it were and distinguished from all future elaborations as, say, an urbanistic idea, set down in a masterplan and interpreted at some later date by sundry architects each in their own way.

To concentrate the essence into a concept means summarizing in elementary form all the conditions of a particular task on a particular site as assessed and formulated by the architect. Trusting on the insight, sensibility and attention he accords the subject, the concept will be more layered, richer and abiding and not only admit to more interpretations but incite them too.

It is the conditions as they obtain for that particular task that foster the idea for a design and the concept distilled from it. Those conditions dictate that the end-product satisfies that idea and that its special qualities get expressed as 'hallmarks';

this way the idea encapsulates the DNA, so to speak, contain-ing the essence of the project and guiding the design process from start to finish. The concept, then, is the idea translated into space – the space of the idea, and bearer of the character traits of the product as these will emerge upon its develop-ment.

Designing, basically, is a question of finding the right (read appropriate) concept for the task at hand. But all too often concepts, however dazzling they may be in their own right, are dragged into the proceedings and pitched at the world with no thought given to whether the task in question has anything to gain from it.

Our work needs placing in the context of society, whether we like it or not, venturing beyond the safe haven of architecture where we designers together attach meaning and weight to formal inventions. Admittedly, things always look good in the country of the blind, but beyond its borders the takers are usu-ally few and far between. Genuine spatial discoveries never ensue from the mental cross-breeding in the small world of architecture. They have always been inspired by the wider hori-zon of society as a whole with its attendant cultural changes, whether or not incited by social and/or economic forces.

With each new task – and this implies components of a build-ing, each and every one of which can be regarded as a distinct task – you should always ask yourself what purpose it serves in society, what idea it represents and what, finally, is the issue it seeks to resolve.

You have to fathom out what is, and is not, required of a par-ticular task; which conditions are germane to it and which are not. You need the right species of animal, so to speak, that fits, or meets, those conditions that apply specifically to the task in question. Whether we are designing for savannahs with tall trees or for more swampy terrain will determine whether a giraffe or a crocodile is the most appropriate choice of beast. But architects are usually all for designing a giraffe for a wet-land region and a crocodile to keep the tall trees company. What conditions, we should be asking, form the immediate cause and the departure-point for the direction a design will take?

The assumption that an idea underlying a design needs to fit the task does not mean that the concept can be deduced from it. It all depends how you interpret the conditions. For spatial discoveries you have to move beyond the bounds of the task, in other words beyond the surveyable area, to be able to see this in a wider framework and then interpret it through induct-ive reasoning in its enlarged context.

The idea that points the design in a particular direction needs to be strong enough to free the task from the confines of its conditions and overcome the clichés entrenched in it.

It is important that the concept guides the elaboration of each distinct component if there is to be cohesion between the idea of the whole and that of the components. Every design of con-sequence presents a coherent narrative, built up as it is from components that have something to say individually and in con-cert rather than contradicting and counteracting each other.

Only by thinking through the project consistently and sensitively can the architect safeguard overall quality and prevent the design from being no more than a gimmick. Just think of the number of prize-winning competition designs, chosen for their sterling underlying concept, that come a cropper when fleshed out. What marks out a good architect is that his schemes only improve by being worked out in detail.

The eventual design is always an interpretation of the concept. Another designer would probably have made something else, as everyone has their own individual world of associations to throw at it.

A concept has to be challenging, must incite responses. It must leave room for multiple interpretations and say as little as possible about solutions in a formal sense, or about form, and concentrate all the more on the space.

Thinking in such proto-forms presupposes an abstraction towards the syntactic, such as pictograms which encapsulate the essence of a message. Concepts, then, are ideas expressed as three-dimensional ideograms.

In the practice of design, a guiding idea is seldom forthcoming right away. First it's noses to the grindstone on the strength of a few vague suspicions and only after persistent kneading of your material, and with a better overview of the field of conflict, do your objectives begin to assume shape. The biggest danger is that of the rash solution which you find yourself stuck with before you know it, a groove that is all too difficult to escape from. By contrast anything seems possible when drifting without a fixed course but it won't lead you anywhere.

The concept may be a compass, but it is hardly the final destination of the design process. The end-product can be nothing other than a development and interpretation of that concept, the way one might apply or render an overall vision. Thinking in terms of concepts, models, strategies etc – deriving as this does from seeking out the essence of what you are occupied with – does mean that there is a danger of that abstraction all too quickly leading to simplification. The issue is how to couch complexity in simple formulas. Who has never been lured by the bait of simplicity and who would not be inclined to reduce or rather distil until only the essence, the basic idea, remains?

■ THE COMPLEXITY OF SIMPLICITY (OR THE PITFALLS OF REDUCTION) Simplicity is more easily associated with true, pure and serene that with barren, dull and poor. Every architect strives after simplicity, even if only because 'truth' would seem to equal simplicity. Saying 'I want to make something very simple' is construed as an expression of extreme modesty.

Unfortunately not everything that is simple is also true, pure and serene.

Many architects think that leaving things out is a surefire way of getting to heaven. The seduction of 'less is more' often leads all too easily to 'all skin and bone' – at excessive cost. Once you have acquired a taste for omitting things you are in real danger of succumbing to anorexia architectura. The 'art of omission' consists of leaving out only those things that are irrelevant,

in the way that a sculptor (Michelangelo, by all accounts) was once asked by an admirer how he could possibly know that a beautiful woman was to be found inside the unhewn stone. Of course the answer is that he must have had the form of the finished figure in his mind to begin with. You can only reduce a thing when you know what and what not to leave out; you have to know exactly where you are headed: you have to have a concept.

Omission is a dangerous business and whether less is indeed more depends entirely on the concept you had to begin with; this is what decides what can go and what must stay, not some assumed will to simplicity. Simplicity is not an end in itself, you arrive at it during the design process while searching for what is essential to your concept.[1] Leaving things out is less a question of reduction and far more a process of concentration. It all depends on what you want to express – not with the absolute minimum of means, but as clearly as possible without being thrown off course. It is obvious that you can say more with more words, but what the poet does is to arrange just those words in just that order so as to express what he wants to say as clearly and as precisely as possible.

'Where economy of means is concerned, architects could learn much not only from engineers but also from the poet: the way in which he selects his words and structures them into sentences to achieve maximum power of expression and beauty of sound: 'la poésie est une chose aussi précise que la géométrie' (Poetry is as precise as geometry, Flaubert). What we term poetry is particularly that utmost precision of thought, which while reducing its means can actually increase the layers of meaning.'[2]

Each time for the formgiving architect there is the tightrope to be trod between too much and too little, between 'underdesigned' and 'overdesigned'.

In that respect the engineer can serve as an example to the architect; after all, his aims are simpler and fixed firmly in advance. His task is easier, say organizing a certain span with a minimum of material, or with the least structural height. For that matter, you usually need complex constructions and measures to achieve outward simplicity. Here, too, simplicity can fool you. For instance when rebuilding Mies van der Rohe's Barcelona Pavilion it proved a supremely complicated business to reconstruct the slender slab of cantilevering roof and uphold the appearance of simplicity. Again, the expressive lightness of the roof of Jean Nouvel's concert hall in Lucerne must have required moving heaven and more especially earth. The structural tour de force rids the building of its objectness. With its seemingly wafer-thin roof and the way it spreads out across the surroundings, the building conjures up visions of a gigantic bird that has just landed, having chosen this monumental waterfront site between the mountains as its territory.

197

198-199

■ CONSTRUCTIVISM Showing how a building is constructed is a spectacular invitation to all-embracing form. Although this does express the essence of constructivism it does not necessarily result in space.

Form expressed along constructivist lines is a demonstrative show of the pride its makers had in making and achieving structures that were unattainable (and less necessary) before then. They were therefore the symbol of a new era of new and unprecedented possibilities. And of its space, though the sense of space was ultimately due to the elegance of ease rather than the heaviness of effort. Which is why we prefer the poised quiescence of the ballet dancer to the tensed muscles of the weightlifter.

Attractive as it is to show how things fit together, and legitimate too, if only to keep them from getting too abstract and therefore unnecessarily obscure, there comes a moment when the aspect you wish to express begins to dominate all the others.

In addition, structures and constructions have the tendency to visually become increasingly complex and more and more difficult to understand, so that their expression imposes rather than informs.

This holds not only for expressing how a structure is made, but also as to its purpose, which is more likely to be concealed in such instances than revealed.

Just as modern technology is no longer self-explanatory in a visual sense, so functions and allocations, volatile as they are, are suffering a marked decrease in identity as time goes by.

We will have to accept that buildings, like household and other appliances, are showing less and less of their contents and their workings, and starting to behave increasingly like urban containers.

Architects are continually competing to make the most beautiful box. With control over the contents looking likely to disappear, the form of the packaging has become more important that the form of the contents. 'L'esthétique du miracle', as Jean Nouvel puts it.

With the expression of how a thing fits together and what its specific purpose is pushed into the background, the concern for objectness cedes to an expression of the spatial idea – activating, enfolding and unfolding both construction and function – and the spatial characteristic this brings to bear. The more we are able to make, the more pressing the question of what our intentions are. First you have to have an idea of where you want to go before setting up a strategy to achieve that aim.

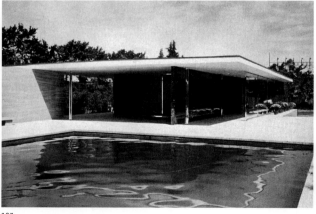

197

198

199

Brancusi [200-207]

No-one was more capable than the sculptor
Constantin Brancusi of compressing such a
complex world of ideas into his pieces, the
smaller of which must have looked at first
sight like objects that had been found in
passing (objets trouvés).

Brancusi had that rare ability to take seemingly simple forms and so charge them as to
arouse a myriad associations in those who
observe them. One such association,
depending on the eyes that are upon it, is
foregrounded, 'pulling' the form in a particular direction.

Though his sculptures do admittedly have
titles, these do nothing to inhibit the
observer from seeing them as something
else. They can often be birds, wings and
propellors but also objects conceivably from
another planet or materialized from outer
space; aquatic creatures, dug-up parts of
some machine, perhaps agricultural implements, primitive art, objects found on the
beach, lots of those. And because there is
no longer a distinction between ancient
and futuristic, organic, fossilized, solidified, eroded and cast, the notion of time
and place is extinguished. According to the
'naive' painter Le Douanier Rousseau,
Brancusi saw the opportunity to make the
ancient modern and the modern ancient.
Wood, stone and metal gain an almost
machine-like expression when worked by
hand, naturally rough or smooth and shiny,
each one of an incomparable purity of
material and form; almost nothing and
almost everything, arch-forms, no more
and no less.

Brancusi manages to achieve the maximum
complexity in the simplest form, both furi-
ous and calm, much like the ballet dancer
who controls the most prodigious tension
of so many muscles and tendons to transform it into a single elegant gesture. In the
way that they still have to attain an explicit
form, so to speak, his objects are in fact
protoforms which become what they are
through interpretation. They are concepts
that are a summation of the complex ideas
which reside in them as layers, to be evoked
by association rather than being explicit.
Brancusi worked in Paris (where a replica
of his studio has been built in front of the
Centre Pompidou as a well-intentioned and
informative panopticon) but he came from

201

Romania, from the country, where even today you can still find the agricultural objects and folkloric motives that were an ever-present stratum in his work.

Being a sculptor and not an architect, Brancusi was principally concerned with objects that require the attention of their surroundings. In Tirgu Jiu, near his birthplace in Romania, stands his most famous work, the *Endless Column*, part of a monument that spans the entire town. At one end of the town Brancusi fitted out a park with numerous elements while at the other end stood the column – kilometres from the park in other words, yet still on axis with it. Depending on how you regard it, the column either consists of stacked identical elements or of a single element with identical indentations – yet in either case it is an accumulation. With neither a below or an above, without beginning and without end, rising skyward like Jacob's ladder, it gathers together ground and sky.

Brancusi was continually making accumulations of elements, each bearing and borne by the other, every one a plinth for the next, each a base and a sculpture for another. Unlike classical sculptures placed on a pedestal to elevate them to a higher plane, here all the elements are equals, relating to one another as dependent yet autonomous components.

202

203

204

205-207 Traditional sources, Romania

Museu de Arte São Paulo (MASP), São Paulo, Brazil [208-215]
Lina Bo Bardi, 1957-68

The MASP in fact consists of two buildings horizontally organized. The large horizontal gatelike opening between them has a free span of 75 metres. Upper and lower buildings are linked merely by a glass lift with which you leave the lower building, where almost the entire adminstrative department is housed, for the upper where the permanent exhibition of paintings is displayed in one unbroken expanse. Originally each painting was hung off its own glass panel standing in a heavy though movable concrete foot with the relevant information on the rear of the panel. This supremely uncustomary manner of displaying art works, hanging freely in space so that visitors can move between them in a route of their own choosing, is of a stunning simplicity and furthermore unique. Meanwhile this sublime way of exhibiting has, for quite inexplicable reasons, been replaced by a more traditional layout.

The way this long space, with a glazed wall to either side and enormous square columns only at the short extremities, appears to hover in the air is of the same lofty order outside as was the original exhibition arrangement inside.

The prodigiously broad columnless gateway links the space of the traffic thoroughfare running parallel to the complex on one side with a parklike terrace on the other, that looks out over the lower-lying part of the city. This view is further accentuated by the gateway of urban dimensions, as well as by the expansive entrance to the terrace which you reach by walking beneath it. The area above roofed over by the upper building is of such size as to encourage mass gatherings and of course outdoor exhibitions, both of which might extend into the open area beyond.

When underneath the building, you feel absolutely no sense of oppression due to the immense presence above you. The large free-floating space reveals nothing of the undoubtedly stupendous structural forces operative within the material of this building, though permanently invisible. There is nothing of this to be seen from the outside. The underside, the ceiling of the 'gateway',

208 Study in which skylights illuminate exhibition space

209

210

211

212

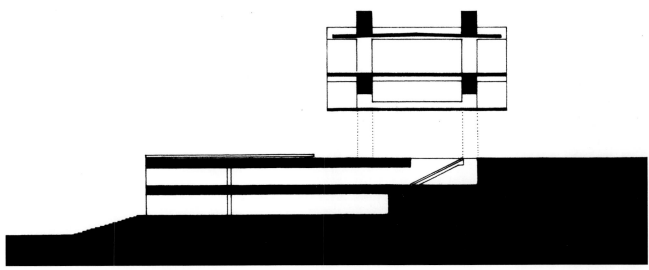

213

gets its lightweight look precisely by being perfectly flush with no exposed beams and suchlike. It is just this understatement, evidently, that makes a 75-metre span look trifling whereas a major show of strength would have been a constant reminder of how difficult such a construction actually is. By underemphasizing the build-up of the museum complex, the attention is more strongly focused on the totality and the main principles underlying the spatial concept. Just as the basic idea is clearly discernible in the end-product, here concept and development are virtually identical.

214

215

Pirelli towers, Milan, Italy (1986) [216-222]

In this competition design for a masterplan for the Pirelli factories in Bicocca (Milan) it was the existing built development – which needed preserving – including a classical cooling tower, that prompted a concept to match the proposal called for in the brief. At issue was the question of how a provisionally unknown number of companies and institutions were to be accommodated in the immediate vicinity. The response consequently takes the form of an urban blueprint, a framework of conditions, that can be filled in by so many architects, each with their own signature.

Taking the lone cooling tower as a stepping-off point, the idea emerged of a cluster of towers on a common platform with parking and feeder roads; a sort of mini-Manhattan of autonomous towers in relatively close proximity in a confined area. You then find yourself asking whether the shape of the potential newcomers might not derive from that of the cooling tower. At the moment that the cooling tower (or at least its form) starts to lead a life of its own in your mind, with its original function set aside, another association is likely to penetrate your consciousness. This then seems so obvious that the idea stays with you. Didn't the painter Morandi spend his entire life depicting

216

217 Giorgio Morandi, *Still life with White Can*, 1950

arrangements of bottles, jugs and pots; round, straight and often polygonal, as though seeking to portray a city? My thoughts have often turned to cities when looking at his paintings.

Suppose that all the towers, whatever their differences, were to resemble in some respects a bottle or a jug; it might then be possible to achieve an urban unity though without unduly strict rules as to the outward appearance of each tower.

Next you would have to make a general study of just how good the possibilities were of accommodating an efficiently organized office building in such forms. There would

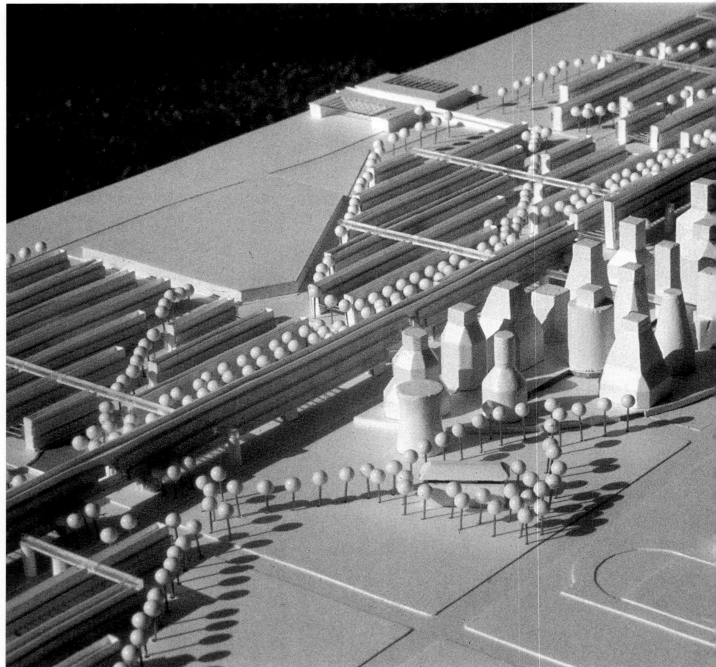

218

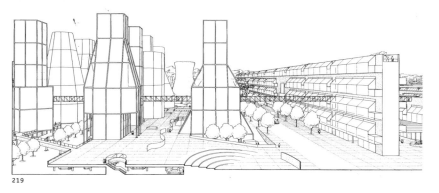

219

220

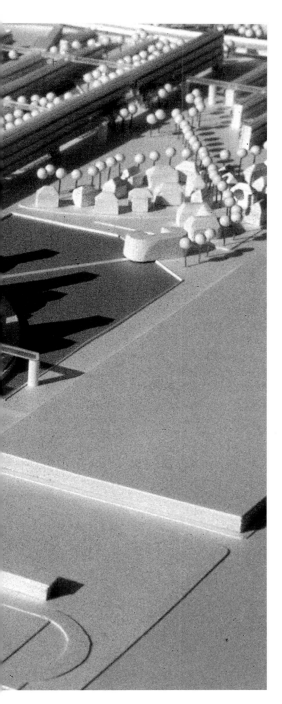

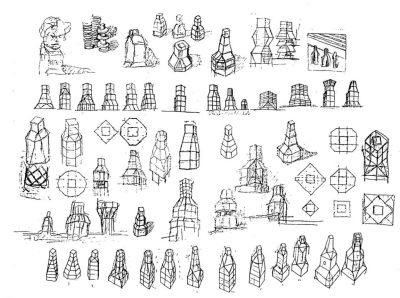

221

need to be a number of basic conditions ensuring that there was sufficient similarity among the designs but also enough freedom of interpretation to achieve a wide variety in practice.

You could start with a large number of possible variations simply by stipulating a maximum footprint and at least one indent which would serve to reduce floor plans over a certain height. This is not to impose restraints but most of all to create a degree of leeway, also for the less motivated developers, inciting them to interpret the basic concept so that it expresses their own particular brief.

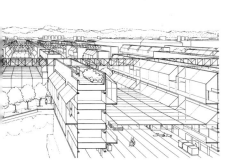

222

This design takes a banal standard office type and opens it up with what in itself is an obvious design intervention.

By splitting the building open lengthwise, in a manner of speaking, to generate two corridors, each with rooms on one side only so that the exterior space can visually enter between them, a new concept emerges, one better suited to the need for communication obtaining in a building of this nature. This intervention not only creates visual contact among the building's users, it takes the view from the central space of the world outside and works it up into a design theme.

The passages widen into a pair of atriums reaching up three storeys and roofed partially with glass. Each atrium leads in both directions to a terrace abutting the sunken floor areas of either the restaurant or the reception hall cum waiting room. All rooms give onto galleries running along them.

These atriums are where the external space penetrates into the building.

The result? Freedom from the suffocating effect of the endless labyrinth of corridors with room after room on either side characterizing the average office building. Once outside your own room you can take in the entire building at a glance and also be seen by others whom you might find yourself dealing with in the future. This way, a building's spatial organization can have a positive impact on communication. Having this face inwards strengthens the feeling, more so than the view out, of genuinely working together with others.

The primary aim when designing this building was to use a spatial intervention to escape from a cliché as persistent as it is difficult to erase, one that invariably informs office buildings the world over yet functions neither socially nor workwise and in fact is merely the cheap way out.

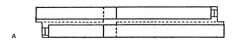
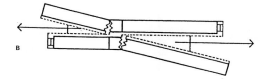
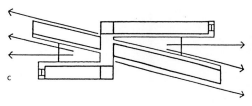

223 Space generated when a normal office plan (A) is broken open: the corridors widen into a hall (B). The parts are then shifted out of alignment: the hall areas open up (C)

224

225

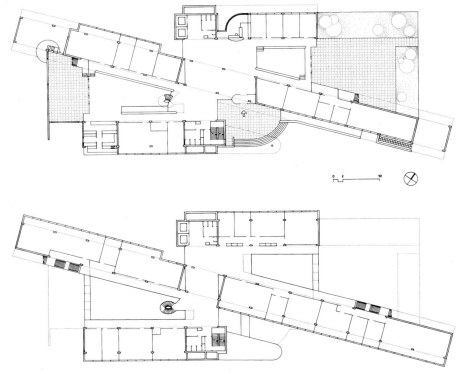

226

227

228

229

■ **HEAD AND HAND** Do we think while we draw or draw while we think? Does the hand guide the head or the head the hand? Was there an idea before we began designing or did the idea arise during the design process?

At first sight this would appear to be a non-issue.

Of course you draw as you search and search as you draw and this way you immerse yourself in the task. The longer you work on a task, the more clearly focused its essence becomes. While proceeding you subject all manner of references to scrutiny and so ultimately arrive at an idea and an approach. 'Begin, and the results will follow'.

The artist, unlike the architect, can perhaps count on one of the themes he has been nursing for some time to yield results in the end. In films of Picasso painting, he gives the impression that his ideas emerged spontaneously to be just as easily erased and replaced by new ones. Later, when his endless series of sketchbooks was published, it transpired that each motif in his paintings was carefully prepared beforehand and often even practised, as a performing artiste would do.

The architect's tasks, other than those of the artist, are more specific in the sense that each task makes its own conditions requiring an appropriate answer. Unlike the artist he is not in a position to throw random ideas about.

The architect's ideas concern less autonomous concepts which in general can only be applied to the most specific circumstances, that is, if those circumstances did not produce them in the first place.

The danger of 'just beginning' to draw and design in the hope and expectation that something will come of it, is that before you know it you are resorting to well-trod paths or clichés. This is virtually unavoidable, as it happens, for it is impossible to envisage something that was not there to begin with. You are borne on by what you already knew, because you yourself, but more particularly others you admire, have already left a trail. The composer Hector Berlioz relates that, as possibly the only composer unable to play the piano, he was at an advantage compared with his colleagues who were in the habit of composing at the keyboard, so that like it or not they were drawn by their hands to already familiar sequences of already familiar chords.[4]

'[T]he tyranny of keyboard habits, so dangerous to thought, and ... the lure of conventional sonorities, to which all composers are to a greater or lesser extent prone.'[5]

We know that Mozart heard entire works in his head before committing them to paper. This enabled him to turn those endless journeys in bumpy carriages to his advantage. Why shouldn't architects design buildings 'in their head'? Are plans and sections really more complex than the voices of, say, twelve musical instruments, each with its own timbre, such as need weaving together in a symphony?

First you must have something in mind (heard or seen), call it an idea; only then can you note it down – although of course it is never quite as simple as that. Drawing can bring out an idea, give it a clearer outline if you like, but it must have been in your subconscious to start with.

It should proceed more like research. The researcher does not start anywhere, at random, he does not begin without an idea, a hypothesis, about what he expects to find, and where. That he may well ultimately end up with something other than he sought is another matter.

'The architect's design process should, as such, be viewed more as a method of research. It should then be possible to make explicit the steps of the process, so that the designer is better able to realize what he is actually doing and what reasons are guiding him. Of course sometimes you may discover something seemingly out of the blue, but those moments, for the architect at least, unlike the artist, are scarce. Mostly, when you muster up enough courage and take the trouble to be conscious of it, the underlying thought process will prove to be less mysterious than that of the pure artist. We work according to strategies to achieve specific aims, preferably with as limited means as possible. We make use of practically all the resources and techniques which the researcher uses in, for example, operational research.'[6]

But for those who flinch at the usually strict rules that scholars wield with such gravity, we can look closer to home.

'The working method in the design phase in many ways resembles cooking. Even when the cook works without a recipe, he has a fairly clear idea about what his aims are, and before he can start he must gather together the necessary ingredients. If certain spices turn out to be missing from his kitchen cupboard, then the outcome will be a different dish from what he had in mind. In the same way the architect, bearing in mind the requirements his design will have to meet, can draw up a shopping list of ingredients, as it were, with which he intends to set to work.

'Cooking consists of a fairly complex set of actions, undertaken in an order that is apparently without logic, at least without any logic that might correspond with the logic of the end-product. For instance, some ingredients have to be soaked beforehand, or dried, cooled, heated, thickened, or liquified, be kept for a long time on a low heat, or stirred vigorously for a short time on a hot burner, and all these actions are undertaken in an order that bears no resemblance whatsoever to the order in which the final product is eventually served on the table. Similarly, the design phase proceeds in an ostensibly chaotic fashion, and we must not try to impose an artificial order onto the different stages, because it doesn't work like that. What we can do is to keep in mind, throughout the design process, the final product as we envisage it in its totality, and thus ensure that the initially fragmentary image slowly but surely comes into sharp and complete focus.

'That is why you should, ideally, concern yourself with all aspects of a design at the same time, and of course not only with how everything is going to look, but especially with how it is to be made and how it is to be used.

'While absolute simultaneity in the work on all aspects of a design is impossible, it is at least possible to spread our attention evenly and alternate our focus of interest with due deliberation, so that all the screws, as it were, can be tightened in turn – a little, not too much at a time – until the correct allover balance is achieved in the work as a whole.

'The greatest danger constantly threatening us is that, fixated as we often are on a small problem whose solution eludes us, we spend too much time on that one problem, more because of a psychologically felt necessity than because of a demand inherent in the design. And paradoxically, when an excellent solution eventually presents itself, it often has a disastrous effect on the design as a whole. After all, the more convincing that (partial) solution is, the stronger the temptation becomes to adapt the rest of the design accordingly, which inevitably results in lopsided development.

'There was once a painter, who spent an inordinate amount of time on a portrait that he was finding impossible to get right. Everyone agreed with him about that, and incidentally also about the fact that one feature, the nose, was outstandingly good, unlike the rest of the face. This nose met all the demands that could possible be made on it, it was indeed the sole component that was truly finished. So it was not surprising that the painter, falling into his self-made trap, kept on altering the mouth, ears and eyes, erasing them time and again from the canvas and starting all over again, in the hope of portraying the right mouth, ears and eyes to go with the already perfect nose. Until another artist came along and saw his predicament. He offered to help, and asked for the palette knife. In one fell swoop he dealt with the problem – to the horror of our painter. He had slashed the only successful feature of the face. Once the handsome nose had gone, the only obstruction to the painter's ability to see things in their proper proportions had gone, too. In the wake of this destructive deed came the possibility of a fresh beginning.

'The complexity of the architect's design process and the underlying thought pattern is in a sense also comparable to that of the chess player, who also has to deal with a great variety of possibilities and choices and mutually influential factors. The chess player who becomes too preoccupied with the possibilities offered by one particular piece is punished with disasters that will inevitably occur elsewhere on the board. And just as the chess player (like the cook with his efficacious but apparently random sequence of actions) keeps track of all the possibilities of the game, the architect too must develop a manner of thinking that enables him to monitor the range of his attention so as to take in as fully and as simultaneously as possible all the interrelated fields of interest. Only then can he arrive at a design in which the different aspects are properly and fully integrated in the whole. Both chess player and cook succeed in developing new strategies to deal with ever-changing situations, and also the architect must be capable of undertaking his design process according to such strategies, so that the form does not evolve without consideration for construction and material, the organization of a floor plan not without consideration for accompanying sections and the building as a whole not without consideration for its environment.'[7]

'A particular difficulty is faced by the architect … he cannot represent his ideas in reality, but has to resort to representing them by means of symbols, just as the composer only has his score with which to render what he hears. While the composer can still more or less envisage what he has created by checking to hear what his composition sounds like on the piano, the architect depends entirely on the elusive world of drawings, which can never represent the space he envisages in its entirety but can only represent separate aspects thereof (and even so the drawings are difficult to read).

'That is why the average architect usually starts by getting his floor plan technically right, whereupon he may think up an interesting section to go with it, after which he must finally complete the structure with facades that remain within the framework of the possibilities of floor plans and elevations. This unsatisfactory state of affairs is maintained and even aggravated by the fact that the drawing, irrespective of the meanings it seeks to communicate, evokes an independent aesthetic image, which threatens to overshadow the architect's original intentions and which may even be interpreted by the maker himself in a different sense than initially foreseen.

'A complicating factor is that, due to the sheer superabundance of this type of image and our constant comparisons with antecedents, which has given rise to a sort of metalanguage full of such things as lucid concepts, well-positioned staircases, interesting spatial effects – in short an insider's jargon of extensive qualifications which do not refer so much to the actual building as to its abstract graphic representation on paper, i.e. to an expectation.

'However absurd this may sound, we must in all seriousness ask ourselves how many architects are actually capable of reading their own drawings, that is of interpreting them with an eye to the spatiality of the structure that they are supposed to represent, as well as to the social and utilitarian objectives. Most architects read their drawings as an autonomous graphic image, thereby involuntarily placing them on a par with the graphic work of an artist. Thus the architect can be said to be the prisoner of his own drawings, which seduce and mislead him by their own imagery and which do not transcend the confines of the drawing board.'[8]

The space we visualize relates to our drawings as a landscape does to an ordnance survey map. Exactly perhaps, but two-dimensional and most particularly incomplete.

Designing is in the first place thinking, and then drawing as you think. It is not just visualizing something that goes with what you are drawing, but much rather rendering by drawing what you visualize. Other than that, it is a question of organizing your imaginative powers as best you can. Designing is a quest that you want to have proceed with maximum efficiency, purposefully if possible.

Therefore you should not fritter away too much time chasing fly-by-night 'solutions' that shortly after have to be dropped – there was something you overlooked after all – for the next rising impulse. All this leads to is depressing piles of sketching paper. It is better to leave the paper and certainly the computer screen alone and begin by thoroughly exploring the field. Just as detectives in popular TV series need to first grasp the plot before they take off after the villain, so the design process consists in principle of a like period of looking, listening and fixing the conditions.

Prior to resolving the task, you must develop ideas proceeding from your insight into the full complexity of the task, that lead you to a concept, just as the doctor diagnoses the problem before embarking on a therapy. The concept contains the conditions you wish to fulfil, it is a summary of your intentions; of what needs saying; it is hypothesis, and premonition. There can be no quest without premonition; it is a question of finding and only then seeking.

'D'abort trouver, chercher après.' Jean Cocteau

230

5

Social Space, Collective Space

■ Although we have become fairly used to seeing the entire world as our territory, our space is principally that of the city. City means space for trade, culture and entertainment and therefore the best possibilities for social exchange. The more people, the fuller the city, the better. Outside the city we expect to find the open space of the countryside, and there the less people we see the better. This is the place to clear your head, take a break from networks and congestion. Here you want to be alone, or at most with friends. What we call 'nature' – landscape, outdoors – is where you can withdraw, as you would into your own home.

The city is the model for society. It is our universe and arena where we show ourselves in company, sound out social situations, measure ourselves against others.

You shut the door of your house behind you to go into town, to dispel loneliness, check out the action, see what is up for grabs, make arrangements. Cities, large or small, planned and evolved, have always accepted these conditions, each with its own character and facilities, and with great differences in attractiveness.

Cities are inviting, and uniting, the place where everything happens – both place and space.

We are continually preoccupied with measuring, mirroring and pitting ourselves against each other. It is not we that determine who we are, but mainly others, meaning the social system and the roles we play in it. Our environment, built as it is, can not avoid being an influence, even though buildings are as often as not mere backdrops to the action.

The aim every time, one that the city as a whole but also in its smallest built parts should aspire to, is to provide the opportunity for us to inspect, assess, keep an eye on and bump into one another.

In short, it is all about seeing and being seen. The city as spatial model for society is about social space. In making it we have to adjust continually so as to safeguard the coherence of it all.

Simiane-la-Rotonda [231]
Henri Cartier-Bresson, 1970

Among the places people feel most attracted to are those in the heart of the city where one can still see out to the surrounding country. Just this brings them together, even when they had no truly conscious inclination in that direction, and were merely hanging around listlessly. Cartier-Bresson, celebrated for his eye for the decisive moment, 'le moment décisif', recorded that one single moment when happenstance caused these girls, boys, men and dogs to come together in pairs; standing, reclining, sitting. It once again demonstrates his mastery in illustrating the canonical in everyday life.

231

■ HABITAT AND SOCIAL SPACE Wherever there are complaints about the new housing estates cropping up everywhere, that they are too open and chaotic, these are invariably accompanied by descriptions of those old towns with their sheltered streets where you could get your bearings better than in the new estates where there is no street pattern to speak of.

The open city is a typical twentieth-century achievement. The product of general domestic requirements consolidated in a tight-knit and hermetic system of rules just about impossible to avoid, it seems, but irrevocably creating a sense of distance, it simply refuses to function, at least not as a city. The sense of urbanity is lacking and it is hard to feel at home there.

The question is: how do we bring back to it the quality of interior of the nineteenth-century city without impairing the quality of the sunlighting, light incidence, parking space, play space and the like?

Now, at the outset of the twenty-first century, we need new spatial discoveries to bring urbanity back to our new residential districts.

Besides such examples of well-functioning streets as those given in the earlier volume, *Lessons for Students in Architecture*, here are a few more of social space in its most elementary and explicit form, surviving through the centuries in the most wide-ranging situations.[1] In a sense they can be regarded as 'arch-forms' of collective exterior space with the best possible conditions for social life, be it of close-knit groups and so not really comparable with the situation as it affects modern city-dwellers. One example that is most definitely tailored to suit prevailing conditions is our residential court development in Düren in Germany, which can be said to synthesize the principles of the perimeter block and those of the open city.

Streets, Nias, Indonesia [232-243]

Villages ordered according to strict planning standards are the last thing you would expect to find in the middle of the tropical rain forest on a remote island to the west of Sumatra. Two rows of majestic wooden houses in two storeys and with large roofs stand consistently lengthwise along the street. The street itself is entirely paved with smoothly polished stone slabs whose provenance is unclear. Even less clear is how they were made to fit together so perfectly on site. What, finally, was it that prompted all this prodigious effort?

Most of these villages (many of which are still intact) stand on flat mounds, tables in fact, and can only be reached up stone stairs set at the extremities of the villages and often of a great height. The village is comprised of a number of houses limited by the size of the mound, a number established beforehand and organized according to ritual religious criteria. The departure-point is the central position of the larger house occupied by the headman of the village. The only central street where everyone looks out onto is as much collective as private space in accordance with a complex system of zoning, little of which remains visible to today's tourists. Outsiders were expected to walk exclusively on the central strip and only approach the houses when the occupants had given their consent. The villagers themselves could make use of

232

233 Hilinawalo-Maenemolo. Section

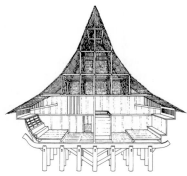

234

SPACE AND THE ARCHITECT

235

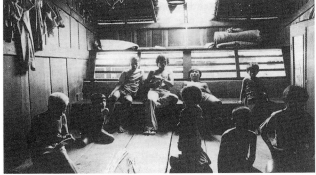

236

the entire surface of the street right up to the houses, though once again according to strict rules and depending on the occasion. Although the traditional system of meanings regarding each place and the behaviour expected there lives on and undoubtedly is revived in certain circumstances if only superficially, there is little of it to be seen in everyday life. This only brings out further the exceptional quality of these streets as elongated village squares and communal dwelling spaces. Used as grounds for ball games as well as for drying seeds and plants, a stretch of street may suddenly become draped with washing that is soon dry from the warm stones and is gone again quite as suddenly.

One would doubtless be hard put to find anywhere in the world a street where private, public and collective use intertwine and mesh in such a taken-for-granted way as here.

Here all efforts combine to give shape to the most ideal street space imaginable: the unbroken surface of smooth stones on which rainwater soon evaporates, the absence of traffic so that children can play anywhere they choose, the stepped profile where villagers sit together on and around megaliths, immense ancient stones that keep the ancestors in their midst and also accommodate those confined to the central area. An essential aspect is that all houses are set lengthwise in an unbroken line on either side of the street.

The large living rooms are on the first floor overlooking the street where they are provided with continuous horizontal slits through which the occupants keep constant watch on what is going on outside. This way it is possible to follow the movements of passers-by the full length of the street. The houses, which are all organized along the same lines, have an open understructure used as storage space between the timber columns. Above it rise the large living rooms fully equipped for visual contact with the street and continuing up into the majestic roof.

Between the houses are narrow alleyways containing stairs to a landing. From each landing you can enter the living rooms of the pair of adjacent houses, and thence to the rest of the house at the rear. All houses, then, are accessible from two sides via the living room, effectively generating internal

thoroughfares along which the children in particular can pass unhindered through all the houses and are therefore able to closely follow the movements of strangers from one end of the street to the other.

Given this informal internal street parallel to the external street, we can identify a dual access system that basically divides the house into two zones: the rear with its strong sense of privacy and the more publicly accessible living room on the street. Here everyone walks in as they please and it can soon be packed with visitors. At such times the living room literally becomes part of the street.

These villages, most of which are separated by several hours' travel, lie like stone islands in the green mass of the rain forest, connected only by a chain of narrow jungle paths along which all goods are transported. There is nothing in the way of a road link. Your arrival at a village is announced by a monumental stone stair, sometimes naturally eroded but just as often incomprehensibly taut and perfectly constructed. Recalling ancient Mexican temples, it forms a descending, stepped continuation and advance notice of the meticulously paved central street.

237

238 Steps, Orahili

239

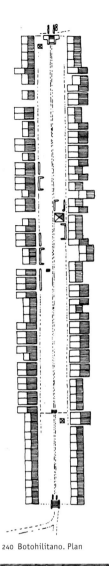

240 Botohilitano. Plan

241

Whereas the wooden houses are subject to deterioration and needed repairing or replacing, this welcoming carpet of rising stone steps represents the timeless structure that also includes the ancestors in their megaliths. As much collective space as the horizon of social life, it announces in no uncertain terms the end of your journey along the jungle path.

242

243 Steps, Bawometaluo

Hakka dwelling-houses, Fujian, China [244-256]

These unique ring-shaped buildings are found exclusively in Fujian in South China, particularly around Jongding, either individually or in groups, and each constitutes a complete self-contained residential village. Exceptional though they are, there are still several thousand of these structures in existence. They were built from the seventeenth century to the present, with diameters varying from 17 to 85 metres. Besides the round variety, there are a great many square ones and all manner of intermediary forms. Although inward-facing and closed to the outside world, they make a less impenetrable impression in the landscape than one might expect. They are inhabited by communities of entire families of Hakkas

244

245

246

247

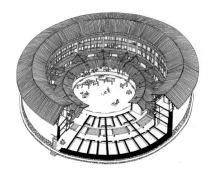

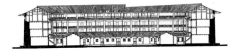

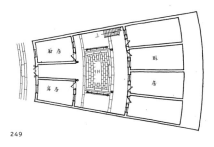

(strangers) who migrated to this region from the north looking for better living conditions. In these fortress-like buildings they could protect and defend themselves against onslaughts and often lengthy sieges. Otherwise the surrounding walls are entirely blank with perhaps the occasional tiny window placed as high as possible. Constructed of bricks of dried clay, the walls are one and a half metres thick at the bottom and taper as they rise. All dwelling units are located against the outer wall, whereas the central area is either open or built-up to some extent. On the ground floor are the living and eating quarters and kitchens, all ranged in accordance with Chinese tradition round small internal courts giving onto the open central area. The bedrooms, like the storage rooms, are located along the galleries above and curiously can only be reached from two or four public stairs. In other words, with certain exceptions you are unable to proceed directly from your living quarters to the bedrooms except by way of the front door, across the public space. Evidently there is less need of privacy, though these are, after all, large family groups, in China the

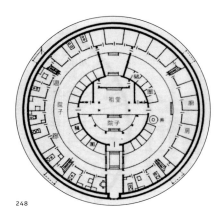

248

249

250

251

252

basic units of the social structure. Privacy, besides, is a privilege of the rich who are more in a position to indulge in it, as they have less need to rely on one another. The central area, whether open or closed, is collective. Here the harvested crops are prepared with some degree of collaboration and stored in barns. Besides rooms set aside for production, there may be schools, boarding houses and general café-like spaces where you can meet together. Finally, there

are the remains of religious places, in the shape of open corners resembling miniature squares along the galleries, where modest ceremonies are enacted. In some complexes there is space for a temple in the centre that doubles as a theatre. Presumably these religious activities are still not accepted by the authorities and have been reduced during the last fifty years to their present marginal form. Nor do we know exactly how much more prosperous these communities were in the

past, and the fate of the landowners who must have lived and ruled here in earlier times and presumably built these houses. Divided into living units that all emerge at a differentiated communal area, these housing complexes are in effect fully-fledged towns which like medieval settlements could hold out almost indefinitely against attackers. Their shape suggests a comparison with a built-up amphitheatre such as the one at Arles.

379-380

253

254

255

256

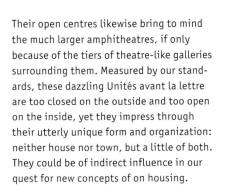

Their open centres likewise bring to mind
the much larger amphitheatres, if only
because of the tiers of theatre-like galleries
surrounding them. Measured by our standards, these dazzling Unités avant la lettre
are too closed on the outside and too open
on the inside, yet they impress through
their utterly unique form and organization:
neither house nor town, but a little of both.
They could be of indirect influence in our
quest for new concepts of on housing.

Düren housing complex, Germany (1993-97) [257-266]

This residential complex consists of some 140 units in various dwelling types and with a shared meeting area, all beneath a roof that doubles as an almost rectangular frame round an open central courtyard.

The continuous roof suggests a perimeter block, yet the units placed beneath it are held clear of one another, leaving openings everywhere that access the inner courtyard on all sides – not exactly the hallmark of a perimeter block. Again, whereas the central court of a perimeter block would be taken up with individual gardens, here it is pre-eminently a community space with a street running through it and space for parking cars. All entrances to the houses are on this inner side which has taken over the function of the streets traditionally around the outside of the block. In this inner zone there is room

257

258

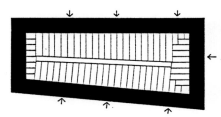

259

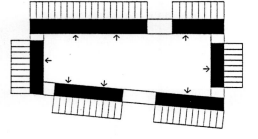

enough left for playgrounds and for community activities that can be watched from all sides, as can the children who play here. The private gardens have shifted to the outer side, confirming that the principle

of the perimeter block with gardens inside and bounded by streets has been roundly turned inside out.

What we did for one block in Düren was developed in subsequent projects into an

urban design principle, with streets turned into gardens and the internal courtyards into enclosed city squares.

Thus the perimeter block could be reintroduced, be it in this reversed state. This

260

261

262

263

precludes resorting to the none too urban character of the open row principle, but it could also provide an alternative for streets, as overloaded with traffic and parked solid as they are. And not to forget the pedestrians who have to share the streets with the traffic, to say nothing of play space for children.

Though the open row development of our new-build estates may provide enough open space for traffic, pedestrians and greenery, there seems no way to combine it with the containment and order brought by more or less enclosed housing blocks with their clear street pattern and concomitant sense of urbanity.

By construing the inner courtyards of housing blocks as streets widened into urban squares with a pre-eminently public character, and placing these built 'islands' in an open, green environment with private gardens and public parks, it should be possible to assure a clear and accessible urban pattern.

264

265

266

Residential court projects (1995-97)

[267-276]

Our residential court projects are an attempt to find alternatives that can lead to a greater spatial cohesion in the modern city without needing to fall back on the traditional perimeter block.

There are a number of examples which, although each is different, can help us form a picture of urban squares when these are within a city block turned inside-out. These examples include Places des Vosges in Paris, the Amphitheatre at Lucca[2] and the Palais Royal[3] in Paris.

The following projects at widely dissimilar locations continue to explore the principle of the inside-out city block as an urban core set in mainly green space.

■ Veerse Poort residential scheme, Middelburg, Netherlands

Here in Zeeland Province the town of Middelburg, its ancient centre surrounded by water and fortifications, has seen expansions in various directions over the centuries.

Our scheme is for a new residential district that is to be an urbane offshoot of the town's core on the one hand and perpetuate the green of the landscape up to this core on the other.

The brief additionally stipulated that about half of the dwellings were to be detached units standing in green space. The remaining units are grouped in seven urbanized cores consisting of inside-out city blocks with a predominantly stone presence. These and the central stretch of water are the nucleus of the new suburb. The gardens have been moved outside the blocks where they provide a green zone locking into the public parkland and containing the one-family houses. Construction of the project has since begun.

■ Theresienhöhe, Munich, Germany

The brief to develop the former exhibition grounds in the centre of Munich called for retention of the large green wedge thrusting into the city and ending in the distinctive oval-shaped green field of Theresienwiese. In addition, the urban fabric which in effect cuts off this green wedge from the oval void, needed suturing. Here, too, these conflicting aims could be reconciled by leaving the green zone intact round large city blocks embedded in it like islands. One criticism of the scheme was that this

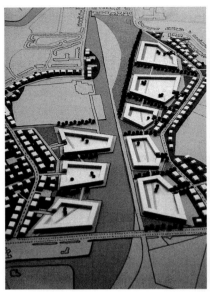
267 Veerse Poort, Middelburg 1995. Model

traditional

turned inside-out

268 forgetting the streets

269 Palais Royal, Paris

270 Place des Vosges, Paris

271 Place des Vosges, Paris

272 Amphitheatre, Lucca, Italy

273 Palais Royal, Paris

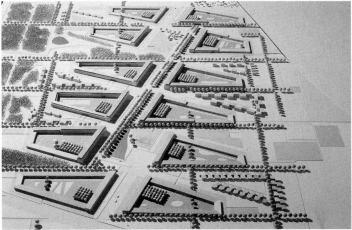

274 Elisabethaue, Berlin-Pankow 1998. Model

275 Theresienhöhe, Munich 1996. Model

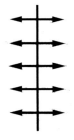
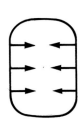

276   A   B

would negatively affect the image, so characteristic of an urban centre like Munich, of clear-cut streets between solid blocks, and that the city's explicit urbanity would therefore suffer too. Evidently the scheme was seen more as a Siedlung or suburban housing estate than as city.

But with today's dwelling criteria there is no avoiding the greater distances between buildings, and there are no more picturesque inns or shops on the corner. In short, that image of the city is an illusion however you look at it, and we must quickly find other images to prevent such illusions from producing one failure after another.

■ Elisabethaue
  Berlin-Pankow, Germany

Whenever former open country is built up, one condition is always that as much as possible of the old character has to be retained. So the result can scarcely be described as undiluted urbanization. The close proximity of green open space is eulogized as the one quality of such habitats.

Here too we sought to design contained urban spaces lying like islands in an area where everything is done to maintain the continuity with its surroundings.

The project for Berlin-Pankow is accessed by a central spine with branches leading off to the residential courts. This made it possible for the surrounding nature to penetrate the scheme without being cut off by main roads.

The projects for Middelburg and Munich placed emphasis on the parkland in the centre so that the preferred response was a circular access system with branches leading inward.

Besides accessibility for motorized traffic all three schemes provide networks of paths for pedestrians and cyclists cutting clear across the residential 'islands' and through the blocks, thereby dispelling the illusion of complete enclosure.

276A

276B

■ COLLECTIVE SPACE, SOCIAL USE By far the most examples given in *Lessons for Students in Architecture* of spaces where mainly social activity takes place are of streets and squares, urban spaces in the public realm; the living rooms of the city. But in fact such social spaces can be found wherever we live and work, where we interact. It is at those places where we invariably end up, where we meet, in short where the action and the adventure is; so they can just as easily be within the walls of free-standing buildings and structures. This is a fundamental reason for organizing buildings along urbanistic lines.

That which we call public life is enacted not only in the public part of the city, but just as much in publicly used buildings. Besides streets and squares which are brought into use on special occasions, there are, for example, theatres, discos, stadiums, museums but also shopping centres and stations which are converged on by large numbers of people. *Lessons* gave a number of examples in both categories, as much public areas or buildings as private ones temporarily made public. Often the accessibility is so ambiguous that the entire relationship between building and street dissolves; take the arcades that look like public streets but can be closed with gates, and where it is hard at times to know whether you are inside or outside.

The fact is, public and private, whether inside or outside, are relative concepts. Only the containment of buildings vis-à-vis the openness of the street presents a barrier in the continuity of this system of successive transitions. In practical terms, the city is divided into monitored areas, buildings, and the relatively unmonitored area beyond, the street. We must keep striving with architectural and urbanistic means to uphold the openness of the private 'bastions' and the continuity of the street so that the collective doesn't get reduced in the interest of consolidating the private. This is something you can see happening everywhere due to the public domain being suppressed.

Whenever architects and planners through the ages have occupied themselves with space it has almost always concerned buildings for social life, in other words where a sense of the collective is expressed and where large numbers of people converge whether spontaneously or along organized lines. Such buildings are necessarily of large dimensions and thus contrast starkly with places of habitation.

Should there be a need for roofs to keep out the elements, it is the structural means, facilitating the required span and enlarging the scale as a result, that give these edifices their imposing appearance. The history of architecture was domi-

277 Rockefeller Plaza, New York

278 Plaza Mayor, Chinchon, Spain

279 Via Mazzanti, Verona, Italy

280 The street as mosque. Achille Chiappe, Marseilles, France

281 Apricale, Italy

nated by religious buildings until the nineteenth century and the emergence of the large sheds, arcades and stations which would take on unprecedented dimensions in the twentieth. These then began vying with public open space.

Whereas people once gathered together in churches, but also in public baths or in the Stoa, now they do that in shopping malls. Our sense of space is attuned to things that impress through their sheer size.

'Collective space is neither public nor private but much more and at the same time much less that public space.'[4]

Large spaces, whether inside or outside, where large numbers of people congregate, may not only impose but also give a sense of like-mindedness or even of fellowship through their role of 'overarching' common interests.

The feeling of togetherness that collective spaces manage to arouse can be dissimilar in social terms and we would do well to note that difference. Churches as well as mosques, although less unambiguous, are almost exclusively organized about a central point where the message is proclaimed, and with the eyes and the ears of the congregation turned to it. All attention is directed primarily at one point, which therefore figures as

the centre of the space. There is less concern for one another mainly because those gathered there only see each other's backs.

In theatres and auditoriums and also in stadiums the attention is likewise centrally oriented. So essentially these differ little from churches in terms of social patterns.

In all these situations the building is an all-inclusive construct that encourages a shared concentration and a harmony among those attending certain organized events. Important though this is, at least as important for social life are the streets and squares, cafés, lobbies and other examples of collective spaces whose spatial setting has a catalytic effect on social contact, not just targeted at one and the same activity, but so that everyone can behave in accordance with their own intentions and movements and so be given the opportunity to seek out their own space in relation to others there.

Great though this feeling of togetherness can be at organized events, these invoke social contact at a distance only. Yet it is social contact that turns collective space into social space. What we need to find are space forms that are so organized that they offer greater opportunities and cause for social contact. Spaces that enlarge the chances of encounter and have a catalysing effect on seeing and being seen, and so contribute

The examples on pp. 134-137 show a distinction in social patterns according to the following criteria:
- inside – outside
- with an audience (in the round or on one side) – without an audience
- organized – unorganized
- attention centralized/concentrated (282A) – attention polynuclear/dispersed (282B)

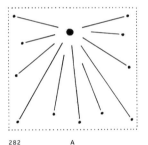
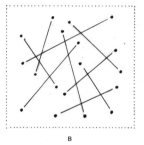

282   A   B

283 André Kertész, Children playing on the parvis

284 The Dam, Amsterdam, during an official ceremony

to expressing what it is that brings people together; in short, they should provide the thing that makes us seek out the city. In the foyer of a theatre or auditorium people move in rhythm with their own whims either to grab a coffee, to look for someone or simply to be seen. Here, the attention is spread according to a polynuclear and random pattern that will change from one moment to the next. Except when specific events are organized that offer temporary inducement to centralized behaviour, that random pattern – as we find it in discos, cafés, hotel lobbies and museums as well as in foyers – makes a more favourable environment for social intercourse and, for this reason, is closer to the idea of the city.

Social space is a model for the city; a potted version of the space of the city.

Buildings where large numbers of people come together take to functioning as tiny cities. So they ought in fact to be organized and designed as such. We are talking not just about so-called civic buildings but also common-or-garden office buildings, regardless of whether or not these private institutions are open to the public. The more people who come together for performances, meetings or parties in large spaces, or indeed to work in small rooms behind closed doors, the more city-like the organization should be.

Such collectively used buildings require an internal structure of streets and squares with a division into relatively 'public' parts, and parts for insiders only that are distinguished from the network of streets as buildings-within-a-building. Such an arrangement enables you to find your way about even without prior knowledge.

The collective function of this area is eminently expressible with spatial means and can be so formed as to be appropriate for all kinds of utterances and actions that best confirm the feeling of solidarity as that of a community and as a corporate identity. The spatial concept needs to make use of the common characteristics of the group in question. Are many visitors expected? Do they convene often? Is there a busy internal circulation? Where do they drink coffee? Inside the building you can feel you are 'in the city' even without the presence of shops.

A collectively-used building can stand in independence as an object with a pronounced entrance, or open itself up so that the city is carried into the building, so to speak, and the building can be regarded as an indoor continuation of the city.

In the first instance, then, one tends to think of the arcades of the nineteenth century or the 'public' shopping malls of our own time. There, public space does penetrate inside but

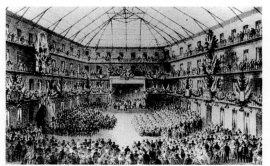

285 Familistère, Guise, France

286 De Drie Hoven nursing home, Amsterdam

287 Fine Arts Museum, Boston, USA

288 Screen in Feyenoord Football Stadium, Rotterdam

289 Arkaden, Berlin, Renzo Piano

without negatively affecting the private space. Again, the relationship between inside and out dissolves but not beyond the entrances to the different buildings.

So the building as city is only partly about arcades and such-like, though it does have something to teach us as regards form and materiality.

What we are advocating is that buildings that are used collectively in some degree are organized more like cities. The underlying argument is that though they are not actually public, they function in a practical sense as a part of the city – much more so than, say, a dwelling-house.

So there is every reason for allowing buildings that play an explicit part in urban social life to express that function to the city at large, and (one sincerely hopes) without recourse to turrets and domes. The main issue is to make them look inviting, and to draw attention to the fact that they can be accessed by the public. It is of the essence, then, to make as much as possible of the internal urban organization legible from the outside.

290 Bibliothèque Nationale, Paris

291 Place Clemenceau, Vence, France

292 Central Station, Glasgow

293 Galleria Vittorio Emanuele, Milan

Budapest Railway Station, Hungary
[294-298] Gustave Eiffel, 1876

Though linked to the name of Eiffel, this station is little different basically from other nineteenth-century examples, of which those in London and Paris are the best-known. Railway terminals take you past the rear of the city and into its centre. They are the end-points and immediate 'gateways' to the city, to a much greater extent than stations along the line.

Here the station concourse is no more than a large roof among all the other roofs, and covers the final section of track. It is almost part of the streets beyond, barely separated from them by a glass screen virtually flush with the street elevation, into which the station slips with little fuss.

A four-millimetre thick sheet of glass separates the station concourse from the city square with its trams, buses and cars. On alighting from the train into the city's bustle, the visual contact is complete and overwhelming.

The station itself is reduced to a large hall, with the necessary ancillary facilities housed in built-on flanks which differ little from the city buildings around them. Unlike the major examples, especially in England where the stations were crystallizing points of urban amenities and grew into complex structures of great size, here we see the act of entering and leaving the city by means of this new and first large collective mode of land transport – the train – stripped back to the most direct and minimal spatial organization befitting it, and expressed here as a new prototype of city gateway.

295

296

297

298

299 Gellért Baths, Budapest, Hungary

Public baths [299-310]

Perhaps the most evident examples in the history of built social space are public baths. These we find not only in the Roman and Ancient Greek civilizations and in Islamic countries but also in Hungary. And we have not yet mentioned the medicinal baths located all over Europe.

The Roman public baths were public meeting places which under the mantle of physical culture and relaxation, presented the opportunity for the most informal encounters. The most famous are undoubtedly the Baths of Caracalla, not least for their ingenious installations for hot water and steam – so modern to our eyes – integrated into the structure of the building.

If business appointments are not uncommon in the sauna culture of Finnish origin, in the Roman *thermae* with their estimated 10,000-15,000 visitors a day, the social contacts must have had a far greater scope and intensity than in the temples, theatres and amphitheatres which were geared to communal events with arguably less focus on the individual and person-to-person interaction.

In our roofed swimming pools the emphasis is on practising sports, on achieving and learning, while the open-air variety, like the beaches, is resorted to only when the sun is there to encourage unduly letharthic and drousy behaviour. Indeed, the succession of baths with various degrees of warmth and the concomitant massage treatment are intended to incite an element of activ-

300 Sir Lawrence Alma Tadema, *The Baths of Caracalla*, 1899

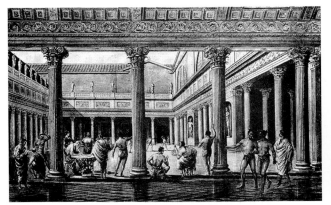

301

302 Baths of Diocletian

303 Turkish baths, Bursa, Turkey

ity, making personal contact so much easier. In Islamic culture purification has religious significance besides being a hygienic measure. This enables the women in particular to finally shake off their domination by the men and exchange ideas and raise more intimate matters. Turkish baths are still being built today, be it on a more modest scale and less accessible than the Roman *thermae* whose evident presence and exuberant use must have made such a mark on the city and on city life.

A separate category of baths is that of the mineral springs to which medicinal powers were attributed and where thermal baths were founded. This celebrated nineteenth-century tradition and early form of tourist

304 Turkish baths, Jean Lèon Gérôme

306 Baths of Caracalla

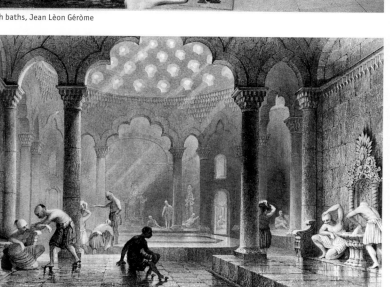

305 Turkish baths, Istanbul, 19th century

attraction persists in places like Vichy[5], Baden Baden and Marienbad (now Marianské Lázně).
In Switzerland, high up in the mountains in the village of Vals, Peter Zumthor has added a new type to this category. Here the indoor bath, with an outlet to the outdoor bath, is not a clearly shaped basin but a 'water-labyrinth' that cannot be taken in at a single glance, where you often have to wade your way between bulky free-standing stone columns containing water caverns in which a variety of temperatures, showers and other beneficient facilities obtain.

There are, besides, spaces for resting and massages with large windows offering a grand view of the green hillsides. Below the water level is a world of steps and stone benches and handrails along the walls where, in the light of underwater lamps and between fountains, bathers cluster together like water lilies. Here you are overtaken by the decadence of a pampered and hedonistic body culture in this so 'natural' world of pure materials where tiles, symbol of hygiene, are not present for once. Its romantic, almost cavelike look is equalled only by the sleek, restrained materiality. This conjures up visions of Roman *thermae* and the life these held. If the social contact here is not quite of the same order as it was in the Baths of Caracalla, then (leaving aside the isolated setting far from city life) this can be blamed on the lack of a tradition. No reproach can be laid at the architect's door; he has fulfilled all the conditions and done everything to make of this unique thermal bath a surprising city of water.

307

308

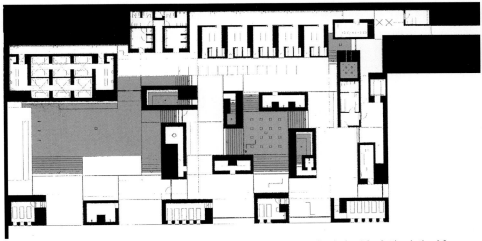

309 1 Showers 2 WCs 3 Sweat stone with Turkish showers and sweat chambers 42° C 4 Indoor bath 32° C 5 Outdoor bath 36° C
6 Fountain grotto 36° C 7 Fire bath 45° C 8 Cold bath 12° C 9 Sounding stone 10 Flower bath 30° C 11 Rest space 12 Massage

310

Theatre complex on Spui, The Hague (1986-93)

[311-320]

The theatre complex on Spui in the centre of The Hague forms a cornerstone of a concentration of cultural buildings also including the concert hall cum dance theatre across the street and the city hall cum municipal library.

Next door is the Nieuwe Kerk, a seventeenth-century church (with a central plan, curiously enough; see pp. 212-213) that is also used for concerts. The theatre complex adds a film theatre, a video centre, an art gallery and a theatre café to its pair of auditoriums seating 350 and 120. There is in addition 1300 m² of retail space plus 76 apartments on the upper floors. One elevation of the residential levels curves back in a quarter circle away from the building line so as to bring the distinctive Nieuwe Kerk out to full effect rather than hide it from view. This urban-

istic principle became decisive for the basic form.

The heart of the complex is the large theatre foyer. This can be seen and entered from the street, with only a full-height, full-length glass front separating the two. This foyer space is a glazed continuation of the forecourt and indeed acts as a sheltered urban plaza. It is constantly host to myriad events including concerts, meetings and receptions distinct from the shows in the official theatres. The ambience here is usually more informal, this being much easier to achieve here than in an environment specially designed for such events.

Set a few treads lower, with evident ramps ascending to the auditoriums and the long low wall guiding the public to the cloakroom, this sunken section is bristling with visual information to focus the attention

on what there is to see and hear; all this makes the foyer function better.

The film theatre opens both to the foyer and directly to the street with the bar up against the elevation. The projection booth thrusts into the foyer like a recessed balcony. This central place serving all three film theatres is visible from the street in an allusion to Duiker's Cineac in Amsterdam of 1933. The Cineac was the first true cinema, conceived as a 'window on the world', where the glass wall rounding the corner revealed the film projectors to those passing by in the street.[6]

Sited along the street and facing outwards, this café/foyer with its 20 m² of display window is nothing if not inviting.

The theatre complex as a whole is a city centre in miniature with an unprecedented number of possibilities. It is part of a com-

315
319
320

311

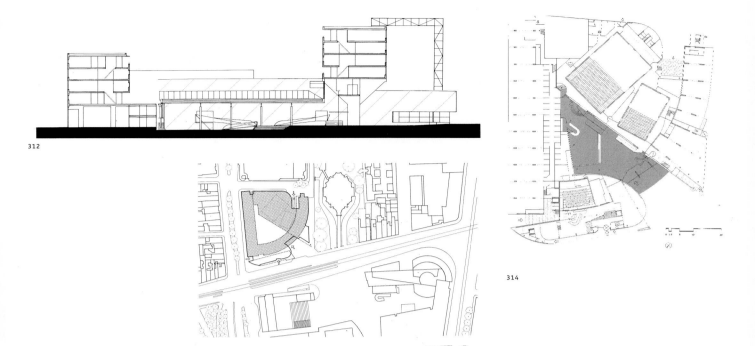

312

313

314

315

pressed cultural package taking up no more than 500 metres of street. According to Rem Koolhaas, you won't find that even in Manhattan. A cursory stocktake elicits besides housing and shops the following: a parliament building, city hall, concert hall, dance theatre, church, library, disco, casino, hotel, restaurants and this Spui Theatre.

316

317

319

318

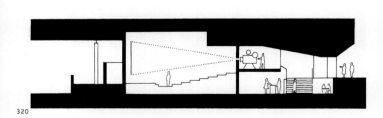

320

Markant Theatre, Uden (1993-96) [321-328]

This modest theatre slips into one wall of the market square of the small town of Uden. The foyer space is expressed on the exterior by a large glass facade resembling a shop display window. In the evening the lights of the foyer shine out on the city, its interior inviting in those passing by. This theatre is no formal, inward-looking building but open and facing the city. A large jutting canopy bridges the area between the tilting glass wall and the line of the urban elevation on this side of the square. This area, officially part of the street, is now just as much part of the building – an 'urban portico' letting in the urban space of the square. Unlike all those highly-placed glazed facades of foyers that look festive from afar, here by contrast it is its nearness that makes this one so inviting.

Placing the main floor one and a half metres

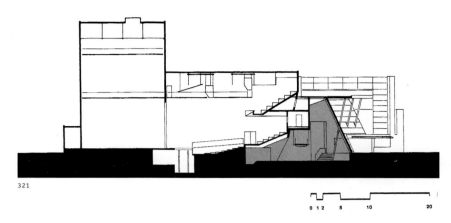

321

below street level (as in the Hague film theatre) only enhances the view in. Not that this in any way disturbs the theatre-goers, who feel protected by the solid expanse of wall.

Catwalks hung from the roof structure and variously leading into the auditorium spatially define the tall foyer space. Apparently crisscrossing the space at random, these footbridges like the ones in

322

323

324

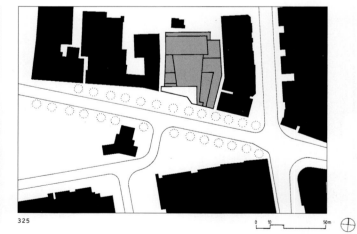

325

326

Breda generate a layered spatiality which makes the presence of others felt everywhere.

The heavily extravert, inviting character of the foyer only serves to stress its informal function. Like a 'grand café', you can walk in at any time without necessarily attending a performance.

327

328

■ SOCIAL SPACE Wherever people happen to meet – by chance or as passers-by – or converge in the act of meeting – whether accidentally or deliberately for gatherings or appointments – we can use the term social space. This can be in the city downtown or in the back of beyond, even in places you would not immediately associate with an architect. It is pretty humiliating the way architects, and urban planners too, are apt to simplify the sheer range and complexity of this phenomenon when it comes to analysing and explaining it. The off-putting connotation of charity suggested by the word social also has some bearing on this tendency.

Everywhere in the collective domain, inside and outside, there is social space to be found. Though expressly formed in some places, it is usually just there – in cafés, restaurants, shops, clubs, stations – wherever people convene for whatever reason.
The city is such a complex phenomenon that any attempts to rationalize it are, inevitably, simplifications.
However great our efforts, it proves impossible to trace the complexity of social life in all its layers and ramifications, much less chart it in a way that may be of service. Here I have chosen 'Amsterdam Global Village', a film by Johan van der Keuken, to show that a small city like Amsterdam with all its limitations has a dazzling array of places on offer, together making it the centre of a hinterland with the occasional long-distance foray across the globe. This four-hour-plus sequence of seemingly random images of unexpected and unanticipated moments from all corners of society shows that social situations and foci of social life are in fact interwoven wherever they are. Together they demonstrate the great wealth that is urban space. As a foil to the city as the largest social space, I would like to follow it with the smallest most elementary artifice capable of keeping people together: the table.

Amsterdam Global Village [329-333]
A film by Johan van der Keuken, 1996

'I shoot high culture, the Concertgebouw Orchestra, alongside street culture, a tramp trying to earn a few cents as a living statue. You have to watch out when making a film like this that it doesn't become a collection of everything we have in Amsterdam. This is why I choose subjectively. I always seek to go against the representative. Which is why my selection is always lopsided. That's why my films often include people with a handicap, someone who's blind, for instance. Nobody is representative, I've made an anti-anthropological selection.
'I never choose extreme subjects. We've shot scenes in a discotheque, but then a run-of-the-mill disco, not some kinky party. The extreme bit needs to come from my own viewpoint. A porter who spends eight hours on the trot welcoming visitors to a metal detector in three languages. I hope that I show more of the everyday by looking at it longer. Filming something – really that's bringing it to its full value.'[7]

329 Johan van der Keuken filming, with Noshka van der Lely recording the sound

■ Santa Claus arrives ■ Oude Schans shot from canal, rain ■ Moped courier Khalid on Haarlemmerdijk and the winter canals ■ Christmas lights being put up in Reestraat, Runstraat and Keizersgracht ■ making echographs at OLV Hospital, Roberto and Aletta ■ Taking the underground to Bijlmermeer, the baby's things in Roberto and Aletta's flat: the baby has arrived! ■ Ganzenhoef market ■ Shots from car of Bijlmermeer ■ Borz-Ali, the Chechen, watching Russian TV (Invasion of Chechnya) with his wife Julia and son Kasbek ■ Christmas lights at night ■ Fireworks on New Year's Eve (Nieuwmarkt area + overview of city) ■ Shots from car of Amsterdam-Oost – broken-up streets – following a woman carrying bread ■ Turkish women ■ Courier Khalid riding in the rain to the arcade at the Rijksmuseum where he meets others couriers and girls ■ Mathilda from Ghana visits Ghanaian fabric shop – Ganzenhoef ■ 2 girls standing in front of two windows, Keizersgracht (from canal) ■ Talk with Khalid the courier ■ Playing cards in table tennis centre ■ Shots from car of Bijlmermeer with distorting TV ■ Mathilda at Ghanaian seamstress's, her daughter watches the distorted TV ■ Shots driving round 'Arena' under construction ■ The Chechen Borz-Ali on the phone in the car (driving over Dam Square, Paleisstraat) ■ Borz-Ali with video image of his dead brother (presumed dead it transpires later) ■ The Bolivian Roberto cleaning at Albert Heijn supermarket, Bijlmermeer ■ Talk with Roberto, air trip from Bijlmermeer to Bolivia ■ Party in Roberto's village, Copnsquia ■ Talk between Roberto and his mother ■ Khalid arrives at the photographer Erwin Olaf's; the photo session ■ Tramp with pointed cap – posing as statue – and his mate; Damrak in the rain ■ Chinese school in Pijp neighbourhood; the calligrapher ■ Shots from water along canal fronts (Oude Waal); sound of a Chinese lute. Late winter ■ Shots driving through garages at night in Bijlmermeer ■ The Ghanaian Mathilda at the mirror – puts on headscarf ■ Ghanaian 'funeral party' in Bijlmermeer ■ Flying above Amsterdam, waterways and canals in the spring sun ■ Shots driving through city centre ■ Cross-street conversation between two ladies at opposite windows in Jordaan area ■ Fishmonger's on Zeedijk ■ The courier Khalid waits in the courier's corner of the photolab while listening to house number 'Move Your Ass' ■ Khalid riding over Rozengracht ■ Khalid riding in the Vondel Park wearing reflecting sunglasses. Above him the spring green of the trees ■ Khalid arrives at Museumplein, the couriers' meeting place. A 'gladiator fight' between couriers and skaters (class struggle?) ■ Backgammon in the chess café – outside, the barefoot tramp (evening) ■ The barefoot tramp woken up in a park just up the street (Korte Leidsedwarsstraat) ■ His barefoot journey ■ Borz-Ali on the phone in the car ■ Talk with Borz-Ali who lives between screens, zappers and mobile phones ■ Journey to Chechnya, into the war zone, through Grozny and as far as his village in the mountains ■ Queen's Day on the water (Amsterdam) ■ Spicy chips in a Jordaan snack bar (Ajax football club on TV – video game) ■ Spicy pitta bread in a snack bar on Damstraat (Ajax on TV) ■ Surinamese sandwich bar in Amsterdam-Oost (Ajax on TV) ■ Coffee shop, dope-dealing. Khalid there to buy 'skunk', Dutch grass (Ajax on TV) ■ DJ 100% Isis carrying her suitcase across Rembrandtplein ■ The entrance to the house-disco 'Chemistry' – weapons check by metal detector ■ 100% Isis arrives at 'Chemistry', crosses the undercroft, opens her suitcase (of vinyl discs) and starts mixing it. House scene ■ Rock group 'Sikter' from Sarajevo (Leidseplein, tram stop) ■ Playing football in a burned-out street in Sarajevo (war) ■ Airplanes, chimneys ■ Smoke, waste and waste incinerator (Western Docklands) ■ A Boeing landing at Schiphol ■ In the corridors where the asylum-seekers wait (Schiphol) ■ Photographs and fingerprints ■ Shots driving of 'Byzantium' and copse near Leidseplein ■ Shots driving past night club display windows – Thorbeckeplein ■ On the stair in the tower. Man climbing ■ Man arrives at the top, hits that carillon. The bell-ringer ■ We get carried aloft by the chiming of the bells ■ Carillon music drifting across the city ■ Shots from the water along rafts, a girl and a boy in bathing suits, reading ■ In a garden on the river Amstel, photo sessions 4 sisters, partly naked. Enter the courier ■ Shot from car of church (Zuiderkerk), sunset ■ Moving shots of Transvaal neighbourhood, Amsterdam-West. Early. (Hennie narrates) ■ Shots from car of Plantage – Desmet Theatre, Hollandse Schouwburg (Story of the Jewish mother Hennie) ■ Hennie and her son Adrie leave their house in her turquoise car and arrive in Transvaalstraat ■ Visit to the flat where they lived during the war until going into hiding (Mrs. Hasselbainks from Suriname lives there now) ■ Talk between Hennie and Adrie, saying goodbye to Mrs. Hasselbainks ■ Shots from car of Transvaalstraat, quiet and early ■ Hennie and Adrie's trip to Zeeland. Talk about the end of the war. They sing a children's song ('Kortjakje') ■ DJ 100% Isis walking at night with her case of records ■ Vondel Park, summer. Youngsters busy doing nothing while Albert Ayler blasts out 'Summertime' on his sax ■ Thai restaurant on Zeedijk ■ Poster proclaiming Thai boxing gala, Amsterdam ■ Flight to Thailand ■ Boxers sparring in Thailand – an elephant passes the ring ■ The match. 'Our' boxer wins. He and his family – a 'filmed photograph'. Mother ■ Boxing gala in Amsterdam (Zuid sports hall) ■ 'Filmed photograph' of Thai boxers. Mother ■ Roberto (the Bolivian) and his small son Aini, who kicks a ball for the first time ■ Khalid riding in a new office district. His thoughts about being a Muslim ■ Khalid takes a photograph to the editors' office and discusses electronic image technology with newspaper editor ■ On the water at night – early morning – an out-of-the-way spot in the IJ inlet – offscreen narrative by Johan (the filmmaker): a man swimming, Neptunus in late summer ■ Bridges in autumn, canalside, brown leaves. Music from Debussy's 'La Mer' begins ■ Over to the Concertgebouw Orchestra. Riccardo Chailly rehearsing 'La Mer' ■ 'La Mer' continues. Winter. Snow, cold. A Christmas tree on the water. Builders' skips ■ Driving movement continuing to canal fronts, window with a woman behind it ■ The woman shuts the curtain, inside the house ■ A multisexual love scene unfurls ■ Seagulls, their screams and wind (Oude Schans) ■ Khalid rides off out of the film (Western Docklands) ■ End titles

➤333

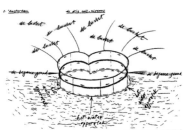

332

330   331

Sociology of the table [334-344]

The table, a raised surface for arranging objects on and sitting round, is an elementary plaza, a surface for everything that takes place between those sitting round it. The table is pre-eminently the space to clinch a deal. The surroundings are there too, but at a distance. The table top generates a form of concentration that makes it difficult for you to switch off or turn away. It keeps the group together. A field of attention, the table is also an arena, a place for games and drama. It articulates the sense of togetherness or maybe the lack of it. Likemindedness, discord, misunderstanding, agreement wash across the table and it is here that the rules of the relationship between and understanding among people are established and where things are discussed, negotiated or sold.

A table is a socially veiled means of getting into conversation, in some situations with more impact than with standing encounters; a mechanism whose effect is either wordlessly intentional or innocently unintentional. Government leaders prefer to sit more informally, in a salon or by the fire, except when it's contract-signing time. That requires a table. This is round if the question of equality is expected to cause trouble. In the case of long tables the person sitting at its head prevails. It is he or she who has the best view of the proceedings. In the case of fixed tables the

334 Centraal Beheer, Apeldoorn

335 Photo Brassai

338 Van Gogh, *The Potato Eaters*, 1885

336 Picnic, Geneva

337 State banquet, Windsor Castle

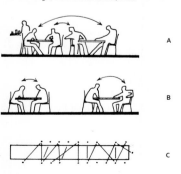

339 Communication at table

head ends can be closed off so that no-one can rule the roost from that position. Excessively long tables divide themselves automatically into smaller sections due to breaks in contact, depending on the conversation. The sense of unity, however, remains. (339C)

At large-scale dinners or party games the table needs dividing into so many individual tables, grouped so closely together as to be experienced as a single table. Should this not be the case, then the sense of togetherness dissolves. This is why the distances between them must be so slight as to prevent discrete islands from forming and so that contact with the table over your shoulder is as strong as that with those sitting across from you. (339A)

Background music in restaurants serves to create distance between tables. You want your own conversation, distinct from that of others, though they have to be there.

Parties and celebrations where there is food served without there being enough tables for everybody, might give you the advantage of being able to choose your company yourself. However, eating standing up, with one hand clutching your plate, is a clumsy, unstable, piecemeal affair. A table necessarily reduces the level of informality and keeps things and people together.

340 Paris

341 The G7 ministers confer

343 Photo André Kertész

342 Potato eaters, Bolivia

344 Village square, Bussare

It takes a conscious, purposeful attitude on the part of designers to give the space inside a building – whatever is left between walls, floors and columns, in other words between everything that is constructed and made material – the quality of social space. Important though it is to make sufficient place-like areas that invite short- or long-term stays with 'official' or informal seating facilities, this in itself is not enough. If a building is to function properly, it is essential that it is organized so that people do indeed encounter one another.

When organizing the design, you can go a long way in influencing visual relationships and possibilities for encountering or avoiding others. Strategic sight lines, places for sojourn and intersections of circulation routes articulated by inserting voids, landings, bridges, light and dark places, transparency, views out, views through and screens to conceal and protect – these are some of the means architects have at their disposal. This is an essential and enduring design theme.

Besides such fundamental design premises there are also practical procedures without which you are lost. Partitioning, for example, as requested in each case by the fire brigade – a disaster for spatial continuity – rules out all feelings of 'urbanity' that an interior space might have had.
The issue here is to safeguard spatially the 'great gesture' alongside the many smaller rooms and places inside a building. Without falling into the trap of seeking to replicate real streets inside buildings, it does make sense to capitalize on the associations aroused by particular architectural means. In *Lessons for Students in Architecture* I described how different materials and resources can strengthen the feeling of being inside or outside. This holds equally well for the ambience that natural light in particular can create.[9] As an example, overhead light entering in long strips can stress the difference between a passage and a street.

Raise the standard storey height and a sense of spatiality emerges that suggests a larger, more urban character.
This feeling of 'urbanity', as antithesis to the sense of a degree of enclosure and security that unconsciously belongs to private rooms, also has to do with the presence there of others. Space can announce the presence of people even though those people are not present physically.
You can also influence the bustle or peace and quiet in a building by having many people seem fewer, or by making fewer people more manifest.
Analogous to the idea of a 'promenade architecturale', as Le Corbusier describes how a space is experienced while passing through it, you can use spatial means to strengthen and dramatize the dynamic of moving people so that more theatrical (i.e. intensified) situations arise that tend to draw people closer. The way the space is organized can increase the chances of encounter for those in search of others or someone in particular, maybe without them wanting to admit it or even being aware of it.

Space through its organization can have an attracting effect and bring or hold people together like a kind of electromagnetic field, by creating the conditions that best focus their attention on each other and keep it there.

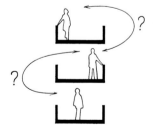

345

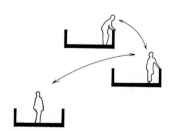

346

Ministry of Social Welfare and Employment, The Hague (1979-90) [347-355]

This office building almost amounts to a demonstration of how a building can be organized as a city.[9] The office units are housed in a string of more or less independent buildings comprising the periphery, wrapped round a communal space extending throughout the building. This central space is the main artery where all the general facilities are to be found – toilets, meeting rooms, coffee bars – and, most importantly, where all internal circulation takes place. The entire building has a single entrance and is in fact hermetically sealed off in line with the security requirements – perhaps too much so, for it is more of a fortress than we intended.

Arriving from the entrance lobby in the main space, you take the escalator to the left or right half of the building. From there you branch out, taking one of six free-standing stairs and lifts leading up to the various corners of the complex. There are also large central lifts in both left- and right-hand portions of the building.

The streetlike quality of this spatial backbone is enhanced by the glass roofs and the outflows to terraces for general use. Whether entering the building or leaving one of its departments, you invariably find yourself in this central zone. This is where you meet others, either by chance or by appointment.

In most buildings, you have rooms and corridors and little besides. The only place for accidental encounters is the restaurant. Here by contrast the central zone that breaks down the division into floors and spatially fixes the entire internal organization is typical of the building as a whole, triggering social encounters and encouraging everyone not to stick to their own room or department.

Informal social contacts are not only important in terms of breaks or relaxation but also serve an intellectual purpose. This is familiar to everyone who has spent far too long trying to solve a problem, only to find that the colleague they inadvertently bumped into was the very one who could have helped them to sort it out long ago. If only they had thought of that sooner! This is where a building's spatial organization can offer positive conditions. This large central space is in effect an atrium like the

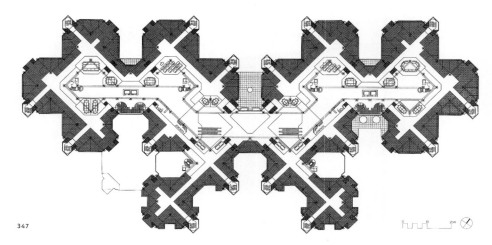

347

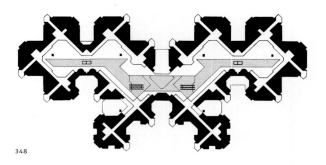

348

349

ones found in so many large buildings. All too often it is just a static visually-oriented space with few real attractions.

It is essential that such buildings are so organized in 'urbanistic' terms that all activity is concentrated in this internal high street. Everyone inevitably returns to this supremely logical connecting route between the different shared facilities, much as you are drawn to urban streets or squares that provide everything that makes a city a city.

Layouts of cities are in effect flat – only rarely is a city accessible on a level other than the ground plane. Here in this build-ing by contrast the various layers are inter-linked by voids, thereby adding a dimension to the space of the centre. You might say that the familiar evocative images from Fritz Lang's film 'Metropolis', where we feel surrounded by the dynamic of a major city, served as an association for this scaled-down model of a multi-level urban space. The various interacting levels of this cen-tral zone are not identical or repetitive. Our idea was that every level should follow its own course, so that you skirt the level below on your way across to the other side of the void. No two bridges across the void are vertically aligned, but slip past each other to generate the most favourable sight lines, up and down at an angle, to increase, at least visually, the chances of encounter-ing others. The upshot of this three-dimen-sional high street was that roughly half of the total surface area of the building (luck-ily excluding the voids) proved not to be for offices. If this seems more than a little inefficient, it is more than made up for by the many activities accommodated there and so not requiring separate space else-where, such as meeting areas, places to sit with clients and coffee corners.

We removed as much of the brief from the official domain as we could to informally house it in the 'street'. This space also takes up a considerable proportion of the internal circulation, there being almost nothing in the way of corridors literally in the narrow sense of the word.

Although the building was primarily designed as office 'cells' it lends itself admirably for more open configurations should the need for these arise.

The 'islands' of offices are so divided as to leave a quarter of their centre open to widen the passage at that point. This produces an extra place for each island that can be allocated accordingly. Corridors have been kept as short as possible and save for the odd exception in the understructure they are in principle no longer than is necessary to reach between two adjacent linked islands. All doors to rooms slide open and shut, providing openings that are larger than usual. We suspect that these doors will come to be left open more often than if

351

352

they had been the customary variety, increasing the feeling of solidarity between those on the island. Looking at the average office today, one is struck by the fact that in general most of the doors are permanently in the open position – evidently they are there just in case. Sliding doors create a considerable amount of extra space, no luxury in a room of minimum size. Besides the central coffee bar near the restaurant there are coffee corners scattered throughout the entire central zone; subcentres at strategic points that act as meeting places at 'neighbourhood level', to continue the city analogy. These facilities are equipped as kitchenettes – with a fridge and hot plates – and so designed as to function as buffets when manned by serving personnel and as self-service counters when not. This set-up deviates fundamentally from that of the coffee bars in Centraal Beheer[10] (since removed, as it happens) and in Vredenburg Music Centre (since modernized).[11] Here in the ministry they have an open configuration and a low table that invites you to pull up a chair. In both situations, with and without personnel, they are fully functioning. Equipped with small movable tables, these places act much like pavement cafés in a city. They are mostly found at wider parts to one side of the circulation routes, islands generally located near clusters of meeting rooms, though 'passers-by' may easily find themselves drawn there too.

354

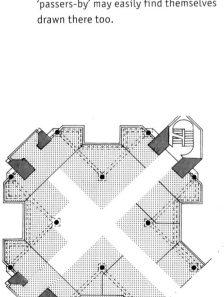

353

355

Foyer, stairs and bridges,
Chassé Theatre, Breda (1995) [356-367]

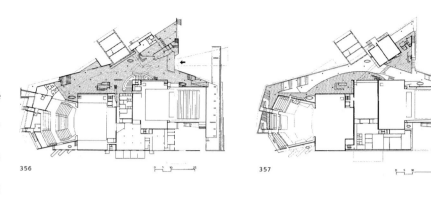

356

357

358

The foyer of a theatre or music centre is perhaps the best imaginable example of a collective space functioning as a city centre in miniature. It is not just visited for the performance but also to observe one another and meet friends and acquaintances in the interval or after the performance. The space has, of course, to be primed and equipped as a multiplicity of zones, places of differing qualities. The wider the diversity of what is on offer – different types of seating, lighting, colour and decoration, each with its own ambience – the greater the choice and therefore the flow of visitors constantly en route, maybe even unintentionally looking for someone.

As this particular foyer has an element of amorphousness imposed upon it by external factors, this almost automatically led to a great variety of corners. These are spread over three storeys suspended as discrete balconies, linked to one another in a continuous circuit by flights of steps and walkways.

Just as important is the fact that these areas are linked visually and so fully connected as to present together a layered spatiality, where you are surrounded by others but for a void, so to speak. Balconies are always placed at such a distance that the occupants of each have a view of the others.

The exceedingly broad stairs reaching from the ground to the first floor are in effect ascending floors when people stop to talk or even sit on the steps. These stairs have not only a function as circulation but also are a place to linger, a thoroughly serviceable foyer surface in fact.

The stairs leading on up to the balconies in

359

361

362

363

364

the main auditorium divide into two half-way up and slide over each other so that the traffic flows cross. Whether ascending or descending you often have unexpected views of the opposite flow, unlike on single broad staircases. Protruding sculpturally through the facade in places, they simulta-neously provide a succession of views out. From outside you can see something of the accessibility mechanism of the many ter-race-like balcony units – in and out of alignment, horizontally and vertically – in the main auditorium.

365

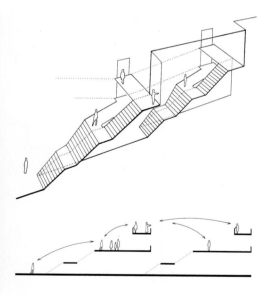

366

367

Montessori College Oost, Amsterdam (1999) [368-373]

A school for secondary education is populated by children of an age when generally speaking they prefer to get out of the house whenever they can to hang out with others of their age; something they are more likely to do in the street than at school. Not only that, at the Montessori College there are no less than 56 nationalities, most of which have difficulty adapting and little motivation, not least because they speak little or no Dutch.

For that reason alone we should be designing schools that make a less hair-raising impression than the customary labyrinth of passages that most closely recalls hospitals and the like.

Though we architects have scarcely any influence on the actual teaching, we can try to make the setting in which this is done as inviting as possible. In view of all the mental effort required of them, pupils should

be made to feel as much at home there as in their familiar stamping ground: the city. Consequently we have organized the space of this school so that it conjures up associations with the city; a wide range of places with a multitude of possibilities where you can hang around, assemble or meet up. The emphasis here is very much on performances, parties, handiwork and artistic offerings, as well as all the things that can take place there outside school hours. In organizing the layout of this school of 1200 to 1600 pupils we deliberately proceeded from this city paradigm by amalgamating as much as possible of the space beyond the containment of the classrooms into a large 'urban' area. The upshot is a large plaza, linked spatially to the void of the classrooms block. Oriented to the south, this void terminates at the top in a full-length semi-roofed terrace.

We were successful in almost entirely avoiding compartmentalizing the 'collective' area; so there are no self-closing doors to constantly remind you of an intricate branched system of internal corridors. To do this it was necessary to locate all rooms in the periphery, with galleries alongside connected to external stairways. These galleries are not just emergency exits but flank all classrooms where they double as balconies as well as contribute to solar control.

The front and rear of this hundred-metres-long building are shifted a half-storey. This downplays the distinction between floors and makes for better communication between different physical and organizational components of the school. The difference in height needing to be bridged is then a mere half-level; it also improves visual relations between one level and

368

369

another. All study areas overlook a single communal hall. Extending the entire length and height of the building and naturally lit from above, this is the internal traffic artery off which are all toilets, cloakrooms, coffee corners and other communal facili-

ties. This 'social space' has a streetlike character, though one that combines ease of circulation with those necessary places on which pupils can descend before, between and after classes if only briefly. In a set-up where the pupils change class-

rooms from one period to the next, they move like nomads through the building, continually 'visiting' and with no territory of their own. It is this very area, then, that should be inviting.

The stairs between levels are deliberately made broad like seating in an amphitheatre. Here lessons can be held outside the classrooms; they are also ideal places for pupils to meet, drawing them there like a magnet. For that matter, wherever there are steps in the city you can see just how popular such informal short-term seating is. These study balconies each bridging a half- level were modelled on the hall of the Apollo Schools.[10] In this school, about seven times as big as its Amsterdam forerunners, the amphitheatre or rather grandstand principle has been rendered as seven balconies suspended at various heights in the void. Stairs, landings, voids and open spaces everywhere are so related spatially as to express to the full the presence there of others, inviting encounters and impromptu discussions.

370

371

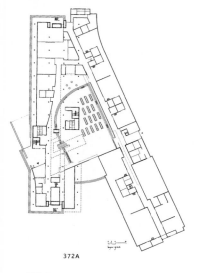

372A

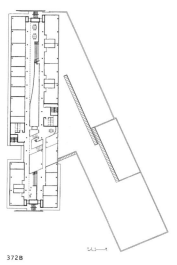

372B

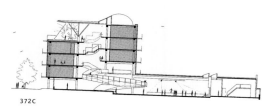

372C

■ BUILDING CONFIGURED AS CITY A theme I keep returning to is that of organizing the interior space in accordance with an urban hierarchy. This proceeds each time from a central space in a more or less articulated form ranged round which are the rooms for living and working, all reached from the central hall. A crucial aspect here is that all internal circulation should be confined to this central space so that everyone keeps returning to it and the paths keep crossing.

This call for configuring buildings as cities was first made five hundred years ago by Leon Battista Alberti in his *De re aedificatoria libri*:

'... for if a City, according to the Opinion of Philosophers, be no more than a greate House, and, on the other Hand, a house be a little City; why may it not be said, that the Members of that House are so many little Houses; such as the Court-yard, the Hall, the Parlour, the Portico, and the like?'[12]

'And indeed vestibules, Halls, and the like Places of public Reception in Houses, ought to be like Squares and other open Places in Cities; not in a remote private Corner, but in the centre and the most publick Place, where all the other Members may readily meet: For here all Lobbies and Stair-cases are to terminate; here you meet and receive your Guests.'[13]

Aldo van Eyck would later couch that same intention in more general terms but, for me at least, far more persuasively. Alberti undoubtedly saw both house and city as universal models, but aside from this metaphor his text can be read as little more than a call for articulation and partitioning as an important element of both building design and urban planning. We should take note that Alberti's urban planning was enacted on an extremely limited scale by modern standards. For Van Eyck, house and city are each an extension of the other in a continually articulated world and at the same time a transformation of each other (tree = leaf).

Seen as part of the social paradigm of the city, the dazzling symmetry of this saying unfortunately fails to hold true. A house, and more especially a building for collective use, we may regard as city, as 'urban', or even as a fragment of a city, but not as a tiny city with its suggestion of functional completeness.

Regarded in a sociological light, to see the city as a house is too limited and, more to the point, too narrow. City for us implies an openness to the world, the availability of choice, space. Excitement, adventure, risk and danger are part and parcel of it. House by contrast presupposes containment, protection, somewhere to yourself; where you can relax, rest, reflect and gather your wits together. The privacy behind the front door of your house is a real luxury, one that is seldom found in the past when it was the privilege of only the most wealthy.

So, we would prefer to forget the city as a house – unless it is a permanently open, though necessarily protected, house – if that city is to function on the social front.

Space for collectivity is essentially open and unprotected. Social space, as still found largely in many central-city areas, is the very nub of the public domain. We today can continue to draw from a still considerable if rapidly shrinking supply of classic examples of cities which – whatever their differences – can be traced back to the type of the central concourse or main street on which the most important buildings stand surrounded by dwelling-houses.

Buildings more organized to that model would acquire indoors the quality that seems no longer attainable outdoors – at least judging from most modern cities of buildings and structures which are too far-flung, too autonomous.

Although we must keep working with might and main to give our exterior spaces something of the enclosure they once had, it remains of the essence that we make our buildings more urban whenever possible and even conceive of them as a model for the city.

The space left between built elements both inside and outside is not automatically social space. We must keep searching for space forms that make our buildings mechanisms where everyone crosses everyone else's path, a mechanism that is more than a human storage system whose contents are condemned to solitary confinement.

Dubrovnik, Croatia [374-377]

The ancient walled town of Dubrovnik is
organized in a way that can be understood
at a glance wherever you are, without
recourse to a map or aerial photograph.
Placa, the main street, slices the oval town
plan lengthwise like the vein of a leaf.
Stepping down to it at right angles are
narrow parallel streets of houses in a Roman
grid, their highest point on the side of the
town wall.
You invariably end up in this main spine
which does not really lead anywhere but

374

375

contains shops and other town services. Its
clear form and shiny marble paving unmistakably mark it out as the town centre.
You could easily imagine this main street
as the central connecting passage and backbone of a large building, the main artery of
internal circulation with smaller passages
issuing from it.
Walled in and freed from its surroundings,
this town with its modest dimensions and
air of intimacy is a long way towards
becoming such a building. In its clarity and
unambiguity of organization, it is the 'arch-
form' of a building, more so than of a city.

376

377

6

Anticipating the Unexpected

Buildings, in my opinion, should be interpreted as cities. At least they should exhibit the same distinction internally between the shared realms – the streets and squares, so to speak – and the more detached or contained spaces – the 'houses' and other 'buildings'. The structure of streets and squares this generates inside the building coincides with the internal circulation obtaining there, so that everyone gets to where they want to be along routes that intersect with others. Such a structure makes a building fundamentally and pre-eminently suited to social exchange between its users or inhabitants.

This wider, 'urban' spatial response to buildings is significant also in terms of durability. A city lasts much longer than a building because, although components are changed or exchanged, there is a tendency to respect its public infrastructure: streets and squares remain while buildings alter or are replaced. Whenever you revisit a place after a long absence everything is different; there are different shops, different names, strange new buildings, the streets are fitted out differently. But your memory finds support in the broad lines that remain: street corners, views through, profiles – in short, all elements that maintain the space structure of the city.

It is impossible these days to conceive of a building capable of resisting the urge, the compulsion even, to alter in the wake of ever-changing ideas, ways of working, forms of organization, property transfers, modifications in zoning and function, expansion, reduction, extreme demands made on efficiency, burgeoning prosperity or simply the need to look different. These are forces no-one can keep in check.

A building that is unable to admit this much freedom of movement has a bleak future ahead of it.

That buildings age more quickly now than ever before has deprived architects of the basic certainty of making meaningful decisions, let alone believing in anything like an immutable basis. Yet it is just this instability among architects that causes the useful life of buildings and structures to extend no further than could be envisaged at the design stage. By kicking away all the certainties, as modern thinking is keen to do,

there would only be 'throw-away' architecture left. It is only by proceeding from the one principle that change contains the seeds of permanence that this dilemma can be resolved. Though there is something of a paradox here: that only the enduring resists change, and resists the unexpected.

The only buildings in a condition to meet social change are those organized more along urbanistic lines, in other words having at their disposal, like a city, a main structure of streets and squares as an ordering hand essentially unaffected by changes in use form. For all buildings, what matters is that they are equipped with a good access structure so that all rooms are stitched together by an elementary spatial 'skeleton' encompassing the entire building.

So it is pre-eminently the collective space of buildings that fulfils the task of a continuous ordering network, providing that this space is clearly and deliberately conceived as such. For a building's construction it is essential – and this is where the analogy with the city ends – that the main loadbearing structure not only follows the collective space but expresses this with maximum clarity. For if anything requires expressing in architecture and construction it is the idea of collective space, and then in a building order that articulates as much the totality as an oversailing gesture as the small components comprising this totality.

A clear spatial structure or infrastructure promises durability, and because of it makes more space in which to capitalize on the need for change. This gives rise to space for time, and space for the unexpected. An essential aspect of this train of thought is the fundamental distinction made between a strong – enduring – if not constant component, a 'structure', and more variable – temporary – accretions or rather infills complementary to it.[1]

An essential part of structuralism as this relates to architecture is its capacity to make a distinction between 'competence' (a form's potential for interpretation) and 'performance' (how it is interpreted in a given situation).

This entails that we can distinguish between structures and their infills. Forms of a relatively great durability have the

378 Amsterdam, structure of canals

capacity to support and give direction to infills of a shorter life-span. An amphitheatre, for example, is able to incite vastly different uses in deviating circumstances, during which the amphitheatre as form – and this is the remarkable thing – is as present and 'available' as ever. It has the capacity to adopt different roles and present different faces yet remain itself. Its form is continually open to new interpretations and, consequently, new applications.

These days the structuralist-influenced mode of thought considered here is all too often regarded with scepticism. The misunderstandings on this front, not just fuelled by architecture criticism but invoked by us architects as well, are difficult to erase.

It is a mistake to seek to define structuralism as a 'style' with an explicit and emphatic, often coercive design marked by the small-scale and a predilection for prefabricated elements that tend to combine in the most complex possible forms. This 'style', it is claimed, is unable to admit change and thus is rendered obsolete by the instability of the world today. This confused reading is most of all caused by a one-sided exposition of two twists to this tale. First, there is a overly partisan emphasis on individual interpretation, meaning the possibility of allowing a form to be filled in and so appropriated by different users and occupiers each in their own way. But for a form to be open to interpretation suggests equally that it can be applied differently under different circumstances on different occasions and therefore is able to withstand time. An interpretable form retains at all times the potential of being able to play a different role under different conditions. Second, there was too sharp a focus on forms that were all too soon understood to be limited components of a building. There was in addition too much thinking in terms of the small-scale, and the urbanistic component of the story remained chronically underexposed – and this while the examples I took, along with the amphitheatres where in fact it all began for me, were just such large-scale forms, such as the structure of canals in Amsterdam and the gridirons of Barcelona and New York.[2]

For that matter, the gridiron story that keeps cropping up throughout history, achieves its absolute peak in the layout of Manhattan.[3] This is the example par excellence of a plan that permits filling in adequately from block to block and in every epoch. There is no other city plan that takes such a childishly simple underlay of rules and manages to generate such a convincing dialectic of order and freedom in a process continuing through time.

'The gridiron is like a hand operating on extremely simple principles – it admittedly sets down the overall rules, but is all the more flexible when it comes to the detailing of each site. As an objective basis it plots the layout of the urban space, and this layout brings the inevitably chaotic effect of myriad separate decisions down to acceptable propositions. In its simplicity the grid is a more effective means of obtaining some form of regulation than many a finer-meshed system of rules which, although ostensibly more flexible and open, tend to suffocate the imaginative spirit. As far as its economy of means is concerned it is very like a chessboard – and who can think of a wider range of possibilities arising from such simple and straightforward rules than that of a chessplayer?'[4]

When we attach the concepts of competence (the potential at our command) and performance (the use we make of our potential) to architecture, then we are distinguishing between what is relatively speaking fixed and so enduring (the long time-cycle) and what is constantly subject to change (the short time-cycle). And if we wield this distinction with a certain tenacity this gives us the space for the unexpected, a space we need if we are to brave the lack of stability of our world.

There are so many examples of buildings which, after having lost their original use form, could be recycled because their 'competence' proved not only suitable for quite another infill, but even went on to provoke it in some way. Thus we see warehouses eminently suited to receiving offices or houses, not just through their abundance of space and sturdy construction but also their elementary organization. Here it holds, that the less emphasis in the original scheme on the architectural

379 Amphitheatre, Arles

expression of their function, the more accommodating this proves to be for new functions or applications.

Having a concrete skeleton is enough to considerably increase the chances of survival of, say, a housing block whose dwellings one seeks to combine, over those of a building with concrete party walls.[5]

In the distinction between 'strong' enduring forms and 'softer' forms with a shorter time-cycle, we possess a principle with which we can combat uncertainty in architecture and planning, leading as this is to ever greater chaos. What we have here, then, is a thematically determined and determining principal line which, etched into a scheme like a horizon, not only lets in change but fundamentally accepts it.

'Structuralism is nurtured on the paradox that order, rather than limiting freedom by using the correct structural theme in fact incites freedom, thus making space for the unexpected.'[6]

The projects that follow all possess to some degree an overarching form. This encapsulates what takes places 'below' without saying anything too specific about it. This way there is in principle the possibility of changes of every kind occurring at any moment without the identity of the larger whole essentially being affected in urbanistic terms.

By making a fundamental distinction when designing buildings and structures, between a relatively abiding principal organization and a 'softer', more time-sensitive zone for filling in later, the client's brief – ever more frequently formulated as it is by specialists in that field – is put firmly in perspective.

By this I mean that though the conditions of the brief are met, there are still doubts as to whether it makes sense to be seduced into taking all too fundamental decisions about the concept underlying your design. If you do, the chances are good that a fabrication, as much en passant as passé and masquerading as truth, will end up with a permanent form.

Architects have been led to believe that the brief, couched by or on behalf of the client they are accountable to, is sacred rather than an 'administrative minumum' which has to be met if the two of you are to remain on good terms. We are all too easily carried away by this belief, as an excuse to not have to

think ourselves; and so we are cheated with an excessively specific idea of a building that is already fast losing its relevance and its usefulness. For then the new director and the new cook and the new occupants arrive on the scene with another idea entirely and there is no room in it for your odd-ball scheme.

The more precise and specific the brief and the closer to it your concept of the building, the greater the certainty that the building will become unusable sooner than expected. Underlying the administrative programme, where everything is portioned out into compartments of so many square metres with an interminable fuss about net and gross surface areas, and consisting chiefly of a litany of supposedly individual interests – beneath this is another programme, to wit, that of your social and cultural responsibility as an architect. This is less easy to draw up let alone quantify but involves a longer time span.

Instead of sticking scrupulously to the brief, the way you might pack a suitcase, you can better try to penetrate to those conditions which, even if coloured by changes of trend, fundamentally remain the same and are valued by everyone in one way or another as a collective feeling, though those same experiences are constantly being reinterpreted over time. For instance, we all require views out but need some degree of physical protection too. Everyone unconsciously seeks a certain equipoise between views on the one side and 'cover' on the other. For all the fact that the thing we sense as spatiality is ours to establish as individuals, this spatiality has always belonged to a web of universal experiences, and it is collectively unconscious conditions such as these that we must seek to dig up and use as departure points for our ideas.

We discussed earlier the difference between an apparatus and an instrument. 'A properly functioning apparatus does the work for which it is programmed, that which is expected of it – no less, but also no more. By pressing the right buttons the expected results are obtained, the same for everyone, always the same. A (musical) instrument essentially contains as many possibilities of usage as uses to which it is put – an instrument

380 Amphitheatre, Arles, France. A fort in medieval times, it was subsequently built solid and functioned as a complete town until the 19th century

381 Amphitheatre, Lucca, Italy, scooped out as a plaza

must be played. Within the limits of the instrument, it is up to the player to draw what he can from it, within the limits of his own ability. Thus instrument and player reveal to each other their respective abilities to complement and fulfil one another. Form as an instrument offers the scope for each person to do what he has most at heart, and above all to do it in his own way.'[7] A good instrument can be played even with a change of music.

A building seems in essence closer to an instrument, musical or otherwise, than to an apparatus (excepting obvious 'servant' components). Like an instrument it consists of a multiplicity of conditions that together represent a particular potential. That potential – or 'competence' – is the leeway the building has and can be addressed by providing appropriate readings for a multitude of situations.

It's competence is the capacity to accept change and the unexpected – the new as this resides in the concept – through its ability to adapt to the new and simultaneously have the new adapt to it. A building derives its competence from the combination of immutable, or enduring, factors or conditions it is predicated upon.

You need to develop a special sense to make the distinction: between that which belongs to the basic conditions and that which is added and of a more temporary and interchangeable value; between the abiding, thus belonging to a long time cycle, and the transient and replaceable.

These basic conditions, which can be nothing other than a reflection of collective conscious or unconscious needs and wishes, are in general under-represented in the brief, paradoxically because they often seem too obvious but also because usually it is the litany of individual wants and needs that dominates unduly.

An administrative programme is relatively speaking the best equipped for safeguarding, or freezing, individual interests of a single moment. Bizarre as it may seem, the more democratic the situation the more this is the case, in that everyone has more to contribute, with the inevitable consequence that the greatest emphasis comes to rest on all manner of quirkily fashionable and often fly-by-night fictions which fade all too rapidly. It is the architect's task to see right through the programme and single out the more 'collective' layers and attune his concept to them.

Spatially the most basic expression of the collective component is in the shared realm that we manage to keep open between the private, more contained realms.

It is true that private and collective zones are reciprocal and complementary units, but in the design process the collective has necessarily to prevail. It is, after all, the stable factor that can cause the building to endure and should inform it conceptually from top to bottom.

If a building is to have maximum competence, the underlying concept must, before anything else, secure the collective realm. Besides a smoothly functioning circulation and a clearly organized infrastructure, it is important that the correct network of social space is safeguarded. By analogy with the city, emphasis must be on collective space: the streets and squares that define the 'buildings', that is, the more private areas, and are defined by them in return yet in such a way that these private areas can change while the collective space stays intact.

It is the ability of an urban entity or a building, or any other structure for that matter, to be able to accept and stand up to change – what we called competence – that the collective realm leaves space for. When it is used in a new situation for entirely different ends, the experiences and associations that that space manages to evoke in the new situation and the new meaning this generates, together determine the new role it is to play.

So in every new situation the concept holds the space as if physically, so as to make the most of it.

What I am attempting to do in this book is to demonstrate that the opposition of specificity, signification, destination and place to indeterminacy, flexibility, movement and freedom is born of a too narrow reading of the space belonging to the architect, or the lack of space in his thinking; by which I mean the degree of pliancy to free what was once determined, or signified, so that it can be signified anew.

382 Stadium in Osaka, Japan, used for an exhibition of houses and as a theatre

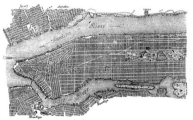

383 Manhattan, New York. Gridiron structure

384

So in terms of data carriers we should not seek to design as if it were a film or a record where the emulsion or grooves retain just one particular non-erasable flow of information, but more as a video or audio tape which is erasable and can be reloaded many times with new information. So though you can typify a magnetic tape as flexible, it is, at least in principle, geared to repeated signification, to being imbued with new information, and because an empty tape literally has no significance it emphatically invites signification. It is this implicit capacity, or competence, that we see as a space, ever available and signifiable in new situations.

Everything we make, construct or leave open should in fact actively invite not only whatever it was made for in the broadest sense, but also change and the unexpected. This is the space that the architect can impart as a potential to everything he designs and makes.

Space fundamentally is not yet destined, not yet signified but signifiable and thus has the capacity to be destined and signified (in the situations that arise). Space is a potential, a commodity that can be acquired repeatedly and in different ways, like the potential of an engine able to be activated in ever new situations; or a mathematical equation in which different quantities can be filled in that satisfy the basic task. Just as a change of formula brings a change of idea, so a potential and thus the space it represents is limited at least in the sense that it is dependent on the concept underlying the scheme in question, which one might regard as its basic task.

What we call space is on the one hand the shaky equilibrium of the signifiable, as yet unsignified – in that sense virginal – but on the other it resolutely invites this treatment and thus is in effect pre-disposed, pre-destined; there is this tug-of-war between the potential for signification and the use of that potential: I call that making space and leaving space.

An essential aspect is that that space is always present in what we do, as a permanent challenge.

Designing is not about whether a thing is determined by the signification attached to it, or indeterminate and free to receive other meanings. The core of the matter rather is whether that signification when stripped away and placed in new circumstances can be resignified, and if so to what extent. We not only have to always give space to things, but do it so that they retain it for all time. For this you need to see the space mentally, to read it in other ways than what is there; to decode as much as code; to unlearn, even more than to learn.

385 Warehouses in Amsterdam converted into houses and studios by Bureau van Stigt

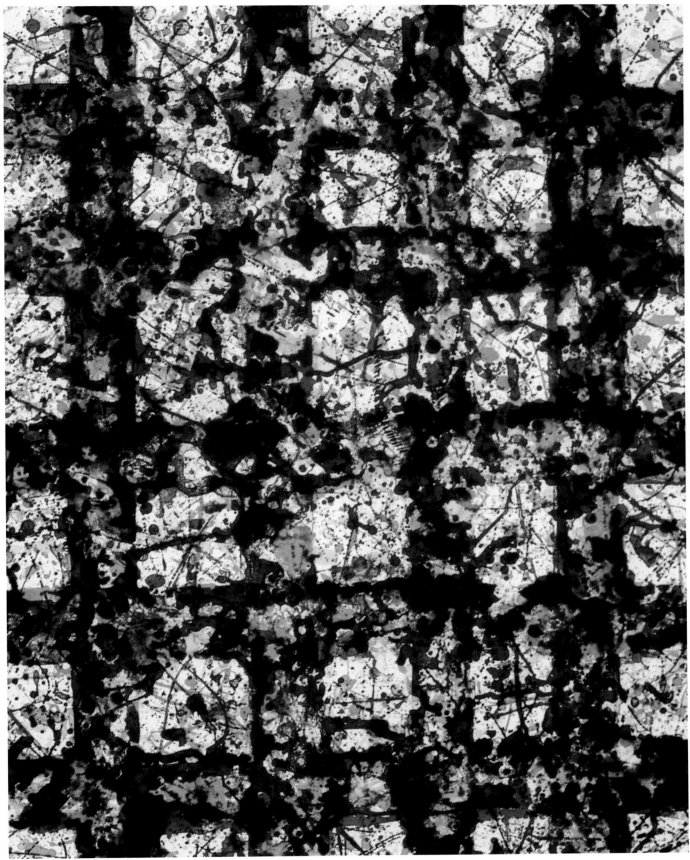

386 Sam Francis, *Untitled*, 1978

387

388

389 Access before (top)
and after 1995

Extensions to Centraal Beheer, Apeldoorn (1995) [387-394]

The Centraal Beheer complex, consisting of the original building designed in 1968-1972, later expanded with the office building next door and long joined to the main building by a bridge-like passage, became unmanageable in every sense by today's standards due to the many entrances that came with the original concept. An ever greater need arose for a system of clear main 'streets' to give the new entity, now almost double its original size, a clearly organized access system. Moreover, the great increase in the number of visitors as a result of changed ideas on company organization, made a single clear, inviting and more representative entrance all the more necessary.

By linking the two buildings with an elongated glass atrium building we could then provide a main entrance on the access road. This 'entrance building' containing the main reception area from which the various departments can be reached, also boasts the main space, a central 'city square' for receptions, festivities and performances – facilities that were lacking until then in both buildings. Also housed under the glass envelope is an entirely free-standing triple-height building, a 'bookcase' of mammoth proportions consisting of a concrete skeleton freely infilled with meeting rooms varying in size from vast to tiny. Because this construction is wholly internal and held clear of the external wall and thus unaffected by conditions outside, any eventual change in the internal subdivision or allocation is merely a question of changing the organizing structure. Such eventualities were taken into consideration from the word go; given the dynamic of the company of today, the building will always be in a state of flux.

The original external wall of the neighbouring building, by then consisting of badly discoloured concrete panelling and doing duty as an internal wall of the atrium clamped onto it, was amazingly transformed by the Swiss artist Carmen Perrin. She had it painted black, prolonging the mullions of the glass envelope in the wall by means of masking tape removed after painting, as if the wall were a light-sensitive surface. With the resulting 'negative' grid reflecting that of the glazing, the envelope is now complete. Finally, the windows in the old

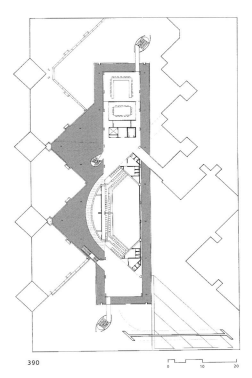

390

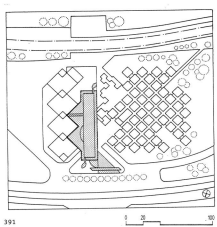

391

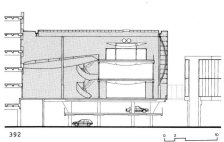

392

facade provide interruptions in the painting, blank spots that interfere in the grid
as random perforations.

393

394

Gebaute Landschaft Freising, Munich, Germany (1993) [395-405]

The overgrown strips of roof characterizing this scheme derive from the need to spare the landscape from being disrupted by intensive development. They oversail the multiformity of the complex which, due to each of the companies to be domiciled there desiring an 'identity' of its own, would no doubt result in a disconnected if not chaotic whole.

This piecemeal and fundamentally out-of-control development is made subservient to curves determined using coordinates that could be fixed in the development brief.

In some respects this scheme is a variant upon Le Corbusier's Obus plan for Algiers of 1932, in which the landscape – in that case the coastline – dictated the shape of the 'sols artificiels' or artificial floors which are not only primed to receive a varied infill in a technical sense but involuntarily draw all the constituent elements together.

The same thing happens in principle to the built development, bound by only a few simple urban rules, within a gridiron system, a development which precisely because of the basic ordering system – unequivocal as it is – can enjoy a greater freedom than would have been possible with a less stringent development brief.

An essential condition here is that the urban ordering system not only determines its infill, but that conversely the infill itself helps to define the nature of the structure. Structure and infill should each be in a position to anticipate the other.

These schemes, and the grid in particular, show clearly what might be the most concise summary of structuralism in urban design: 'an ordering theme, as much determining the infill as determined by it, doesn't restrict freedom but is in fact able to incite it.'[8]

Such megaforms filled in over time, comparable with railways, roads or other constructions that gather together a great many individual participating entities into a matter of general concern, can be regarded as a sort of public facility.

Even though it need not be the government that takes the initiative – a private syndicate could also finance such an enterprise – this becomes increasingly difficult as the part of the construction needing financing in advance increases.

395

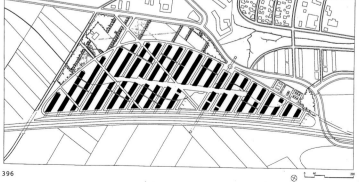

396

397

399 Sketch by Le Corbusier

400

401

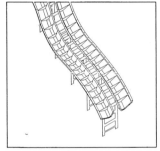

402 Spine

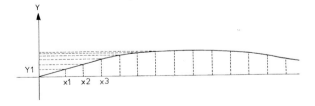

403 Coordinates

398

This is why, after an ingenious spine-like
402 flexible system of prefabricated elements
had been developed for an initial scheme,
the next step was to arrive at a sound set of
rules that would enable the individual
building initiatives to be joined together
to generate the stipulated rows of develop-
403 ment. This should ensure that the complex
can accommodate flows of people over the
roofs and, quite as explicitly, of water as a
'common right'.
As self-evidently simple as such utterances
about collective right of use always have
been in agriculture, this is a complex issue
in our society, as strongly focused as it is
on individual private interest. In our society
all forces operate independently, and it is
these forces that keep splitting larger entities up into discrete objects.

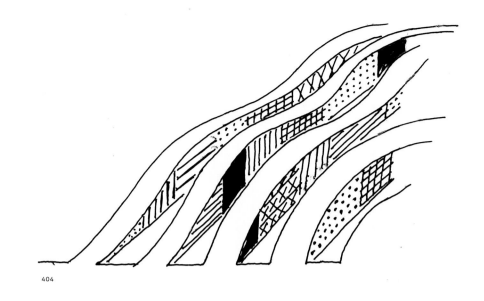

404

405

Competition for the Bibliothèque de France, Paris (1989) [406-413]

A library, certainly an extremely large one, is not just a centre of culture for the city, but visited by so many people it will, like a city theatre or concert hall, come to serve as a social centre.

It is usually quite an achievement finding your way around a library particularly when you are unfamiliar with it. This is why clarity of organization is of crucial importance. Because such a vast concentration of books in such a wide diversity of academic fields cries out for channelling into areas of learning, as the brief in fact suggests, the building is interpreted as a multiplicity of library buildings, grouped in serried ranks on the elongated plaza space, the whole covered with an expansive glass roof. Like a vast arcade, this glazed street draws the city

into the building, flanked by the end elevations of the prism-shaped library departments set square to it.

These individual library buildings are perspicuously accessible from the interior street, where pavilion-like facilities lie like islands containing cafés, information, catalogues, shops and all the other services you would expect to find in, say, railway station concourses and airports.

Within the various sub-libraries, i.e. the internal buildings, peace and concentration can prevail. These sub-libraries can differ enormously one from the other. As building units they are glass containers whose interior is open to change. They are provided to this end with a greater or lesser number of floors that can themselves be subdivided

with partitions into smaller spaces, with the departments more open or inward-looking according to wish. They can also be changed when a new staff takes over, or combined to receive a department that is gaining in importance.

Level with the glass roof, above the library buildings, the entire complex (save for the book stores) is contained in a triple-height framework of general (office) levels. In contradistinction to Perrault's realized scheme, 'turned inward like a monastery', this design opts for a concept that invites the city in, under the large, all-enveloping glass roof beneath which seemingly autonomous libraries are so articulated as to safeguard the overall clarity of organization. The largest dimension of the glass roof con-

406

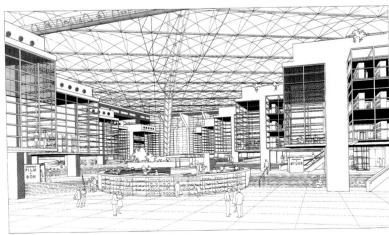

407

curs with that of the Grand Palais while the Bibliothèque Ste Geneviève provided the measure for the buildings arranged beneath the roof.[9] This magnificent elongated space shows in practice what your instinct tells you is the correct unit of measurement.

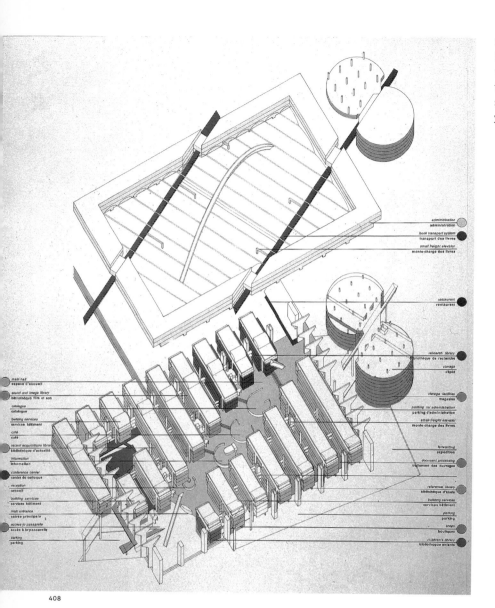

administration
administration

book transport system
transport des livres

small freight elevator
monte-charge des livres

restaurant
restaurant

research library
bibliothèque de recherche

storage
dépôt

storage facilities
magasins

parking for administration
parking d'administration

small freight elevator
monte-charge des livres

forwarding
expédition

document processing
traitement des ouvrages

reference library
bibliothèque d'étude

building services
services bâtiment

parking
parking

shops
boutiques

children's library
bibliothèque enfants

main hall
espace d'accueil

sound and image library
bibliothèque film et son

catalogue
catalogue

building services
services bâtiment

café
café

recent acquisitions library
bibliothèque d'actualité

information
information

conference center
centre de colloque

reception
accueil

building services
services bâtiment

main entrance
entrée principale

access to passarelle
accès à la passarelle

parking
parking

408

409 Grand Palais, Paris

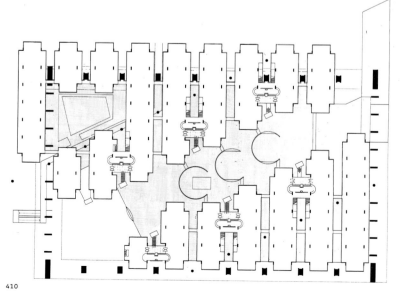

410

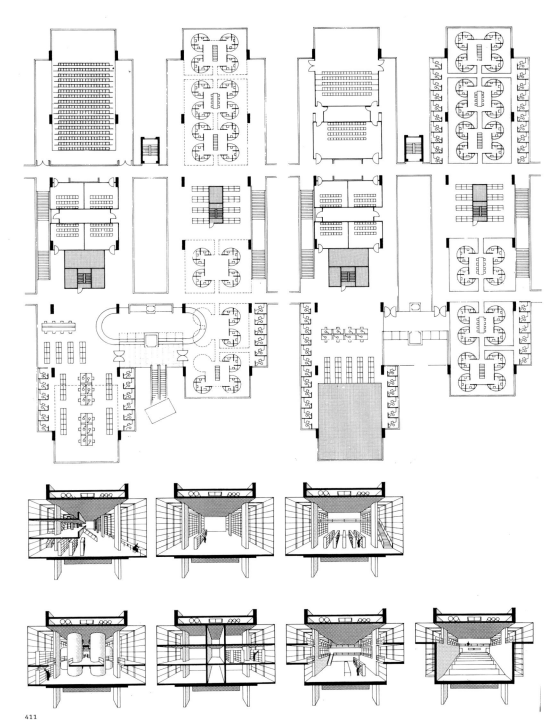

411

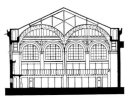

412 Bibliothèque Ste Geneviève, Paris, section

413 Bibliothèque Ste Geneviève, Paris

Carré d'Art, Nîmes, France [414-420]
Norman Foster, 1987-93

This white painted metal building with its facade of slats and demonstratively wispy columns makes a delicate impression against the sharply chiselled Roman pillars of the Maison Carré opposite. Standing together on a single plaza each articulates its worth to the other.

The accessibility of this modest Roman temple and the completeness with which it reveals itself at a glance with its colonnades forming part of the square and only a limited *cella* as interior, is matched only by the impenetrability of Foster's box which is only comprehensible on entering it.

This you do through a fairly banal entrance to find yourself in an imposing hall consti-tuting the central bay of the building, which proves to be buried in the ground and projecting from it in equal measure. The central bay, which to all intents and purposes divides the building into three both in height and depth, contains the main stairs and lifts and seeks to draw in a pro-fusion of daylight through the large skylight as deep into the building as it can, pene-trating down to the subterranean levels. This is presumably why the floors are made of translucent glass.

The rooms of the museum and mediatheque lie along both sides of this arcade-like courtyard where, largely because of their explicit heavy concrete structure, they come across as discrete buildings which you enter from the exterior central zone. The concept of the elongated open and well-lit central zone running through the entire block and doubling as the main stairwell where all internal traffic circu-lates, combines the functions of a vertical axis and a horizontal main street that slices through just about the entire build-ing, endowing it with a great urbanistic clarity.

It would have been even better had this main street inside the building been acces-sible from outside through an entrance of urban dimensions such as the ones many arcades have.

414

415

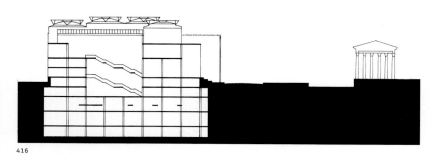

416

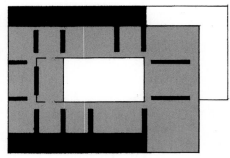

417

418

419

420

Havelis, Jaisalmer, India [421-431]

421

422

In Jaisalmer, an old town in the middle of the Thar desert in the Indian state of Rajasthan, are a number of large palatial residences that stand out through their opulent sculptural decoration on the street frontage. These Havelis, most of which are now empty, have quite a history behind them. In the eighteenth century Jaisalmer was important as a stopping-off point on the great trade route extending from the Middle East to China.

If the exuberant and ornamented sandstone facades are spectacular, so too is the internal layout of these houses. All spaces are grouped on four levels around a number of central square courtyards delivering light to all floors of the house and airing to the full all the surrounding spaces opening onto it.

The living areas consist of square central zones around which are room-sized niche-like side areas one step up and opening onto the central zone.

The house spins out a succession of clear uniform spaces inside a carefully crafted and seemingly geometrically cast stone structure able to receive a diversity of programmes and the fitting-out these require. Besides accommodating one or more families one might imagine the Havelis just as easily containing offices, shops, schools or a museum.

Today these buildings are domestic landscapes occupied by people considerably less rich and moving like nomads with their possessions from place to place, constantly searching for a cool spot.

'Every space changed its purpose with the passing of the day. While the sun was still low, the members of the family went about their business in the highest spaces. As the day became hotter, they would move down into the darker and cooler spaces. During the night, the sun warmed roof terraces provided a good place for sleeping. If the night was particularly chilly, a fire at the bottom of the central courtyard warmed the immediate environment. Thus the houses' inhabitants and their activities percolated through the spaces with the daily climate determining the cycle.'[10]

Numbers of adjoining houses are linked by their roofs. The roofscape this generates with its incomparable sculpture of walls,

423

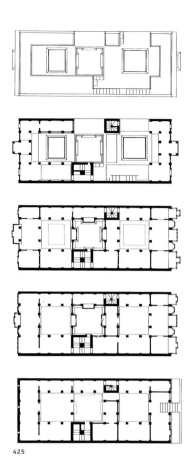

425

426

424

stairs and terraces combines with the square recesses of the internal courts in a system of plaza-like spaces strung together, each with a city of roofs. At present in Bombay, one of the fastest-growing cities in the world with sky-high rents, office spaces are let to more than one party, each for a limited part of the day. Its users, who share the same address, telephone and writing desk, alternate during the day and at night it reverts to a place of habitation.

'Bombay, colonial city centre: First floor, third door left. Along an open-air gallery I enter a mid-sized architecture office:

427

Where the gallery widens about 6 sq. m. there stands a big metal box with a heavy lock.

'Entering the office, eleven people are sitting with one window and one door in about 25 sq. m. Within this space a shelf, close to the entrance door, divides the room into two, into the entrance room with the secretary and a meeting table and then the working room. The ringing of two telephones as constant background noise and a never-ending storm produced by ventilators, keep the paper flying.

'Although the office is rented out for an enormous price per sq. m., the landlord comes now and then to make his phone calls. 7 p.m., time shift. The office closes, the metal box opens and a five-person family starts preparing their dinner on the gallery, where they later also sleep. In the early morning everyone wanders back into the metal box and the family leaves for work.

'Here, on about 30 sq. m. you find a family living, an office running, a landlord checking his estate. Meanwhile, numerous guests arrive, the chauffeur is waiting, tea and food is delivered and the cleaning service is doing its job, all during the working hours.'[11]

One more example of migration across the floor surface. During the day, the lack of space makes for a constant alternation of users.

Just as life in Bombay compacts timewise due to a shortage of space, so in Jaisalmer, where there is too much space, life by contrast rushes apart.

428 Used as a school

429

430

431

Venetian palaces [432-438]

The large Venetian dwelling-houses, the palaces, many of which line the Canal Grande, were consistently informed throughout the succession of styles by the same spatial concept. As a type, roughly speaking, they occupy a place in architectural history that is utterly unique, if only through their siting directly on the water. In outward appearance they might be compared in some respects to the canal houses of Amsterdam, the 'Venice of the North'. But there the siting on the water is always indirect and although in seventeenth- and eighteenth-century Amsterdam water as a major supply route had no small measure of influence on how the city and its components were organized, the overriding issue was the transport of goods. People were conveyed almost exclusively along the quaysides and so the water had no bearing whatsoever on how the buildings were entered. (A unique exception to the Dutch canal set-up is in Utrecht where spaces set below the public street were used to store goods transported over water.[12]) Venice is the only city where the main entrance is right on the water and the houses are accessed by a boat that literally sails inside into a loggia, or rather waterfront portico, with the doors to the house proper set back somewhat. The Ca' d'Oro (1427) is perhaps the most sublime example of this building type. At the back, or in this case at the side of the house is a second, ancillary entrance. This has been known to burgeon into a rival for the main entrance so that you then have two more or less on a par. On entering the Ca' d'Oro a hall gives onto a stair leading to the *gran salone* on the first floor. This encompasses the entire depth of the house, its balcony directly above the entry loggia offering a magnificent view across the Canal Grande. Emblematic of the Venetian palazzo is the great depth with respect to the breadth and unlike the courtyards familiar to us from the major palazzi in Florence and Rome we see here a division depthwise into three with the gran salone the broad central bay flanked by two narrower strips of a succession of rooms all giving onto the elongated central hall. It is this central area of a most generous height certainly by our standards, and often repeated on successive floors, that indisputably dominates the house with the rooms to either side in abeyance to it, no matter how spacious these are. It would be hard indeed to find a more perfect example of Alberti's house like a city, particularly if you imagine the central halls being used for receptions and feasts like a main avenue with the other rooms strung off it like detached buildings. The way the Ca' d'Oro and so many other Venetian palazzi are configured like cities to a simple and perspicuous principle, implies an organization that is just as relevant and applicable today. (Though we would probably be inclined to create a greater spatial link between the various floors with voids and stairs.) This main structure, as universal as it is familiar, is eminently suitable in a wealth of situations for as many different uses. In such cases the outward characteristics of style are nothing other than 'form interpretations' of a timeless spatial order, whatever their part in the look of the successive periods. Although secondary to the spatial organization of these palaces, mention should be made of the unique way these interpretations of form are expressed in the front facades.

Independent of the 'style' in which this is done, the central 'street' zone is invariably expressed externally as a clearly more open area, often almost entirely of glass and sporting balconies. The rooms to either side of it all have their windows shifted to the side walls with between them the windowless section traditionally reserved for fireplaces and chimneys. This produces the supremely characteristic 'hop, skip and jump' rhythm in the facades that is exclusively the preserve of Venice.

432-436

432

433 Ca'd'Oro, Venice

434

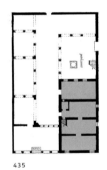

435

436

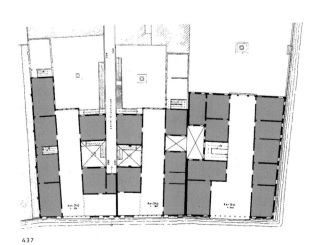

437

438 Canal Grande, Palazzi

Orphanage, Amsterdam [439-440]
Aldo van Eyck, 1955-60

The history of this 'house for children', in actual fact a tiny city, has been a story of changes from the outset. Even before the building was appropriated a discussion raged over how the programme was to be housed in its various units. And when in 1987 the insensitive regime of its then occupants, who were all set to demolish large parts of the Orphanage, came to an end, the building became a place of learning with the arrival there of the Berlage Institute. Then came evidence of the building's great power, or rather its capacity, to take these changes of occupancy in its stride. Although now wholly used as an office building and with little of the former ambience left, a complete disaster it is not. However unfortunately its interior has been treated, as a structure it is still very much in control. Indeed, anything that has been added can simply be removed again. That said, most of the sensitively crafted original interior has gone, a loss that would now seem irrevocable, like so many stunning edifices now vanished from our cities. And yet potentially the space this building has persistently managed to generate as an open structure is present still, ready and waiting for a more propitious age.

439

440

SHELL AND CRYSTAL

This assemblage of open tent-like squares, their contents renewed, is back in circulation to shape the vision of yet another generation of architects. Proof of the complexity and clarity of organization with which formal order and daily life sustain one another, it is both palace and settlement, temple and igloo, crystalline and shell-like. In plan it recalls Fatehpur Sikri, Topkapi, Katsura, Alhambra, yet remarkably is of quite another order and as utterly new as it is familiar.

Immersing himself thoroughly in the mental world of the building's youthful inhabitants, the architect succeeded to a quite extraordinary degree in transposing this world into spatial qualities. It is through such profound identification with its users that the building has become a manifesto against the habitual lack of interest among architects in those who are to occupy their creations. It is a manifesto advocating a sorely needed change of attitude in the profession, namely to use every architectural means to be generous in one's concern for what people expect of their surroundings, both physically and mentally.

It was this 'story of another idea' that made such an impression on architects of my generation, a message that has since made its way to every corner of the earth.

Being thus faced with the sheer variety of what can be done with space confirmed my awareness of just how far the architect's concern could and indeed must extend. Such a radical determination of form, custom-made for each purpose as it is in this building, has been a major inspiration to me to achieve in my own work a more open, more 'interpretable' method, paradoxical though this might seem. The architectural 'order' of the Orphanage provides the lingua franca for a place-by-place interpretation of the demands made by everyday life, to such effect that it convinced me of the need to perceive a building (using the paradigm of *langue* and *parole*) as an interweaving of 'competence' and 'performance'.

The building's 'structure' is still wholly intact, but it has been gutted and thus robbed of its original dialectics. Those who have not seen the actual building – complete, as it used to be – and only know it from photos, are not in a position to truly experience the space of this magnificent 'model of architecture'.

The problem with buildings is that they are too vulnerable, too subject to deterioration, and too big to fit in a museum. It may be possible to preserve limited fragments of them as relics, but those can give but the vaguest reflection of the space they helped to achieve. Break up the bricks and the space escapes – that is, the experience of space, the respiration, the spirit, the taste, the feeling, the idea, the thought.

A void besets our collective memory and our sight.

The brief period of optimism colouring the history of Dutch architecture, the period of Rietveld, Duiker, Van der Vlugt and all those others round and about them who played such a major role – this period is drawn into our own age by Aldo van Eyck's Orphanage. Conserving and sensitively attending to this building so essential to our development, is not just the smallest gesture we can make to its architect, but every bit as much a question of our responsibility to the latest generation of architects, of relaying to them the story of this optimistic architecture. (1987)

Now part of the building at least has been stripped of every improper use and returned to its former glory. With modifications and refurbishments as inventive as they are unerring, Hannie and Aldo van Eyck themselves have shown that the building's spatial possibilities can serve an institute for architectural instruction as well as they served a home for children. Though not designed specifically for its present purpose the building obviously more than satisfies what is now expected of it. Its succession of visually linked spatial units clearly offers a choice selection of workplaces whatever purpose it may serve.

The Orphanage is not merely back with a new use. It has proved itself a most stimulating environment to work in, giving a new lease of life to the story this optimistic architecture has to tell. (1993)[13]

Kimbell Art Museum, Fort Worth, USA [441-447]
Louis Kahn 1966-72

441

442

On approaching this museum, sited just outside downtown Fort Worth, it initially comes across as a mosque-like monument left over from a long-vanished culture. The prominent barrel vaults vertically terminating the resolutely horizontal compact mass immediately conjure up images of North Africa, of which the mosque at Kairouan is the best-known example. That is where Le Corbusier must have got those vault forms that keep cropping up in his work. Like Le Corbusier Kahn seized the opportunity to strip these age-old familiar forms of their ancient attributes and reinterpret them from scratch though without losing sight of their archetypical strength. The main public entrance consists of a single large space, sliced into parallel strips by long vaults; at least it looks that way from the outside. Once in the building, it turns out that the space is not parcelled perpendicularly by vaults at all. For a start, they are shells not vaults, and they only begin three metres from the ground, above which height they carve out oblong units of space. Below that level there are unhampered views through so that the space as a whole is much less directional and has a much less coercive presence than it first seemed to have from outside. The most important quality of these shells, apart from their great span, is that they reflect daylight entering in measured quantities through a narrow slit extending over their full length. The shells articulate the building into a number of identical spatial units that are not determined as to function and can be freely subdivided to suit every exhibition and in theory could receive another allocation entirely.

443

444

Rather than following the programme, the building was merely inspired by it and ultimately is illustrative of a more universal idea.

This built structure, as visually dominating and as permanent as can be, is a setting for the most varied and unexpected use.

Kahn saw the opportunity of gathering into his structure other functions such as a restaurant and shop, with occasional interruptions in the shells to accommodate tranquil inner garden courts.

Finally, it is worth noting Kahn's decision to erect the building in elements whose explicit synthesis of form and construction articulates an elementary oversailing structure as had been demonstrated earlier by Van Eyck's Orphanage and indeed was a key aspect of the Centraal Beheer office complex built at the same time as the Kimbell Museum.

446

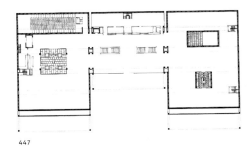

447

445

Academy for the Arts and Architecture, Maastricht [448-450]
Wiel Arets, 1989-93

There can be few buildings in the Netherlands that were made with such scant means;
glass, concrete, a smattering of steel and
precious little else. These elements together
comprise blocks as restrained as they are
severe, aesthetically under control all the
way, without further prettifying and without
frivolity. There could scarcely be less, I
would think, and more would in fact be too
much.

You can of course refine your means and
choose them with such precision that the
effect is greater than if you were to use the
excess of means that architects in general
claim they have to resort to – mostly, it
turns out, because they haven't a lot to
say.

Most of all you need a great deal of care if
you are to tell it like it is with so few words.
First you have to know, during the design
process, what you are talking about; the
story only starts for real with the onset of
building.

We already know that the Japanese can
perform miracles with concrete shuttering,
but that the Dutch can do the same should
be equally clear from this example. And all
that on a Dutch budget too! Here, besides,
Wiel Arets has taken all the insulation and
security fanatics to the cleaner's, emerging
with a building that is immaculate. The
absence of all appurtenances trains one's
attention on the clarity of the space, elementary as is it, like the provocation of
a blank canvas.

It is no more, and no less, than a chain of
clear, bright and above all open spaces
which seem to offer their services to anything needing shelter – like the old warehouses meant for storage but just as good
to work or live in. Impacting on the city
like see-through containers, these academy
buildings are more or less emphatically
there, depending on the light – whether it
be daylight entering or artificial light radi-
ating out – accountable as this is for an
unceasing metamorphosis.

Time will no doubt clothe its invulnerable
nudity and soften and blur its hard architectural edges in an inexorable march of
marks and signs. Like every place of work,
it will adopt the colours of the artefacts
made there and of the people who work

there and who will enter into dialogue with
the architectural space with banal and brilliant effects that will steadily infest and
enrich this academy building.

448

449

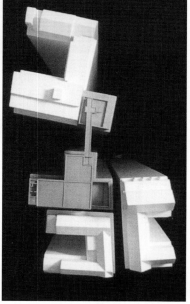

450

University library, Groningen (1972) [451-453]

This design was an attempt to convince the University of Groningen that the nineteenth-century church that stood where the new university library was planned could be incorporated in the scheme as the core of the new complex.[14]

By leaving the nave open, reflooring the side aisles and adding a few new ones, this edifice, important not only for its aesthetic qualities but also for its distinctive presence in the city, could be kept in place. Indeed, by leaving the central aisle open over its full height the library would then have at its disposal an extremely large, and more particularly tall, 'street' of urban distinction that would order the entire complex.

This roofed central street would further enable the holding of such events as theatrical performances, concerts and popular readings while the old church building's structuring effect on the urban context would lend direction and clarity of organization to the whole.

A concept like this would provide a unique opportunity of avoiding the flatness, in every sense of the word, of government-subsidized surfaces and volumes which usually produces something more akin to a storage system than the centre of mental activity one imagines to be at the heart of a university. The presence of the old church space could have expressed the difference in spatial terms between memory and consciousness and with it the range and quality of the university's cultural importance.

By adding onto an existing structure instead of demolishing it and building something in its place, the city not only keeps the old image while gaining a new one but also becomes more layered.

This way, the historical continuity is visually upheld and fostered as a source of inspiration and a guide, rather than the old simply being erased so as to begin anew with a clean slate. Instead of covering up the tracks of the past, these can help to send us in a new direction.

451

452

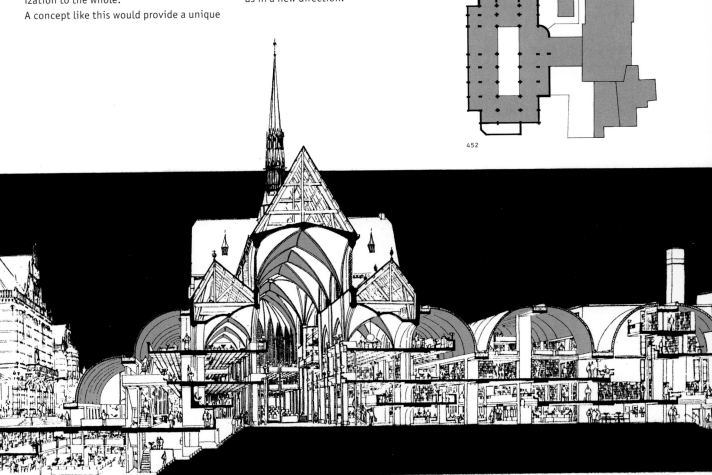

453

Düren housing complex, Germany (1993-97) [454-461]

What was challenging about this compelling urban operation on an apparently 'closed' urban block was the siting of the project, as a landmark in suburbs wholly consisting of scattered development presided over by an impossibly chaotic planning.

The building programme gave rise to an incoherent array of dwelling types that did nothing to alleviate the chaos. In addition, the local planning restraints stipulated a configuration of mundane row houses, a move that in fact could only lead to a further diffusion of disparate fragments.

By then taking these components, planning restraints and all, and so grouping them as to be able to accommodate them under a rectangular roof framing an open courtlike clearing, we were able to create a spatial unity at a scale greater than that of the surroundings.

The roof acts as a shelter, an umbrella of sorts able to house a plethora of building heights and dwelling types. Not only does it embrace all these differences, great as they are, it forges them into a single urban entity. This way, the block could just as easily have been realized by having the units designed by different architects. Then the principle of the roof as an all-embracing gesture, borne aloft by all the components together, would have been expressed even more clearly.

454

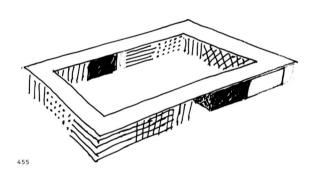

455

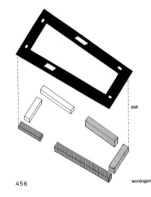

456

457

458

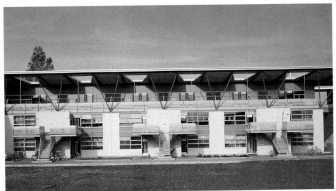

459

460

461

Extension of Vanderveen department store, Assen (1997) [462-473]

A shift in the building line gave this local department store the opportunity to extend its premises (to a depth of just six metres) so as to show a new face to the square which it shares with various rival companies. Here in Assen they are used to relatively closed brick facades, from which we concluded that the stark contrast of an almost all-glass construction would succeed in bringing a metropolitan air to this provincial town. The idea was to have the new portion stand free of the existing block at the front, like a ship moored alongside with only 'gangplanks' linking it to the 'quay'. Indeed, there could be more such 'ships'

anchored around the block. The design proceeded from a 4.5 metre deep building combining a row of slab-shaped columns with cantilevering floors, held clear of the existing department store by a 1.5 metre wide void.

The new building could be made considerably higher than the old block behind it, so that you can see right through the upper floors. This lends extra emphasis to its free-standing status.

This glass satellite is one step in a process of successive extensions; the owners of what can now be described as a department store began with a single modest shop

which was steadily built onto so that now it all but takes up the entire block.

Thus we see an urban block evolving gradually over several decades into a single building, a conglomeration of the original small units which can still be recognized as such today. They were so organized, not only in terms of identifying form but also operationally, that they would keep their independence at least in part.

The new glass addition is admittedly on a larger scale than the existing, but this is a fitting response to the new open space of the square.

Construction-wise it consists of a number

462

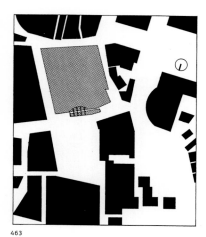

463

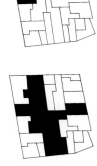

464

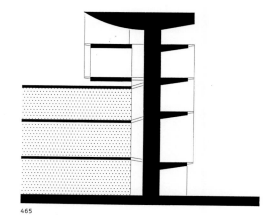

465

466

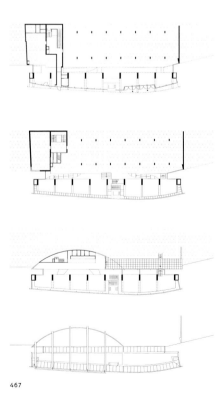

467

468

469

470

471

472

of floors divided into smaller areas by the slab-shaped columns. This vast display window with its glass skin shows off the variety of wares to be found in a department store like Vanderveen.

473

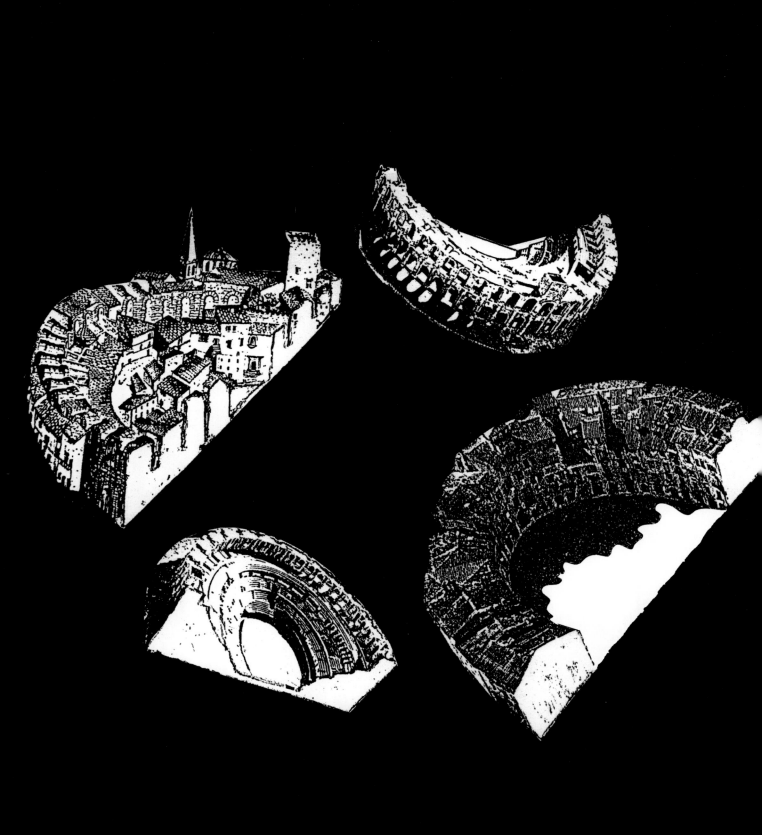

7

In-between Space

Sta Maria della Consolazione, Todi, Italy, attributed to Cola di Caprarola, 1509 [474-479]

Making your way from Orvieto in the southwest through the Parco Fluriale del Tevere up to Todi in the highlands of Umbria, long before anything of that small town comes into view you are struck by the manifest presence of the Sta Maria della Consolazione, a stocky church building standing alone in the rolling landscape, graced with a gleaming dome and, lower down, semidomes on all sides. Set between the hills rather than crowning one of them and symmetrical on all fronts, this central-space church colours the landscape without prevailing upon it in the slightest. Admittedly it attracts the attention, yet the arcadian splendour of the landscape of which it is part prevents the church from stealing the show entirely. Situated as it is in the landscape, the two unite in a natural harmony. Although in perfect accord with its surroundings, standing proudly to one side of and slightly lower than the town like an opening pawn in chess, it illustrates the new paradigm of the Renaissance.

The directionless plan of the church, deriving from the Greek cross instead of the Roman, is the prototype of central-space design and for that reason can only be seen at its best when isolated and viewable from all sides. Accordingly, there was no place for it, literally and metaphorically, in the containment of the town and certainly not on the main square dominated as it was, and still is, by the 'old' church. The central-space plan eschews an approach from one direction to the altar, which in truth has no obvious place here. That one of the four sides was not given an entrance and used as an apse is undoubtedly a concession to church practice.

Not only outside but inside too, the form of the church is non-conformist, out-of-the-ordinary and functionally indeterminate, yet at the same time absolute in the sense that it determines not one but all four principal directions as well as the vertical axis nailing it in place.

This utter typological independence is what enables central-space plans to ultimately slip into any context, providing they do so as a free-standing object. And what could exemplify this better than the Villa Rotonda,

474

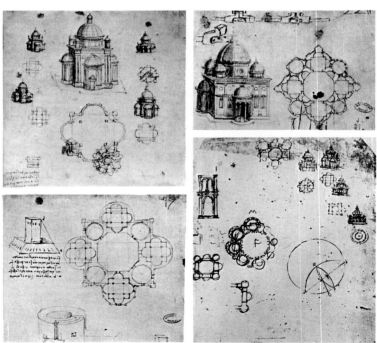

475 Leonardo da Vinci, sketches of central-plan structures, ca. 1489

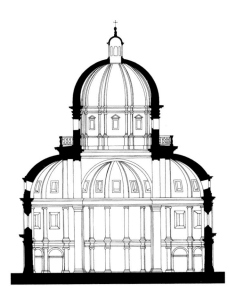

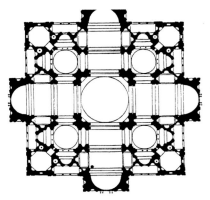

477 Bramante, plan of St Peter's, Rome, 1505-1546

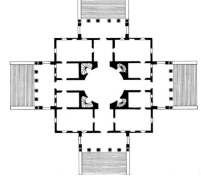

478 Palladio, Villa La Rotonda, 1566-1567

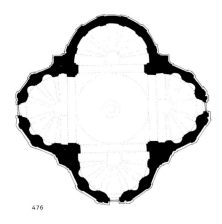

476

479

478 the ultimate descendant and apotheosis of this wayward family.

Sta Maria della Consolazione is probably the purest, most basic prototype and concept ever created from the central-space design principle; it is, as it were, Leonardo's earlier sketches built after all and also the model in built form for Bramante's floor plan for St Peter's as it should have

477 been. This makes it the only realized model of a type that haunted the minds of so many architects round 1500, with the immense richness of Bramante's plan its most far-reaching consequence. Indeed, the interior space is disappointing when measured against the expectations the exterior tends to produce; there is noticeably little of Bramante's touch to be found here, in the sense that it is not the spatial counterpoint of the surrounding landscape; that would have been a little too perfect.

It is the building's objectness that focuses the attention and turns the rest into context. This stresses its significance for the surroundings, introducing, ultimately, a principle of hierarchy. For despite the perfect harmony, that principle tends to subordinate everything around to this manifest object, in the way that a soloist in a concerto stands out from the accompanying orchestra.

In the spaces between
my fingers
lives another hand
Leo Vroman[1]

■ Architects are more inclined to think in terms of volumes, objects and things than in space. Space for them is usually what remains in-between. Space is taken, occupied. All too often the things that are built take up more space than they set free.

In this respect the architect is doing the same as the sculptor, only on an exceptionally large scale. This holds for buildings but just as well for cities.

If in the nineteenth century you could speak more of the 'interior' of the city and the city as a large house, the twentieth-century city is notable for autonomous buildings usually free-standing in their own grounds, each of which tries to attract attention by having the most striking outward appearance whose purpose is to distinguish it from the others with what is purported to be an identity of its own.

Whatever lengths we go to to give the modern city more interior quality we very seldom succeed, and then only when we see a rare opportunity to push aside a mountain of mostly private interests and public rules.

Architects and clients are a double act; both keep wanting to stand out more and more by getting one up on their rivals in outward show, and so you get a desperate war of attrition between objects all wanting to be different in the same way and all end up looking the same, be it along different routes. This desire to strut one's stuff is all too obvious in the architecture magazines where the exterior is invariably foregrounded in all its radiance and general impenetrability.

Architecture photographers are inclined to capture buildings as objects isolated from their surroundings, each time seen from an external viewpoint. This is evidently how architects want their work to be seen, in independence, as a self-sufficient creation they themselves regard at arm's length, and that is the image that travels the world.

The architect wants his entire building in the shot, preferably in sunshine and, apart from some lonely figure doing scale duty, cut off from life and unpeopled. There it stands, a portrait of the architect himself and his client – an achievement that evidently needs the viewer's full attention which may well explain why it has to look so forbidding and hair-raisingly desolate.

There would be little amiss with this attention-hogging were it not for the fact that it blots out everything in the immediate vicinity: objects demand the attention that the space between them fails to elicit. We used to see the 'space between things' mainly as extra quality; as a widening of the possibilities inherent in all the things we design, which as a result become more serviceable, more suitable and better equipped for their purpose – or made suitable for other purposes too.

'The habitable space between things represents a shift in attention from the official level to the informal, to where ordinary day-to-day lives are led, and that means in the margins between the established meanings of explicit function.'[2] Everything that gets built is – necessarily – the objectlike or thinglike, physical, 'bodily' aspect of architecture. We have to look for space where it remains, or has been left, in-between, shaped to this end, constructed with spans or cantilevers, recesses, indentations, coverings, galleries, loggias and so forth. We should not forget either that all these need to be paid for and that this is someone's responsibility. Which is why, generally speaking, as much as possible is kept to a minimum, to what is appropriate only, meaning geared to production, function and user capacity as quantifiable and officially accepted. Circulation and other 'servant' space inevitably gets regarded as extra surface area, for in our pragmatic materialistic world (according to the so-called law of efficiency or direct-benefit principle) all effort should, at bottom, recover all costs. Space is something you have to pay for without being able to measure the yield. Clients think in

480

net as opposed to gross and are soon inclined to regard everything beyond the effective net surface area as a necessary evil that should be held in check. The architect who manages to keep the difference between net and gross surface area as small as possible is soon their blue-eyed boy.

This businesslike attitude is only abandoned (at least in Holland) when it's time to show off, to astonish, and even then clients tend to resort to cosmetics rather than to space.

Everything gets calculated in square metres; cubic metres are alien to the minds of legislators and financial backers. The net of rules and standards is drawing ever tighter in its definition of what is strictly necessary; that is, accommodating it in fixed meanings. Space is categorically excluded from the signified in that definition, and it is just this space of the indeterminate, the unexpected, the informal, the unofficial, that architects should be taking care of.

Space, then, is that which manages to escape the confines of the established, the specified, the regulated, the official and so is there for the taking and open to interpretation.

Most of all, space is between, the thing that building leaves free, and that requires a radical shift in focus. Architects will have to kick their object habit if they are to see things in their true proportions. We have to become less object-happy and shift our view from things, objects and buildings to what lies in-between.

This shift of attention, as obvious, fundamental and radical as it is, means that we are able to assign a value to the area between the objects that define our world, the in-between, as great a value as that assigned to the objects that abut it, and put it on equal footing with them. In *Lessons for Students in Architecture* we looked at 'Das Gestalt gewordene Zwischen' (Buber): the concretization of the in-between, the in-between as object, such as the threshold between house and street which, depending on how you interpret it, belongs more to the house or more to the street and hence is a part of both. Here we are not concerned with such specific instances as the entrance but have broadened this principle to a theme and a paradigm.

The in-between, even if elevated to an object (call it a negative object; defined by its outline and seen from the other side, so to speak), remains an unstable phenomenon. We keep thinking of it in terms of objectness, yet just as its involvement with the things around it persists, so too does its subordination to those things. So long as an entity qualifies as the in-between, it becomes, at the shortest notice, hemmed in, vulnerable, marginal. Secondary, dependent and in the most favourable circumstances, connective. What is formed on the other hand is fixed, solidified, defined, attracts attention naturally, is an object.

There is nothing against objects as such, were it not for the fact that they draw the attention away from their surroundings and focus it on themselves. Space comes about where the things are built and shaped so that they give ground, so to speak, and relinquish their priority by slipping into their context in such a way that built substance and surroundings acquire equal standing, and become as one. Before Picasso's dishes there was Jujol's undulating bench clad with broken plates in Gaudí's Parc Güell in Barcelona, the very city that Picasso had departed shortly before.

'Although Jujol/Gaudí's plates can still be read as such, their autonomy has been seriously impaired nonetheless. The individual pieces are loosed as it were from their original bond to 480-481 engage fragments in their surroundings: there are new relationships to be read besides the unity of the original plate. So you could see this as a form of cubism.'[3]

The Cubists painted people and things in fragments. Like Jujol/Gaudí's shattered plates these fragments, being part of the context, are absorbed and sharply defined by their surroundings. So, for instance, in *Seated Woman with Fan*, an early Cubist painting by Picasso of 1908, it is impossible to tell

481

whether certain planes belong to the woman or to the chair. The two interlock as it were, losing their identity to combine as a new entity.

So here we see people and things fragmented and pushed to the background in such a way that their objectness is called into question. Their makers would prefer them to disappear altogether by rendering them invisible, camouflaging them in fact. The story goes that in 1914 Picasso and Braque, on seeing soldiers marching by in camouflage kit, remarked: 'They've found the very thing we've been searching high and low for.'

All these examples are of situations where people and things are made so dependent on their context that they are determined and signified by that context (i.e., they acquire their meaning from them).

With everything dependent on everything else, there are not only no main and side issues, no context, no surroundings, but also ultimately no *fixed* meanings either.

482 Pablo Picasso, *Seated Woman with Fan*, 1908

Paul Cézanne [483]

In Cézanne's still-lifes with their profusion of fruit in dishes on tables, it is less and less the depictions of those objects that count and increasingly the space between them. Often it is just that intervening space that is indicated and the apples or lemons have become little more than gaps among the colour. We know enough about apples by now, their variety notwithstanding; what they look like, how they taste, smell and feel. They are well-charted territory both inside and out, recognizable, familiar. The space that attracted Cézanne was that between the objects in their relative positions and perhaps their relationship, but above all else he was drawn by the form of the space-between, unnamed and without status. Cézanne was looking for the unnamed, unsignified form. He was able to regard a form as a phenomenon in its own right. By erasing the significations he could give the things back their space and give them equal standing. Without being even vaguely conscious of it, it was he who invented the twentieth-century awareness of space.

483 Paul Cézanne, *Still Life*, 1900

Pierre Bonnard [484]

The painter Pierre Bonnard was hardly a major innovator. Picasso and his friends were unable to take him seriously: his life-long preoccupation was with domestic scenes, whose benign warmth and harmony in sensitively balanced colours illustrated the lives and surroundings of people evidently quite unconcerned with the tempestuous goings-on in the world at large. And yet his work was remarkable in another way than just being aesthetic and benign. For though the objects featured in his paintings – tables, chairs and other items usually found in rooms – are as a rule composed in such a way that they are carefully embedded in their surroundings, it is notable how often the focal points fall between those objects so that all the individual components, so to speak, are suppressed to emphasize the overall cohesion. Though the objects do remain recognizable as such, they have lost their dominance. All elements of the painting attain equal status. He made extremely large paintings which he then reduced in size by cutting them up, seemingly choosing to cut specifically through the objects so that they would disperse as fragments, sideways from the interstitial space. The working method of this modest, reclusive painter was as meaningful as it was bizarre in its strategy of foregrounding the indeterminate spaces between. In that respect his departure-points can be described as cubist.

484 Pierre Bonnard, *White Interior*, 1932

Giorgio Morandi [485]

Like Bonnard, Giorgio Morandi chose to leave to one side the entire dynamic of the twentieth century without taking even the slightest aspect of it as a starting point. He painted predominantly bottles, jugs and pots, everyday objects for use which he carefully grouped. You can see the same objects cropping up in different paintings. He regarded that grouping as the actual work; the business of painting proceeded rapidly. Each combination of elements invariably presents a tight-knit ensemble. The aspect of buildings that his objects possess makes it easy to associate the composition with a city with the area between the 'buildings' seeming to glue it all together. In Cézanne's still-lifes too the area between the fruit constitutes a 'public realm' of sorts, in harmony and on a par with the objects set in it.

What is remarkable about Morandi's still-lifes, however, is that pots that are downright ugly or at least highly inappropriate are, when focused on individually, neutralized as objects within the composition as a whole. If anything is dominant it is the overall image: a city of bottles on a table.

485 Giorgio Morandi, *Still Life*, 1955

■ **KASBAHISM**[4] Make buildings less like objects and they become, shall we say, more open. This resulting greater accessibility comes from reading them as an assemblage of components on the one hand and making them more a part of the greater totality of the city on the other.

This happens when buildings are conceived of as parts of the city, as a conglomeration of parts that enclose urban collective space, and when the oppositions between the building (as an object) and its surroundings are cancelled. Not just by adapting them to each other, but by letting the building infiltrate its surroundings whilst the surroundings in turn penetrate more into the building so that the one tends to become the other.

Decreasing the objectness of buildings makes them less distant in every sense. And as the opposition between built and unbuilt decreases, so too does the difference between inside and outside.

Inside and outside will never truly blend together, any more than degrees of public and private. Requirements of protection as regards climate, property and fire precautions will always insist on more or less clearly defined transitions in the form of controllable entrances.

Building units can however be stripped of their individuality by having them physically engage more with one another and by blurring the bounds of public space so that the units themselves seem to lose their edge.

A first step in this direction came with efforts to physically drive public space through private objects (arcades and shopping malls, for instance, or Le Corbusier's Carpenter Center in Cambridge (USA) and OMA's more recent Kunsthal in Rotterdam).

You can find such an interweaving of private 'substance' and public areas of streets as passages in ancient towns which have evolved through the ages such as those along the Mediterranean Sea (but also elsewhere, particularly if you head east).

This 'kasbahism' has inspired many hill-townlike projects such as emerged in the sixties, the only built example of which is in fact Moshe Safdie's Habitat in Montreal. This was an attempt to attain an urban substance of sorts though inevitably the net result is still a housing block and an object, be it with a frayed edge.

So there are ways to make interior and exterior as well as private and public interpenetrate. This disintergrates the autonomy of buildings free-standing in the void they have themselves caused – an autonomy that is avoided as it is in every historical town centre where even the most important and imposing edifices stand side by side presenting a united front to the equally clearly formed complementary space of the street.

In the following 'classic' examples we will see that the intervening space is on an equal footing with the built space. Each and every one is proof of how a shift of focus can counter too strong a sense of objectness. The projects of mine included here are in a sense indebted to these works, in that all seek to prevent the built elements from dominating, to the benefit of the space between.

486 U-Bahn through a house, Dennewitzstraße, Berlin

487 Le Corbusier, Carpenter Center for Visual Arts, Cambridge USA, 1961-64

488 Matchbox model, 1959[5]

A types of housing blocks

B conditions of housing blocks

C integration of blocks and conditions

489 D boundary between building and city extinguished[6]

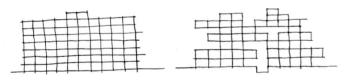

490 Successive disintegration of a building penetrated by streets and squares[6]

491 Taos, New Mexico, USA

492 Moshe Safdie, 'Habitat', Montreal, Canada, 1967

Maison Curutchet, La Plata, Argentina [493-504]
Le Corbusier, 1949

The house that Le Corbusier built for the surgeon Dr. Curutchet is spatially one of his most complex compositions, though its dimensions are modest. That it is an ingenious response to what is a widespread issue is clear from its configuration: the surgery high up on the street side, the living quarters at the rear of the site.

Standing on the edge of a local park in the periphery of the city centre, the building lot is part of a street elevation mainly composed of larger lots. Had the house been organized in the normal fashion, as a solid volume with the surgery downstairs and the living quarters above, its slight mass would have seen it pushed aside somewhat, and the section at the back would have been difficult to use.

Now, however, it is the living quarters that occupy that rear position with only an upper storey at the front. On top of this is a terrace which gives onto the living room in the rear portion. The concrete slab oversailing most of this terrace has the effect of giving the building a greater volume at the street side.

The theoretical volume of this house (the envelope) consists in the main of outdoor space excluded from the mass in such a way that internal and external space fit together like a three-dimensional jigsaw puzzle, so that the external space effectively becomes part of the interior. Using a computer model to render the space left open inside the envelope as mass and the built volume as air, we can see that mass and left-open space are very much on equal footing.[7]

The spatial complexity of this amalgam of built and left-open 'mass' and the sensation of walking through it, are impossible to read off from the familiar and often published drawings. Even Le Corbusier's assistants could make little sense of the sketches. It was only after making a model, according to Roger Aujame, that they came to understand his intentions.

The living quarters are reached by passing under the raised surgery portion at the front and following the incline up to the entrance, to what is in effect a separate three-storey volume. From there a second incline running in the opposite direction

493

third floor

second floor

first floor

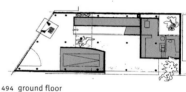

494 ground floor

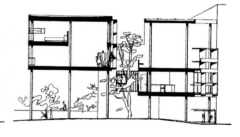

495

leads further up to the entrance to the surgery.

The outdoor area between the two autonomous parts of this structure is graced by a lone tree, as if on scouting duty for the park opposite and recalling the Pavillon de l'Esprit Nouveau of 1925. Here too the tree, seeking an opening between the built masses, soars past the lower portion of the house up to the roof garden adjoining the living room.

That both slopes run from entrance to entrance and do lead somewhere makes this ramp more convincing architectonically than, say, that in the Villa Savoye. There the ramp, though endlessly imitated, has the weakness that it doubles back halfway along, giving the impression of meaningless toing and froing. In La Plata by contrast it becomes clear from proceeding through the

space, just what Le Corbusier meant by *promenade architecturale*.

It seems that Dr. Curutchet never felt at home here. For him it was too light and too open, lacking the shelter he sought. Moreover, there were a number of drawbacks which must have particularly irritated him. The spatial dynamic and the views from the various portions of the other parts outside evidently meant little to him and he took exception to being observed by the outside world. Being a surgeon, he specialized in designing instruments to make them more manageable and efficient. It was his passion for fitness of purpose that brought him, through his sister who regularly visited Paris, into contact with modern architecture with its like concern for functionality, and so with Le Corbusier. They never met, communicating

496

499

497

498

500

only through letters. The construction, though presumably done correctly, was directed by local architects who had their own opinions on how to go about it, which Dr. Curutchet felt negatively affected the quality of the underlying idea. Le Corbusier himself never went to La Plata and could only have seen photographs of the results.

501

502

503

504

Piazza Ducale, Vigevano, Italy [505-509]
Bramante, 1684

The central piazza of the North Italian town of Vigevano, west of Milan, is one of the less well-known examples of a Baroque square. Rather than being a space left over between buildings, it was deliberately formed by the buildings bounding it. The square is enclosed on all sides, a large urban chamber carved out of the surrounding buildings – the negative of a building, if you like.

So far, this example matches the characteristics of the Baroque piazzas found all over Italy, and is often cited as such. But with one of the short end walls – call it the head elevation – dominated by the cathedral, there is more to it than that. At first glance, this wall seems to belong entirely to the church, as the five identical, symmetrically placed entrances suggest.

However, closer inspection reveals that the church in fact has only four doors, the fifth giving access to the Via Roma, the public street beyond it. This is made patently clear if one moves slightly to the right. Then it transpires that the door on the far left is open, with cyclists emerging from it. Is this a public street coolly slicing through the church? The fact is, it only appears as if the church takes up the entire end wall. In reality it is out of true with the piazza, pushed away a bit awkwardly to the right. Looking at the plan of the town centre, we can see that when the piazza was designed, the position of the castle made it impossible to keep on axis with the church, so that the ambiguous situation as it now stands was the only logical solution. Three interpretations suggest themselves:

1 It is not the church facade we are looking at but one elevation of the piazza. The piazza has been put first and the buildings must adapt to it. There is nothing new about this, admittedly, yet it is remarkable all the same that the then all-powerful church deigned to show its face as a mask, set askew to the 'body' behind. The hollow shape, its concavity to the piazza, seems to bear out this theory. The church is less autonomous than if it had been given a convex front; it is as if it appends itself to the piazza instead of standing up to it.

2 You could turn this argument around and say that the church was all too eager to

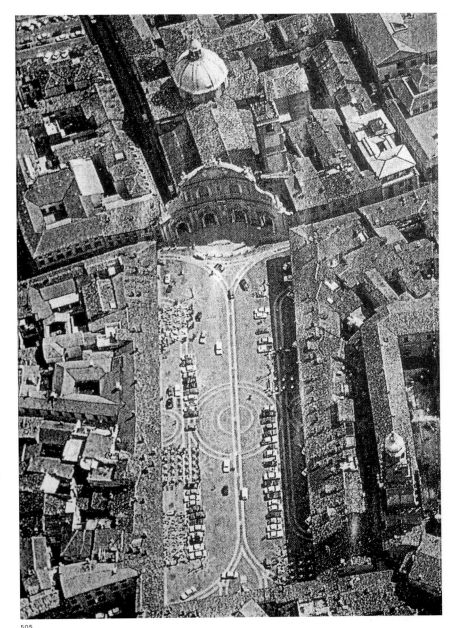

505

506

507

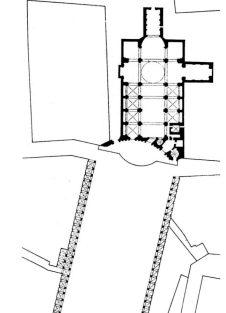

508

509

take on the entire elevation as its front. As a concession it was prepared to go out of its way and adopt the street.

3 If we regard the facade as a free-standing screen between the buildings and the piazza, then these two components theoretically are no longer in direct confrontation. The facade can then be construed as a mediator between what is built and what is left open. The periphery as autonomous screen is not just a mental construct; we can see it in the enclosure of the Place de la Carrière, the last in the succession of squares at Place Stanislas in Nancy[8] and of course in the colonnades of the oval forecourt of St Peter's in Rome.[9] Whereas these examples are of entirely free-standing screens, as against that of Vigevano where the front facade of the church is partly free-standing, they probably issue from the same realm of thought.

What the three above-named interpretations have in common is that the buildings bounding the piazza relinquish or at least play down their objectness. The form of the piazza prevails above the utterances of

individual buildings, yet curiously enough
the church seems more impressive seen in
this light. Be that as it may, all attention
was directed at the piazza which has in fact
become an object, though in the sense of a
negative, like the mould that is to be filled
up by the sculptor, where the periphery
remains the same.

Monte Albàn, Mexico [510-511]

Just as the Athenians built their Acropolis, so between 700 BC and 700 AD the Zapotecs erected their Monte Albàn, an expansive temple complex near Oaxaca, up in the sky on the highest mountain plateau made by man. Besides being the ceremonial centre it must also have been the cultural and administrative hub, an awe-inspiring city of which little remains today save a number of ruins of gigantic pyramids and temples, like long chains of man-made mountains. From the Acropolis one can gain a reasonable idea of how those once magnificent Greek temple buildings must have looked with their sharpened marble contours, maybe awash in primary colours. Of the Monte Albàn complex, however, and for that matter all the other excavated temples in Mexico, there is very little left to see, although reconstructions suggest that these remains are merely the scraped-bare podia of a staggering number of structures at least as opulent as the Acropolis. Perhaps it is their brute severity, almost as if they were shaped by nature, that turns

our attention to the overwhelming bald flat expanses that have not simply remained, but seem to have been deliberately created. On the Acropolis it is the buildings and the Parthenon in particular that hog the attention while the space around them has no specific part to play; here by contrast the structures seem to have been built to so mark off the flat expanses between them that even today they are ready to host grandiose events as if colossal city squares. We know that such events must have taken place here, with a cast of tens of thousands and reaching heights of barbarousness equalling the atrocities perpetrated in the Roman arenas.

Looking at it now, in a state of repose, we can imagine it packed with rather more people that those few tourists who only have eyes (and cameras) for the built elements their guide has so much to say about. What those ruins do more than anything else is to activate the space in-between, which from the moment it has your attention, itself shifts into the foreground and,

510

there on the mountaintop, rightfully assumes the crown. If the Parthenon marks the summit of the high rock of the Acropolis, the large hollow expanse left between the built structures of Monte Albàn is its opposite number in more ways than one.

511

Erechtheion, Greece [512-516]

In the same way that the Acropolis dominates Athens, the former is itself dominated by the Parthenon, the building that prevails over all architectural history in its flawlessness, harmony and perfect proportions. This is what we have all been told and who would cast doubt on the endeavour that led to the incontestable supremacy of this pinnacle of the building art. It is so perfectly made that even the imperfections of the human eye could be redressed by means of so-called optical corrections, a refinement not applied to this degree before or since. If the lion's share of attention goes to the Parthenon, it is difficult to ignore the much smaller 'Caryatid Portico' belonging to the Erechtheion. An utterly unique solution and a truly remarkable discovery, these stone maidens or columns in human form are not

512

513

514

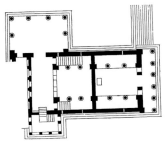

515

just a curiosity but without doubt the greatest surprise that the history of architecture, with its prodigious variety of columns, has to offer.

Whereas the columns of the Parthenon are shaped by the sharpness of the fluting, here it is the folds of the gossamer-like robes diaphanously draped over the figures that have that same effect and although of a freer form they are no less exact. Only the lines have lost their severity. It is as if the hard stone has become soft, as only the sculptor can manage, and the result is indeed as much sculpture as architecture; it is both.

It is supremely difficult to tear one's gaze away from these fascinating female figures who – although belonging together – have their own individual personalities. Yet it is this variety and the infinitely varied column sections that generate unexpected and capricious in-between spaces and, depending on the angle of vision, an endlessly varying intercolumniation. Just this unpredictably changing, variegated interstitial space binds these columns together. Countermanding the consistent and stern circumspection of the Parthenon with its harmonious groups of statues framed by

the building order, this sculptural 'portico' is a complementary opposite as gracious as it is exuberant; more lyrical, and almost palpably close.

516

The space of the theatre of Epidauros, Greece [517-518]

This mega example of a Greek theatre was constructed in a natural hollow, completed by the geometric precision of a marble lining of sculpted rows of seats. The size of the audience able to sit in this furrowed concavity comes close to that of today's stadiums and so belongs among the very largest places of assembly. Its auditory and visual qualities were such as to allow the greatest concentration and involvement in the performance at its centre, as well as generating the broadest sense of collective experience.

Astonishing though it may seem, the acoustics of this space are so good that a whisper on stage can be heard in the outermost ring of seating – and needless to say without amplification of any sort.
The association with stadiums might ini-

517

tially suggest links with the Roman amphitheatres, but these were entirely freestanding structures whose exterior faced the city. What is distinctive about Epidauros is the almost complete absence of an 'outside', altogether absorbed as it is in the landscape or rather having emerged from it. Shaped by landscape and architectural means, here we have a place where an enormous number of people can assemble to witness an event together. Instinctively the comparison suggests itself with the pyramids as its absolute antithesis across the Mediterranean Sea. What was scooped out in the Greek theatre, was piled up in Egypt into artificial hills; there, built forms erected with supreme effort took their place in the landscape.

You might say that pyramid and theatre are each other's counterform, not that they are literally so in either form or dimensions. It is as ideas, more than anything else, that they are complete opposites: if the pyramid is the tomb of a single deceased person, the Pharaoh lying motionless in silence and darkness for eternity, in the theatre all living persons come at some time to celebrate a supreme moment of social enactment.

Both involve the dialectics of individual and community, though one is the reverse of the other.

The monumentality of the pyramid is in every respect outward-facing; there is in fact no interior. The theatre by contrast has no outside, only an inward-facing, self-regarding monumentality.

Both exhibit a basic form of urban planning; one the building, the other the town square. Endowing their surroundings with space, each in its own context, they are part of the landscape, not least through their vast dimensions.

Epidauros is not an object that reveals its qualities on the outside. Its essence is the interior, or more correctly, its capacity to contain, and it is this persistently underexposed side of architecture that emerges here: not what it is, but what it is able to contain.

518

519 *Bord de Seine*, Izis, 1987. 'Because everything is conditioned by the correct human dimension that belongs to our movements, ancient and modern cease to be; there is only what is permanent: the correct dimension.' (Le Corbusier) [10]

Media Park, Cologne, Germany (1990) [520-523]

This project takes the traditional principle of the city block with its formal exterior and private garden courtyards and turns it inside out, so that the fronts face inwards and the rear elevations outwards. Ordinarily it is the front that gets most of the architect's attention, the rear suffering as a result.

'The history of architecture is a history of facades – the buildings seem to have had no backs at all! Architects always searched for a formal order – they preferred to ignore the other side of the coin, the bustle of everyday life. And this is still largely true today, even though the design of public housing has in the course of this century become a full-fledged branch of architecture. There is still that invisible and subconscious dividing line between archi-

520

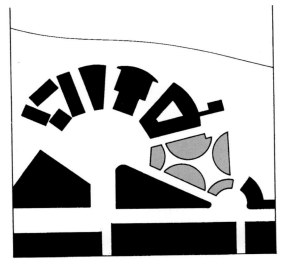

521

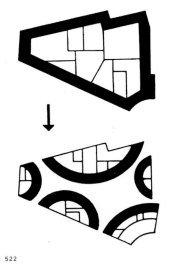

522

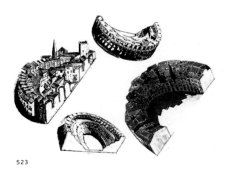

523

tecture with a capital A and without.'[11] The about-turn effected here means that the rear elevations are now exposed and all sides are consequently front facades, while the interior courtyard rejoins the public realm. The whole issue of inside and outside has become irrelevant.

The segments of circle comprising the plan consist of a 'hard' immutable skin, like an arc of amphitheatre such as the examples in Arles and Lucca, built to last and able to receive less enduring infills.[12]

Whereas the enfolding arcs can house the ever essential offices functions, the 'paunches' were originally designed for a

wide diversity of studios for various clients. It is this diversity that makes its mark on the outside world, while the uniformity of the office side faces inwards.

There were several versions made of this proposal, one of which allowed the internal space to be roofed with glass as an atrium. In that case, the result would have been uncomfortably close to a system of arcades and then the disadvantages would have been foregrounded. For in activating all the sides, 'backs' as well as 'fronts', the dilemma arises of where to place the entrances. This project looks ahead to the principle we applied in Düren and other urban planning

reversals. There, however, the inner side of the block was unambiguously chosen as the street side with the entrances placed there, and a predominantly green area of private gardens enfolding the block.

Dormitory, Kurobe, Japan (1998)

[524-539]

This dormitory for employees of the YKK concern is sited close to the centre of the town of Kurobe (Toyama district) between rice paddies and buildings in a disorganized configuration. In this predominantly rural area the dormitory stands opposite one of the YKK factory complexes where it forms a cornerstone of the street, which is to be developed further and linked up to the town centre.

The dormitory comprises a hundred or so dwelling units, fully equipped as one-room apartments. There are, besides, communal facilities including a restaurant and a library. The building divides into a number of discrete parts connected with the most transparent possible means. None the less, this row of modest residential blocks poses a clear urban elevation. Articulating the dormitory into blocks prevents the whole from having an unduly massive presence,

524

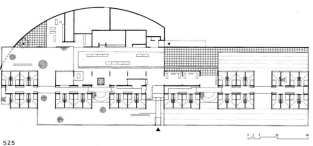

525

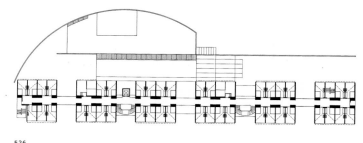

526

making it easier for it to slip into the small-scale surroundings. We also prevented it from becoming too much like a hotel with row upon row of impersonal doors off equally impersonal corridors with only artificial lighting. By splitting the living quarters into six separate blocks linked by bridges, those crossing from one block to another have outside views to both sides. These interruptions give the corridors a street feel.

The six discrete masses are anything but vertically organized detached 'houses' although they may look that way at first. Articulated though they are, they adhere to an organizational unit divided into storeys stitched together by one lift and three stair towers.

This residential portion further includes bathrooms in traditional Japanese style,

527

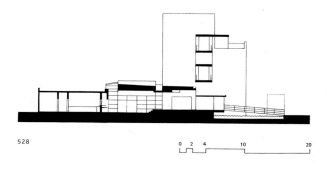

528

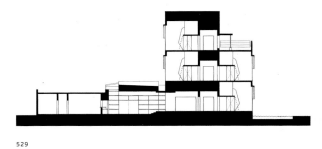

529

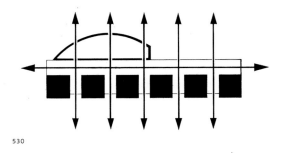

530

531

532

533

534

washing and drying rooms and roof terraces for general use. The individual rooms were made tall enough to receive a mezzanine apiece to be used as a sleeping balcony or a study balcony. This effect of height is enhanced by having the vertically divided glass fronts continue down to the ground. Erasing the normal storey height is not just a question of freeing space. Though the surface area including the sleeping balcony is basically no bigger than is customary for such rooms, it gives the sense of being a complete if minimal house in which you can easily create your own environment, if only because of the question of personal choice introduced by having two distinct living zones.

This means that you can receive visitors without continually having to tidy up; it also makes habitation by two people easier. Parallel to the living units is the restaurant whose line is continued by an elongated zone of garden and terrace. Behind this is a kitchen and service block and the technical area. The restaurant zone forges a bridge between the residential portion and the service block, and gives lengthwise views across the rice paddies to the distant hills. This zone, opened up to all sides, invites all manner of activities and is suitable for parties, concerts and receptions. Also in this zone are the library and more private rooms for talks, and a traditional Japanese room. This project is used to test ways of exploiting solar energy. The sun breaks on the most sunlit side are equipped with solar cells. Instead of tacking on devices willy-nilly it seemed sensible to collect solar energy at places where the sun needed keeping out of the building, and convert it into electricity to help light the interior at night.

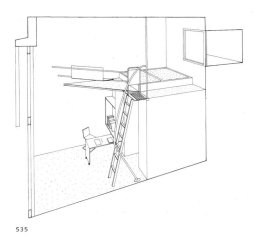

535

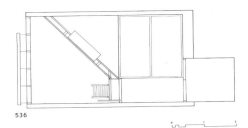

536

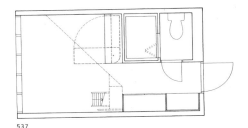

537

538

539

Public library and Centre for Music and Dance, Breda (1991-96) [540-549]

The complex housing the Public Library and the Centre for Music and Dance is wholly absorbed in the existing development of one of the large city blocks which in a town like Breda emerged with the urbanization of what must once have been farmsteads and country houses with large back gardens. The building makes its presence felt in three of the four streets bounding the block. There is nothing objectlike about it in the way it drinks in its surroundings, indeed it can scarcely be called a building.
Each of its facades responds in its own way to the character of the street it faces. It can be accessed from all three streets. This area became the site simply because it had been left over by a combination of property boundaries, spacing regulations and gaps.

540

541

542

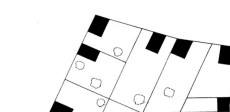

543A A city block compacts

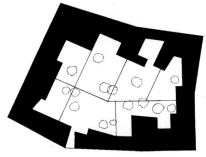

B

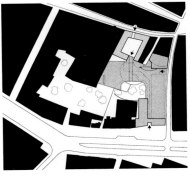

544

A further factor was a group of mulberries occupying the large inner courtyard that, being a rare species, needing preserving through thick and thin.

The upshot is an amorphous patch of built fabric set at a respectful distance from the trees that unwittingly form the hub of the design. The whole is held together by columns following a square grid that bear aloft a roof oversailing all the components; the impression is of a tent with all components assembled in a single large space. The roof has generous cantilevers at places

that partially shelter the adjacent street (as in some Italian cities for protection against the sun). This generates a sense of being indoors, while accentuating the distinctive curve of the street without needing a fully curved facade for that purpose. Spacious views through beneath this jutting roof explicate the various functions and layers and the way they relate.

An inviting exterior is a prerequisite for a library, and you should at least be able to look in from outside. Here a glass facade allows views in of the lower-lying reading

room through to the courtyard garden resplendent with mulberries.

The informality of the whole comes from systematically acknowledging and ceding to those elements and conditions that have determined and shaped the site through the ages. The main library space, unquestionably the dominant feature of the complex, locks into the surroundings on all sides, consisting as these do of mainly old building parts, thereby accepting a subsidiary position.

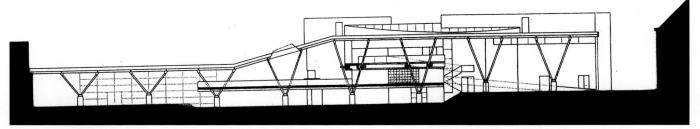

545

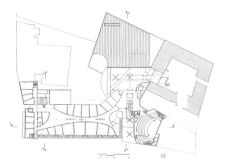

first floor

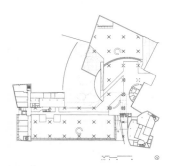

mezzanine

546 ground floor

547

548

549

Chassé Theatre, Breda (1995) [550-559]

'Temple of culture' and 'showpiece' are not words one would expect to apply to the theatre in Breda. Not just because of the extremely tight budget but also given its position on a none too characteristic spot outside the historical town centre. To compound matters, it is wedged between the nondescript municipal offices and the equally unprepossessing former army barracks dating from the nineteenth century. The oblique space left between these buildings was too small to accommodate a newcomer held clear on all sides. Yet because the municipal offices had its wall of fenestration on the side, ruling out direct abutment, a continuous urban elevation was equally impossible.

This cramped site offered little in the way of design freedom, all the more so because the plan was largely specified beforehand by the way the non-public aspects of the theatre were organized, the overriding concern being efficiency in terms of walking distances. Topping the bill in this composition are the two flytowers which basically could only take up a position together along the central backstage area. Visually and urbanistically the flytowers are the most prominent elements, in that together they threatened to dominate the view of the city with their chunky forms in close proximity. This gave rise to the idea of draping the entire conglomeration of spaces and masses, issuing as these did from practical considerations germane to the theatre, with the all-embracing sweep of a gently undulating roof.

This response may be compared with the way the parts of a car engine, again configured to meet purely technical criteria, have a bonnet to draw them together both practically and aesthetically.

The double wave washing over the twin towers and cascading over the foyer zone ensures that no single component prevails externally, making the roof in its capacity of uniting element in effect the building's principal facade.

The only space left for the public area of foyer, film theatres and café was that abutting the former barracks, the obvious solution being to unfurl this zone linearly like a street along the two theatre auditoriums. The head of the barracks building could

550

551

552

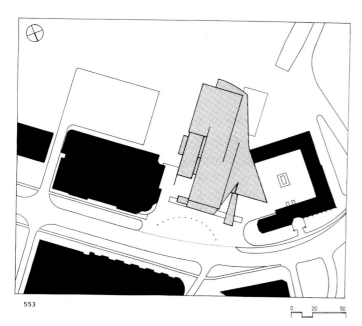

553

0 20 50

then peek in under the large roof as a free-standing edifice from a bygone era. Joining it along this 'street' is the film theatre, stitched to the segment-shaped balcony in the foyer by catwalks.

The foyer zone, then, is more than anything else the space left between the various masses whose siting was necessarily pre-scribed beforehand, hence its amorphous character. The periphery of this streetlike space suggests individual buildings, with the brick head elevation of the old barracks building with its vertical traditional win-dows welcomed as a free-standing element in this interior urban elevation, strength-ening the collage look more usually encoun-tered on the street than in a building. The street effect is further enhanced by the exceptionally high ceiling undulating atop the space in one great flourish and giving the impression of open sky, particularly at night. The tall columns which support this roof, though adhering to a regular grid, nonetheless prove a fairly disorderly bunch in practice, due in part to the differences in length. Isn't a space shaped by its periphery, when all is said and done?

The idea of painting all the columns in a great many shades of red had an unexpected sequel. The proximity of these hues had the effect of drawing the individual members together. This 'forest of columns' turned out to incite the perception of the space to such a degree that the none too cohesive periphery is forced right into the background.

Columns, then, are able to define a space by marking out its depth. They can shift our focus to the in-between spaces, transforming these from shapeless and marginal to the focus of our attention.

554

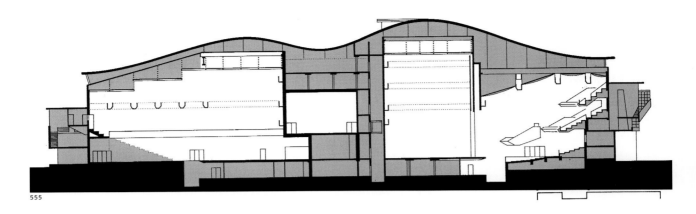

555

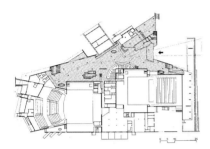

556 ground floor

557 mezzanine

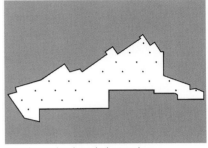

558 columns placed seemingly at random

559

Gebaute Landschaft Freising, Munich, Germany (1993) [560-562]

Industrial parks or 'business parks', whatever fancy name you give them, are in practice parking lots for autonomous buildings, all alike in their longing for variety and all downright conformist in their quest for identity. The result that confronts us everywhere in the periphery of towns and cities is impotent and chaotic in equal measure and as with all buildings stuck away forlornly on their own, no-one has anything to gain from this state of affairs. The authorities, scared as they are of losing lucrative clients, shrink from setting new planning conditions, so that this land-consuming phenomenon continues to spread insidiously. In Freising, a prestigious international competition seemed to herald a change in this situation and for a time it looked as though the plan 'Gebaute Landschaft' (built landscape) would indeed be built, but once again the municipal council played it safe in the end with a 'normal alternative'. The small town of Freising, to the north of Munich past the international airport, nestles in a rolling, mainly agricultural landscape that is gradually surrendering its territory with each new urban expansion; an unstoppable process it seems.

Instead of encroaching further on the landscape with yet another cluster of buildings, we grafted a segment of built landscape onto the site. This way, we have avoided the dubious alternative of 'urban' and 'rural'. The city is devouring the landscape at an alarming rate by building it up, in all too haphazard snippets depending on what the legal position on property, just as haphazard it seems, has made available at the time.

'Gebaute Landschaft' comes across as an artificial hill scooped out or rather erected in rows to give a striking pattern to the landscape.

Here, a variety of settlements can co-exist each in its chosen configuration, providing the curved greenery-clad strips of roof are respected.

These green roofs together present an area of public parkland so that the links in the landscape remain intact. The design for planting the roofs is functional as to drainage and proceeds from a strategy of ecological continuity.

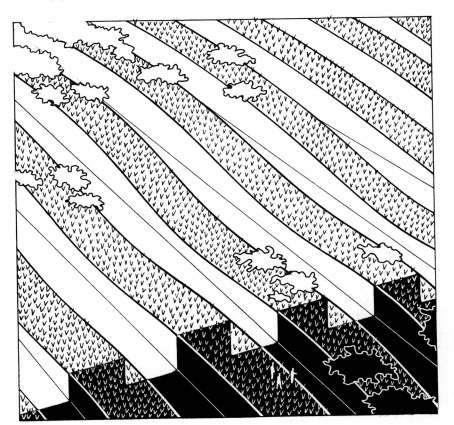

561

562

560

Office building for Landtag Brandenburg, Potsdam, Germany (1995) [563-567]

In this competition design the principle developed in Freising for an entire neighbourhood was adopted again for what was to be a monumental government building. Here too there was a magnificent site, parallel to the river and bordered on the other side by a hill with a parklike character. Was this to be the locus for the umpteenth imposing block, taking up far more public space than is necessary so that the footpath logically following the river would be blocked by it? Buildings often take more space than they give back!

Our point of departure was to express the three principal office wings parallel with the waterfront as gently billowing arch bridges over the connecting hall set at right angles to them. This hall, the central space tying all the volumes together, commences at the main entrance on the street and continues to the waterfront where ships can be moored. Views out are of the water and across it to the city centre. The strip of parkland along the river remains undisrupted, with the footpath continuing over the office bridges as if through a publicly accessible hilly terrain.

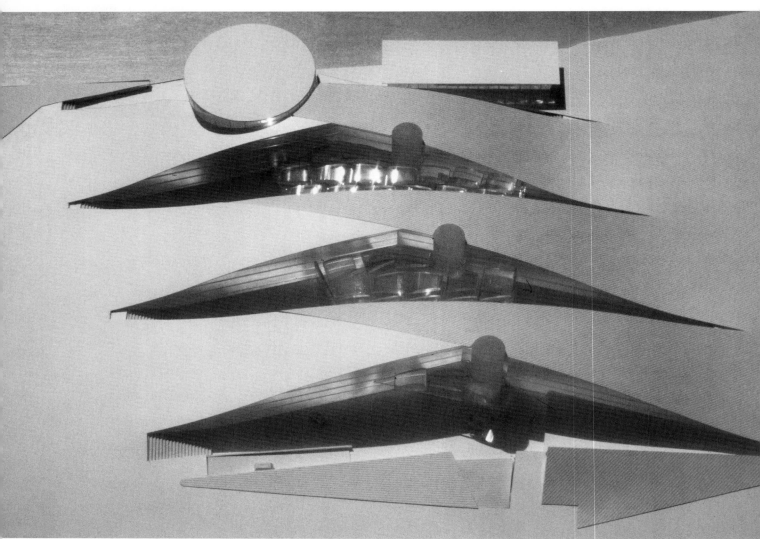

563

564

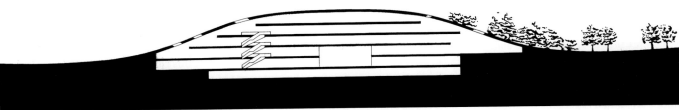

565

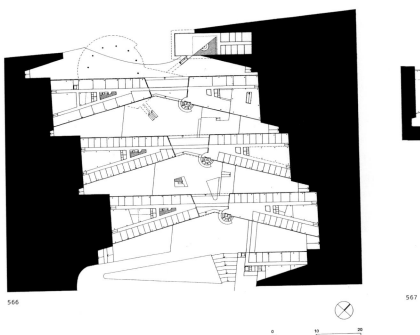

566

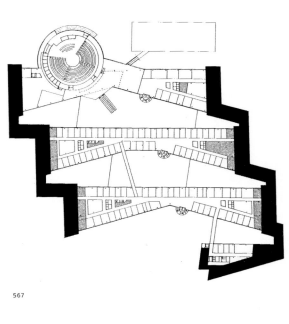

567

■ THE ENVIRONMENT BUILT Whereas the historical city only had autonomous buildings in exceptional cases, preferably those of a social importance and thus for general use, the objectmania of the twentieth century only seems to acknowledge free-standing buildings and the urban character has been fragmented as a result. Both city and landscape are disintegrating. What other way is there to respond to this dilemma than to try to integrate just that which has been fragmented, in other words to look for forms of integration for buildings/built development and grounds/landscape ('building the site'). So now we not only have city as building and building as city but also site as building and building as site.

In spite of the persistent myth of nature-versus-culture, both landscape (in Holland at least) and city are man-made, as compositions of more or less built elements. The controlled character of both demands that we should portion out the built elements evenly and it seems that we are willing to accept components of a more collective import and emphatic presence more easily.

We are all too quickly inclined to see dominant connecting structures such as bridges, roads and high-tension cables as part of the countryside, while regarding blocks of flats or offices as disruptive; far more so than, say, grain silos and other eye-catching objects that we consider to be more necessary, which is perhaps why they strike us less as a blight on the landscape.

While the city consists mainly of brick and stone with green elements in tow, the country is the negative of this though we tend to accept relatively more green in the city than brick and stone in the country. Green enclaves in the city, as it happens, can never be large enough; green after all stands for light and space.

■ MEGAFORMS The more collective the importance of a structure, the easier it is to interpret it as part of 'nature' and accept it as such in the landscape. Aqueducts such as the impressive Pont du Gard seem to be part of the nearby rock formation, if only because of the weathering of the superhuman-sized stones the Romans used. There seems to be little difference here between built and naturally evolved elements. As is so often the case, it was Le Corbusier who got on the scent of the idea of continuous structures that could be laid like 'horizons' through the countryside, their floors bridging differences in height, and inhabitable as belt cities where it would be easy to imagine roads being incorporated. Remarkably, this reversal produces 'negative' buildings that are stripped entirely of their objectness. This is why they slip so easily into their surroundings and that is the great importance of this idea (ignoring in the present context the question of just how successful such inhabited ribbons would be as an urban organism).

Allied to the aqueduct-like ribbon development are the megastructural configurations of the Obus plan, likewise designed by Le Corbusier, that wind through the Algerian landscape like contour lines.[13] Though this proposal opened the door to the notion of a residential infrastructure with individual infills, the fact that this coastal 'viaduct city' deprives the hinterland of a view of the sea is enough to cast doubt on its feasibility, however beautifully it seems to slot into the landscape. A specimen of this type of residential structure elegantly undulating through the landscape, such as the one realized by Alfonso Reidy in Rio de Janeiro, demonstrates the sheer opulence of this large-scale gesture so that you almost forget that it contains mass housing for the very poorest of that city's inhabitants. In Reidy's scheme a central street divides the building horizontally into a superstructure and an understructure. Running at half height through the building like a ship's deck and reached from the mountain slope by footbridges, this street confirms the feeling that the building is no discrete object but part of the mountain. Also

568

569-570

571, 573

568

569

570

found in Le Corbusier, this principle gained international fame through Mario Botta's convincing application of it in his private house at Riva San Vitale in Ticino, Switzerland. The snaking 'deck' of Reidy's residential megastructure gave rise to a further if unexpected spatial sensation of seeing before you the inner bend of the rear of the block and simultaneously having a view through the same building of the world in front of it. In spatial terms this goes a step further than the extra quality of the curved blocks exemplified by the crescents in Bath.[14] This effect moreover strengthens your sense of being on an inhabited mountainside rather than in a housing block.

So the building as landscape trades in its objectness to become a component of a major entity such as a rock formation; theoretically it could dissolve into its surroundings completely.

■ LANDSCAPE AS BEARER OF SIGNIFICANCE In places where there are no overly present objects, such as in a landscape, things and the space between them can prevail on equal footing, together with an egalitarian, non-hierarchic division of attention across the entire 'field' and, consequently, of meanings that tend to impose when attached to objects.

Landscape, in the sense used here, is a more or less articulated expanse with more or less protection (enclosure) and potential for attachment, and therefore more or less suited to be the bearer of meaning, significance, and is therefore signifiable.

The less object-like and the more intermediate, the less expressive – not so much in the sense of less rich in contrast, but less determined, less defined and more open to interpretation.

The smoother an expanse of landscape, and so the less capable of enclosure, the broader the view but the less plentiful the 'cover' (in inverse proportion). By contrast, the greater the potential for attachment and therefore resistance, the further the swing towards physical cover and mental comprehension together with a lessening of the emphasis on view and movement. If a smooth surface suggests movement before anything else, the more 'articulated' it is, the better the conditions for place-making and settlement.

This conception of the landscape idea shows certain affinities with the distinction the philosopher Gilles Deleuze made between smooth and striated surfaces.[15] Put in its most elementary form, his concern is the difference between planes whose meaning is free-floating or nomadic, and 'bearers' whose meaning is place-related or sedentary.

While on the subject, we should attach no more meaning to our references to philosophers than they deserve (architects are crazy about philosophers but tend to attach their ideas too literally to their own enthusiasms). The comparison is an extremely superficial one. Buildings are simply less foldable and pliable than words and images, whether we like it or not. Landscape as it concerns us is a structure shaped by man for purposes of survival and so constructed as to offer the maximum living space and thus the optimum conditions for existence for all its occupants.

Wherever the surface is rolling or sloping man does all he can to make it flat, meaning horizontal, by laying out terraces in steps. This articulation creates better conditions for working the land and it gives more space. We can find all manner of terrace forms in mountainous areas throughout the world. The principle is both simple and obvious: first you remove all the stones and rocks from the wild surroundings and use them to build walls that contain the fertile upper stratum in horizontal lanes. This 'natural' balance of material and ground simultaneously wards off the threat of erosion, which has increased since the original vegetation was cleared, and organizes the water resources. The more water that is needed, the more relevant the horizontality of the terraces.

571

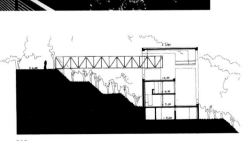

572

573

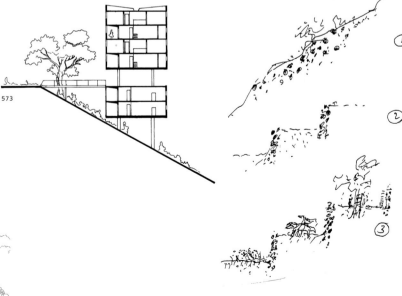

574

574

In the rice paddies of the Far East we can find incredibly refined and sensitive systems, developed from the experience of countless generations, that so determine the dimensions of terraces that the required water capacity can be guaranteed with an absolute minimum of dyking in and, therefore, maintenance.

Terracing is a means of defining territory and also provides clarity of organization and views. Last but not least it presents a close-knit social system through the interdependence of its users who share the upkeep of walls and dykes and look after the water resources.

Each landscape will evolve steadily over time into places; defined, described, won and defended, territorially determining and continually being redistributed and more intensively used due to new resources and standards.

As the capacity for place increases, so does the capacity for sojourn and as indeterminacy decreases, the space – not just physical space but also in the sense of leeway – decreases also.

The same holds for the city at least when sufficient 'homogeneity of heterogeneity' prevails – in this sense landscape par excellence. On that point, the following text dating from 1964 relating to Randstad Holland as an urban landscape is as relevant as ever.

'In Holland, more than anywhere else in the world, the intensive use of the available surface must always be borne in mind, for nowhere are so many people to be found together in so little space.

'In addition, the need for enclosure must be greater here than anywhere, since nowhere is the horizon broken by hills or woods, nor does the flat, soft ground co-operate in any way. Thus, the arguments are evident for close and intensive building in this most open land in the world.

'It is, therefore, the most incredible paradox that people in this town, Holland, are busy wasting space on an extensive scale. These extension schemes for the large cities – garden cities – produce neither gardens nor cities, and there is no possible link when both components are lacking.

'Architects are destroying place while creating a void, where there is already so much void and so little space. In blocks which are spatially set apart at such a distance that the shadow of one block does not even reach another, everyone is an outsider, lost between walls of unassailable smoothness whose impermeability can never accept, but only reject.

'A flat unbroken floor induces one to go on, a smooth wall can only be passed; it keeps its distance, withdraws, and offers no resistance.

'The first stage in the formation of enclosure is the resistance of floor and wall; it is this resistance which causes one to slow down or accelerate, which can influence the rhythm of existence: i.e., the forming of our surroundings into enclosure: town.

'We must create enclosure; enclosure for shelter, shelter for both spirit and heart. The larger the world becomes, and the further men travel, the greater the need becomes for enclosure, and part of our work is to give the widest significance to these two extremes by reconciling them to one another. Our environment is created: chiselled out, coagulated, stretched, extended, like a fold in the ground, so that room is made available for everyone and everything.

'"Town" is the integrity that results from the intensive contouring of the surface: it is the total enclosure, brought about in such a way that the largest possible number of people can be absorbed. Usually, the first lead is given by the contours of the ground itself. Even the most insignificant change – difference in level, incline, hollow (everywhere that dust is arrested in its flow and piles up) – is formative of enclosure and can be the prelude to town... Growth and change are the only constant factors in the image of the town, while every

575

576

577 Johan van der Keuken, *The Twilight of Cubism*, Seillaus, France, 1978

stage of continuous building must be permanent. Therefore every new encroachment must be a complete contribution in itself; a fulfilling of the time, an articulation of the surface. 'Here "articulation" means a disintegration of this surface in such a way as to give it size, enabling it to envelop everything that takes place within. Through this development, walls no longer function as partitions but as bases; the wall as enclosure. As such a process of articulation advances, a town becomes more concentrated, deeper in outline and of increasing capacity. Little room in much space becomes much room. Our starting point in planning must be the provision of optimum capacity.'[16]

■ SPATIALLY EVOLVED PLANES Modern architecture is notably fascinated with continuous curved and often folded and raked planes which in principle offer scant opportunity for attachment. They produce little in the way of interior quality; rather than encouraged to remain in place, you are urged to keep moving. Not conditions for sojourn then, but no commitment either. This flowing architecture excites by the mere fact of seeming in its entirety to be a constructed reflection of our modern way of life, marked as this is by fleeting points of application, as incidents in a dynamic whole.

Not only is this 'liquid' architecture averse to offering quality of place, orientation in the spatial sense vanishes in this fluid too. Particularly at those places where the columns stand at ninety degrees to the raked surface, an effect of alienation ensues with regard to the horizon and your sense of equilibrium. Here, the instability of the modern world is expressed using means that verge on the surrealistic. To compound matters, with floors merging seamlessly into ceilings that are also roofs, all familiar architectural meaning seems to melt away and buildings increasingly take on the attributes of landscape.

The reference to landscape inevitably sounds romantic but also not a little superficial. It may hold true as an implication of expansive, fluid, undulating, dynamic, 'nature' and space, but is undeniably over the top when only nomadic appropriation seems to be at issue.

Architects tend all too soon to mix their reality with metaphor, with the risk that the building's performance on paper and in reality are not always the same thing.

Pleated and folded planes may well express mobility and continuity; a horizontal plane is more likely to invite one to stay. But pleats and folds add information (and therefore meaning) and, like striated surfaces in relation to smooth ones – depending of course on their position with respect to high and low, up and down – are more receptive to meaning and therefore spatial in the sense of their capacity to be read as place, or filled-in and thus determined and designated.

We are saddled with the dilemma that our era has eliminated determinacy from our thinking. The architect, and indeed architecture, has no standpoint to fall back on that can stabilize his arguments for and legitimation of what he makes. There would be no problem here were it not that eventually users remain uprooted in such circumstances of fluidity and flexibility, incapable of becoming occupants. Flexibility may be receptive to everything, but it is unable to incite and thus too noncommittal to act as an underlying principle. Nobody, the most nomadic architect included, can function in the long run other than from a home base, a reasonably stable point of reference in his thinking; a horizon, if need be, that he can ultimately aim at.

Like the desperate servitude of the slave to his dominating and oppressive master, the modern architect is a slave to the instability he should in fact be combatting – if only he knew how.

578-580

578 OMA, Educatorium, Utrecht, 1992-97

579 OMA, Educatorium, Utrecht, 1992-97

580 OMA, Kunsthal, Rotterdam, 1987-92

Pisac, Peru [581-583]

The slopes near the Peruvian town of Cuzco in the Andes were worked by the Incas[17] on an astonishing scale into exceedingly long agricultural terraces resembling gigantic stairs. These terraces are linked together by stones protruding from the endless stacked walls that form minimal sets of steps at regular intervals. These built forms are an intervention in nature. The terrace walls hold the fertile upper layer in place, combatting erosion and enabling effective water management. In an architectural sense you could say that the landscape has become more accessible through this stepped articulation and therefore more habitable.

A structure has come about, both built and of the landscape. To us, it is a potential urbanistic principle capable of launching a multiplicity of meanings, interpretations and elaborations.

583

581

582

Moray, Peru [584-587]

On the plateau, quite unannounced by the surrounding landscape, is a hollow of gigantic dimensions. The walls of the hollow are like the mountain slopes farther on, worked up, we may assume, with undulating lines into lower plateaus in accordance with a complex design of complete and almost complete circles. These shapes are terraces, at times concentric, at others widened, with multiple centres. The hollow itself may be a natural phenomenon but the treatment of the inside, whose precision betrays resolute action, could only have been thought out beforehand, for a reason, and at least to be seen by gods and men. Would the Incas have been practitioners of Land Art? The immeasurably large figures traced by them in the earth at Nasca (southern Peru and northern Chile) can scarcely be anything else. They may not have had aeroplanes or balloons, but they were at least certain that their gods were looking.

A welter of theories exist as to this phenomenon, varying from the seat of the Inca parliament (Rudofsky)[18] to theatres (Benevolo)[19], while the possibility of agricul-

584

tural laboratories has not been ruled out either; after all, the deeper lying the land, the cooler it is, so that variable conditions for growth prevail.

For all our efforts to fathom out the possible intentions of this grand work, a plausible explanation is as yet unforthcoming. All we can do is wonder at this magnificent undulating hollow that is exclusively inward-facing, unlike the extraverted agricultural terraces along the mountainsides.

The widenings where several curves flow together pose a complex system of clearings and places so that one might easily imagine gatherings being held here as much for centralized as for decentralized activities. Like the Greek theatres, this place has no exterior and so is a negative object, arguably the most beautiful one of this size.

585

586

587

Stairs and treads [588-589]

Stairs are pre-eminently intermediate elements. The only reason for visiting them is to ascend or descend to somewhere else. They connect levels, subsidiary like bridges to their job of linking, servant, dependent, space-devouring; they are circulation space and not useful floor area or a destination as such, open-ended and not an end. This is why stairs are all too soon ignored or smoothed over and often stashed away in narrow shafts as obligatory means of linking levels without erasing the physical distinction between above and below. Ascending or descending, from one floor to another, you are moving through a space which, constantly perceived from another angle, is sounded out, bringing about what we call a sense of space. So it is important that a stair so traverses a space that, while moving, your view does indeed make that journey a memorable one.

You might instead construct a ramp but this involves a far greater length if it is not to be excessively steep and thus difficult to traverse. A slope is most effective in extremely large spaces and then only when these are so articulated as to hold the attention even during a long journey. Regrettably there are too few architects who are able to accomplish this.

Le Corbusier introduced his 'promenade architecturale', the idea that you move through a space as if through a landscape, with ever new vistas as on a mountain walk. Ramps and sloping floors compel movement, make lingering difficult. Thus, they have come to typify a 'nomadism' in architecture. But for a stay of any length, we always seek out the horizontal plane. Mountainsides are made into terraces for agriculture, wherever there are human settlements.

The treads of stairs, if the dimensions are right, may permit standing still or become places to sit, and can take on the role of tiers of seats, thereby bringing people together. When hewn or erected in uncultivated space, treads are a primary form of articulation, a place for planting or building in the horizontal sense and cover from behind in the vertical sense – they represent the domesticating and appropriating of natural space.

Stairs can be so developed that they unfold the landscape; creating a sense of space through ever shifting vantage points and views through, they are space-makers par excellence.

588

589

Steps of Machu Pichu and outside stair of Apollo Schools (1980-83) [590-592]

It can not have come about by sheer chance. This regular succession of steps must, like all others like it, have been made by the hand of man. We will probably never know why they had to be at that exact spot, half across an immovable rocky outcrop, and half next to it across material that is a good deal easier to work with.

Composed from two unequal parts that together comprise a functional entity, it resembles a face built up of two halves from different people. You are seeing two not-quite-complete objects simultaneously, and the quality they share prevails as a single composite image. Both have adapted as best they can to the subject and now enjoy the closest proximity without relinquishing their identity.

This set of steps exists because of two components, each of them attributive (though they could each have been a stair in their own right) and together they form the subject. But never an object – and this is what interests us.

590

591

It is an open question whether this remarkable phenomenon would ever have come to
light if the notion of a stair of two different
materials – in this case transparent and solid
– had not at one time arisen in practice.
In the Apollo Schools the brief called for a
stair which, as the general entrance, had to
be broad, inviting, where you could wait for
your schoolmates and perhaps where the
annual school photo could be taken. However, this was not to generate an inhospitable space underneath. For there is the
entrance to the infants' school, and the
place where the very youngest pupils wait
for their parents to pick them up. You could
say that this situation trained our eyes for
the time when years later, on the other side
of the world in Peru, be it in another form,
we would recognize a principle so very close
to it.

592

'Amphitheatre' treads, Apollo Schools, Amsterdam (1980-83)[20] [593-597]

The wide amphitheatre-like steps in the central hall can double as seating for the entire school at informal and organized events. This precludes the need to constantly drag chairs in and out. But these steps also offer an almost endless potential of places for more individual activity. For the children they are long tables to work on. The association with a table due to their height is strengthened by their timber facings. Here, everyone can find a workplace of their own. First, though, off with those shoes. Rule number one: no shoes on the table.

593

594

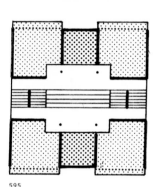

595

596

Anne Frank School, eight-class primary school, Papendrecht (1992-94) [598- 601]

This school constitutes an urban corner-stone of a site otherwise given over to housing. Developing the building upwards serves to free it from the houses around and limits the size of its footprint.

The heart of the building is the main hall where all activity converges. This tall space is oversailed by roofs that articulate the spatial organization and are curved so as to unite the directional lines and heights of the three surrounding volumes.

The classrooms are accommodated in two nearly identical blocks and the remaining rooms in a third block a half-storey taller to create a stacking of volumes round the central hall. The internal circulation takes place over half-stairs round the central well, a strategy that transmutes the entire building into a single capacious staircase with the prefatory spaces of the classrooms as its stairheads. These enlarged landings act as internal balconies and give each class an unhampered view of the others.

600

598

599

601

Stair in video centre of Theatre Complex, The Hague (1986-93) [602-605]

311-320

608

The video centre is in actual fact only a stairwell in the Hague theatre complex. Not threading elastically through a large free space as in Centraal Beheer, here in the cramped though tall exhibition space of the video centre the height is sliced through with a stair pushed as far as possible into the corner. Cut loose, so to speak,

from the upper floors like an installation such as those regularly showing there, it comes across as a permanent component among the temporary exhibits.

Besides forging a link between adjoining storeys, this stair presents a diversity of vantage points from which to observe the art on show. It is a means of encouraging

the specifically vertical use of a space with a severely restricted surface area.

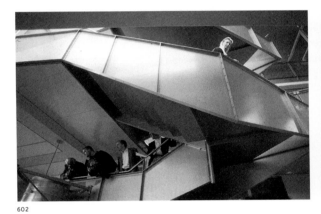

602

603

604

605

Outdoor stair of De Evenaar primary school, Amsterdam (1984-86) [606-607]

In siting this school as a more or less autonomous object in the middle of a local public plaza, and somewhat brazenly in front of the entrance to a currently disused church rearing up like a threatening monster behind it, we proceeded from the assumption that the school and the neighbourhood would share this plaza space.

In other words, it had not become just the school grounds.

This public clearing, set centrally in a densely populated residential area, is used to the full, especially by children whether from the school or from the houses around. The entrance stairway, defiantly extending into the plaza, has a key role to play here. It functions not only as an entrance to and exit from the school but also as seating for those watching the local junior footballers. In addition, this 'obstacle' offers the shelter necessary to make it a meeting place for the local children.

Public space for children should not be confined simply to cut-and-dried playground apparatus. Buildings in the old parts of cities have appurtenances, recesses, nooks and crannies and, not least, undefined space to play in. The planners and builders of today, fearful of irregularities, seek to create a smooth, clean, unassailable world of certainties and perspicuity. It is up to architects to incorporate aspects in their buildings that contribute to transforming this world into urban social space.

606

607

Stair in extension to Centraal Beheer, Apeldoorn (1990-95) [608]

387-394 To traverse this free-standing stair is to follow an oval spiralling movement that gives unhampered views in all directions. It allows you to experience space vertically. During office parties, preferably held here in this atrium, it offers a fine view of performances and other events.
This free-form stair with almost no repeating elements winds sinuously through the space, hovering almost, like a fragile sculpture.
The springy feeling resulting from a greater sag than is normally acceptable, strengthens this effect of floating. The design was made intuitively rather than from calculations. Based on paper models, which give a good idea of the stiffness of sheet steel at the critical points, the stair was in fact modified somewhat during its assembly, bringing design and performance into uncustomarily close proximity.

608

Stair in Maison de Verre, Paris [609-611]
Pierre Chareau, Bernard Bijvoet and
Louis Dalbet, 1932

All in all, this house is a dream, not only of technical perfection but over all else of the physical discovery of a new world. 'To me this house – one single space really, like an articulation of places merging and overlapping from one level to the next, without distinct partitions – was a completely new experience when I first visited it. I entered a spaceship, out of this world … '.[21] Entering on the ground floor containing the doctor's surgery, you then proceed to the living quarters continuing on the two upper storeys (three storeys high at this point). Coming in through a curved glass sliding door with a similarly curving though independent perforated steel screen at the foot of the stair, you leave the surgery zone behind you. The screen slides over the sprung landing that is the first tread.

609

610

You walk upstairs, back in the direction of the front facade of glass blocks, towards the light. Almost at the top you arrive at a landing from which you reach the living quarters up a further two treads. This landing, expressed in the exterior where it announces the entrance portico, is not just a kind of negative 'doorstep' to the living room, but accompanies the change of direction in the route through the house.

The supremely gentle stair, of regal width and with no handrail, has treads clad with rubber that seem to hover in the light entering through the facade.

The idea of such a transparent stair is now commonplace, and we can make them even more slender these days. Yet it is not often that this openness and lightness makes as much sense as it does here in this, the original prototype. On this stair you ascend effortlessly through the space without having even the slightest feeling that you are moving up one storey.

611

Stairs of Grand Bibliothèque, Paris [612-613]
Dominique Perrault, 1989-96

That steps are also able to express inaccessibility and can be characteristic of a deliberately chosen concept of limited access is demonstrated by the enormous plinth containing the public portion of the new Paris library. You must first ascend it, climb up it to then descend into the building.

The image that the city has of the library is dominated by the four glass towers filled with its store of books. Not for books to look out of, but rather to be looked at. This building is pervaded with 'concentration and reflection', as Perrault's design report puts it, and is inspired by a monastery. Clearly conceived as anti-space, it is closer to the pyramids of Egypt than the Greek theatre and certainly not social space for life in the city.

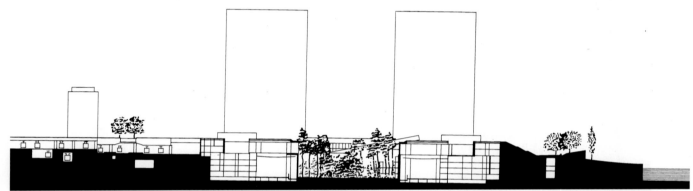

612 'The project is a piece of urban art, a minimalist installation, the "less is more" of emotion, where objects and the materials of which they are made count for nothing without the lights which transcend them. An initiatory walk across the footbridges slung among the branches of the trees, somewhere between sky and earth. Last of all, the soft protection of undergrowth, with its aromas and rustling sounds, reunions with oneself and with another world.' From the competition text for the new Bibliothèque Nationale de France (Dominique Perrault, 1989)

613

Roof of New Metropolis, Amsterdam [614-616]
Renzo Piano, 1992–97

Standing on the bank of the IJ inlet and founded on the car tunnel running beneath, this science museum with its sloping roof is the tunnel's mirror image. The museum itself is a sealed box given the shape of a ship's prow for rather too obvious reasons. But the stepped roof makes the building less building-like from the city side and more of a land abutment-like continuation of the bank, accessible to the public and facing the sun.

This makes it an attractive place to linger, particularly for children who can also find water there, cascading down among the steps. The building constructs an attractive slice of public space like a hill in flat country, offering an unfamiliar and surprising view of the old centre of Amsterdam previously only to be seen from the historical towers in its midst. This way it is contributing to the social space of the city.

614

615

616

Library steps, Columbia University, New York [617]

Placing buildings considered to be important on a pedestal is a regular theme in classically organized architecture. Held clear of the ground, elevated above us, the building is marked out as an object and singled out for our attention. Steps do admittedly suggest accessibility, but only when distance has been created first.

The change of guise into a tier of seating temporarily makes of this stair a place. From being 'in-between' it has become a subject and aim in itself, temporarily relegating the library to the background as a side issue and shifting the emphasis from the established, contained and solidified to the informal, the inviting, the ephemeral.

Just as with the many kinds of stairs and steps that classically-influenced architecture has brought forth, here too it transpires that the capacity for interpretation depends on the situation. What was meant as monumental can, depending on the circumstances, just as easily transmute into the opposite.[22]

617

Stair of Opera House, Paris [618]
Charles Garnier, 1874
Stair of Philharmonie, Berlin [619]
Hans Scharoun, 1963

Garnier's 'old' opera house represents a type of theatre that is no longer made. The same holds for the cascade of stairs attendant on it, if only because of the huge dimensions that make such a spacious stairwell and its contents a building in itself. When the audience takes to these stairs it becomes a theatre in itself and a unique spatial experience for all concerned. The great space around presents views on all sides, upwards too, and, more so than would a level floor, allows the audience to see and be seen.
A more up-to-date example is Hans Scharoun's Philharmonie in Berlin, where you can enter the auditorium on all sides by way of a great many small stairs rising from the foyer. Unlike in Paris, the audience is not shepherded upstairs in a great flood but taken there in small groups. More than that, where two distinct flights of stairs lead to the same landing, slipping in and out of alignment as they proceed, a power-

618

ful sense of dynamic ensues as the flows of concert-goers seem to be perpetually clashing and separating.

619

Carrefour Rue Vilin/Rue Piat, Paris

[620]
Ronies, 1959

There is clearly more involved here than just the concrete stair, a construction in its own right joining the lower-lying neighbourhood to that higher up. At the very place where the difference in level is briefly expressed as an impassable mountain slope there is a window, obviously a vent for the Métro directly behind it where noise and heat make their exit. Here the children cling to the belly of the city. Perhaps there is even a train to be seen flashing by.

Like mesmerized insects stuck to the grating, they are all but out of reach, in every sense. Here at this place, where the layers of the metropolis come to light in a pocket edition, there is real freedom of movement. It makes a vigorous contrast with the desolate perspective of the none-too-exciting street above. Not designed for this purpose and without explicitly offering the opportunity for it, this marginal spot is a place where children can get together undisturbed.

620

Lessons for Teachers

■ A student who had been given an extremely low mark came to discuss the matter with me prior to doing an exercise. (The stronger ones you never see again, it's the weaker ones that keep trailing you.) His work showed a total lack of understanding of architecture. This was a hopeless case who should never have embarked on this training course to begin with and this seemed the ideal moment to impress on him that it would be better all round if he were to do something else. In what turned out to be a lengthy discussion of his work I made it plain to him, patiently and in the proper manner, the full extent of his lack of understanding. From his reaction it seemed that the message had struck home, for he now appeared to fully grasp why he had received such a low mark. Then he came out with it: 'You know, I had in fact decided to pack this study in; but now, after this little talk, I can't wait to get back to work.'

■ Most teachers only accept what they themselves consider to be good and tend to use that as a standard against which to measure absolute quality. It is known that the composer Maurice Ravel, when judging work by young colleagues and coming across a composition he confessed to understanding nothing of, always gave it his approval. 'To be able to condemn a piece you must at least have first understood it, and should it be beyond your understanding it might be gibberish but it might just as easily be a work of genius.'

■ Problems are often regarded as pits in which you get more and more deeply entrenched, to the point of suffocating. You could better address yourself to mountains that need digging up. There are for that matter no such things as problems, not in our profession at least, only challenges.

■ Written accounts of projects, even of the most excellent projects, are all too often tedious in the extreme. This is because they tend to reproduce the design process from the beginning, so that they culminate in the chosen final form, much as a detective story climaxes in the unmasking of the villain. Unfortunately this is not the way projects work. The idea, the quest with forays to left and right, is only interesting when you know where it is all leading to. The thought process does not run synchronously with the events in the report you make of it, no more than a meal is served in exactly the same order in which it was prepared. What, for that matter, would you choose to say if some TV reporter perpetually pressed for time gave you sixty seconds to get across to the viewers the gist of your project?

■ Once a chemistry teacher had to carry out in front of the class experiments set down in the textbook as chemical equations of an unmistakable simplicity. The results had to be spot on, bearing out in practice the theory in the book so that the pupils would, for example, indeed see just a blue residue at the end of the experiment. He explained that they often took him ages to get organized, including bringing in all sorts of elaborate catalysts so that a process all too regularly dogged by contaminants would at least have a semblance of simplicity.

■ Never burden a student with 'You could have done that differently'. And certainly not with 'You should do it such and such a way'. This may show how good a teacher you are, but it's no help to a student. It wasn't your discovery anyway.

■ Jean Arp was wrestling with the problem of how to put together the two blocks of the perfectly smooth wood sculpture he was making so that they would come the closest to a single piece. A visitor to his studio who evidently did not fully grasp the problem, suggested hammering a couple of large nails through them. The holes these would make could easily be touched up so that absolutely nothing would be seen of the operation. Arp, tormented by this proposal – obviously too simple and too logical to dismiss yet too insensitive to accept, could only answer: 'Maybe so, but God sees everything.'

■ A group of students on excursion were received at Alvar Aalto's office. They were invited to ask him questions, and one ventured to inquire as to whether he ever used a module. To which the master must have replied: 'Of course, in all my work.' The next question, regarding the size of module, was inevitable. Aalto's answer? 'I always work with a module of 1 mm.'

■ During a lecture he gave to students in Zurich Aalto told the following anecdote to make clear what kind of architecture he would prefer not have anything to do with: An insurance agent was rung up by a client in a state of complete panic who tried to explain how seriously his house had been damaged in the previous night's violent gale. His account was so garbled that the insurance agent interrupted him with the demand: 'Sir, just tell me whether the house is still standing, yes or no.' To which the stricken victim replied: 'Yes, the house itself is still standing, but all the architecture has blown away.'

■ 'An architect is someone who tries to sell lemons to people who want to buy turnips.' S. van Embden

621 'Separate bills please waiter.'

622 'You have to take into account that the architect is only four years old.'

■ How often you hear people, usually the successful ones, complaining that they 'learnt nothing at school, no use at all, a waste of time'. A certain pride resonates in this condemnation; that they made a success of themselves in spite of it was all their own doing. I myself feel I learnt a great deal from everything the school sent my way. Obviously there was a lot of crap mixed in there but I still found it interesting. I mean, you don't have to believe it all. It is difficult and perhaps impossible to have a point of view without having taken cognisance of so many other potential viewpoints. Nonsense can teach you just as much as sensible things, perhaps more. After all, cut and dried solutions are no good to you when you really want to arrive at them yourself.

■ The painter Edgar Degas complained to the poet Stephane Mallarmé that it had cost him a whole day to try to write a sonnet: 'And yet I'm not lacking in ideas, I've enough of those!' Mallarmé could not resist answering: 'But Degas you need words to make a sonnet, not ideas.'

623 'I didn't actually <u>build</u> it, but it was based on my idea.'

■ Right to the end they were the familiars of every Dutch architect, inseparable, respected for their age, their integrity, their wisdom and their stories about meetings with celebrated colleagues; I am referring to Alexander Bodon and Hein Salomonson.
Up to my eyes in the preparations for a new school of architecture (the Berlage Institute) I bumped into them and was informed more or less in unison: 'Such a waste of time concerning yourself with teaching architecture. All good architects teach themselves; look at Le Corbusier.' I was temporarily lost for an answer. Only later did the deadly truth of their message dawn on me: that was why there are so many bad architects; if they hadn't been so stupid as to go to school they could all have been Corbusiers.

■ 'Oh Monsieur Debussy, that was such a wonderful concert. How on earth do you manage to think up such marvellous music?' 'Oh Madame, but that's easy, I just leave out all the irrelevant bits.'

■ One of Rietveld's clients, no doubt worried that the master would allow him little leeway, was smart enough to ask Rietveld to draw three alternatives for the house he had commissioned, giving him a loophole should the result get completely out of hand. To everyone's surprise Rietveld agreed, quite contrary to his usual practice. When the plans were presented Rietveld gave an explanation of all three, giving the pros and cons of the various options, to end his discourse by pushing two of them aside and choosing the third: 'And so this is the alternative we are going to build!'

■ As a Westerner building in Japan you are inevitably faced with confusing issues of mentality. Takeo Ozawa worked for us for a long time in Holland at our office and represented us magnificently in his own country, explaining our intentions to his fellow countrymen with endless patience and understanding. In his almost daily phone calls to us he kept on coming back to a particular detail which he insisted was 'very difficult'. I was unaware of the issue and kept on telling him, 'Takeo, you are so good, you must be able to get it through'. Still he persisted that it was 'very difficult' and I still didn't understand what he was driving at: it's impossible, we can't do it and it won't be done either. Finally it dawned on him how he should pass on the bad news: 'Listen Herman, we can't make what you propose, it is too good for Japanese people.'

■ Few are the goals made exclusively by the players who slam the ball into the net. He is the one who gets carried shoulder-high, harvests the laurels and goes down in football history, but usually it was a pass, often a perfect one, from an impossible position that paved the way for the triumphant deed. So there is the necessary preparation prior to a decisive step, often just as brilliant, even more perhaps, but less spectacular and most of all soon forgotten.

■ During a late discussion of students' work the cleaners had already started on the room where a small group of us had gathered. In the middle of my discourse on one of the projects I noticed that one of them had stopped what she was doing and stood there listening. Despite what for her must have been a pretty cryptic narrative she listened on. From that moment I felt the challenge of seeing how long I could keep her interested in my professional discourse on architecture. I tried to choose each word – obviously without it becoming apparent to those present – so that it would keep to the level of normal language and be about things that in principle could be understood by everyone, and not in the formal jargon we resort to without realizing it.
It is certainly difficult to couch everything in such a way that everyone grasps it without reverting to a simplistic populism. With architecture you necessarily have to know a little beforehand, but it does seem sensible to aspire to some level of intelligibility. It is a question of navigating between the rocks of populistic simplification on one side and the intellectual smokescreen on the other behind which the indecisive among us so like to secrete themselves.

■ Architects with their affected childlike innocence are often inclined to deny the influences on them. 'Has someone done that before? Is that so, oh I'm not that familiar with **x**'s work.' What is really naive is the complaint that you would rather have thought of it all yourself, and to assume that it is everyone else who is naive. As a student I remember times when the discovery you had claimed to have made yourself all too soon transpired to come from a book about one of your heroes. Instead of acknowledging where you got the idea, the tendency was to obscure the evidence, like a criminal trying to cover up his tracks. But history has a habit of catching up with you, not only as regards what you know but also what you should know.

■ Sammy was passing Moishe's house and saw a lorry standing with an enormous grand piano being unloaded from it. Moishe was out there giving the men instructions as to how the thing was to be hoisted up. Trying to suppress his envy, Sammy said: 'You can't possibly afford that – what's more, you can't even play the piano', a remark Moishe pretended not to hear. A week later, Sammy was passing by again and there's that lorry back in front of Moishe's house. And sure enough, down came the grand, once more accompanied by Moishe's instructions. 'Told you, didn't I,' Sammy gloated, 'there's no way someone like you could keep it up.' 'Is that so?' retorted Moishe condescendingly, 'I'm off to my piano lesson!'

■ 'The master should exalt his pupils, not lower them. Instead of exercising power over them, he should interact with them on the same level.' Friedrich Nietzsche

■ Whenever they hold a concert on Bali, the instruments of the gamelan are always set up long before time, where they attract the local children. Some of these try to play the instruments themselves. This is permitted, though their efforts are surreptitiously observed. Those who show signs of talent are encouraged and invited to play with the orchestra. Seated between the practiced musicians they are instructed until they have reached the same level of competence and then enlisted as regular members.

■ 'I often regret not having learnt architecture instead of music; for I have often heard that the best architect is the one who doesn't have ideas.' Wolfgang Amadeus Mozart

■ 'One never finishes studying, one never finishes, one keeps going without stopping, one becomes more and more of a student.' Le Corbusier

■ 'The tact of audacity consists in knowing how far one can go too far.' Jean Cocteau

■ 'Rodin was willing to have me as a student but I refused: for nothing grows beneath large trees.' Constantin Brancusi

■ 'I have never avoided being influenced by others. I would have considered it cowardice and a lack of sincerity with respect to myself. I think that the artist's personality develops strengthened by the combats it has with other personalities. If the combat proves fatal to it, if it succumbs, it is merely its destiny.'
Henri Matisse

624

■ 'Chopin got his ideas unexpectedly, without looking for them. His inspiration came at the piano – suddenly, completely, sublimely – or resonated in his mind whilst walking and he needed to quickly unburden them on his instrument so that he himself could hear them. But then began the most woeful toil that I have ever experienced. Exertion, indecision and impatience to take fresh hold of certain details of the theme he had heard followed one upon the other: the idea he had conceived of as a single entity he now overly dissected when seeking to write it down and, regretful because he felt he could not retrieve it as it was, he would sink into a kind of despair. He would shut himself up in his room for days, weeping, pacing to and fro, breaking his pens, repeating and altering a bar a hundred times, filling it in and then immediately erasing it, and persistently began again the next day, precisely and despairingly. Six weeks he would devote to one page, to finally return to what he had dashed off with a single stroke of the pen.' George Sand

■ 'The most practiced hand is never more than the servant of thought.' Auguste Renoir

■ 'On one occasion, Schönberg asked a girl in his class to go to the piano and play the first movement of a Beethoven sonata, which was afterwards to be analyzed. She said, "It is too difficult. I can't play it." Schönberg said: "You're a pianist, aren't you?" She said: "Yes". He said: "Then go to the piano." She had no sooner begun playing than he stopped her to say that she was not playing at the proper tempo. She said that if she played at the proper tempo, she would make mistakes. He said: "Play at the proper tempo and do not make mistakes." She began again, and he stopped her immediately to say that she was making mistakes. She then burst into tears and between sobs explained that she had gone to the dentist earlier that day and that she'd had a tooth pulled out. He said: "Do you have to have a tooth pulled out in order to make mistakes?"'
John Cage

■ 'When I first went to Paris, I did so instead of returning to Pomona College for my junior year. As I looked around, it was Gothic architecture that impressed me most. And of that architecture I preferred the flamboyant style of the fifteenth century. In this style my interest was attracted by balustrades. These I studied for six weeks in the Bibliothèque Mazarin, getting to the library when the doors were opened and not leaving until they were closed. Professor Pijoan, whom I had known at Pomona, arrived in Paris and asked me what I was doing. (We were standing in one of the railway stations there.) I told him. He gave me literally a swift kick in the pants and then said, "Go tomorrow to Goldfinger. I'll arrange for you to work with him. He's a modern architect." After a month of working with Goldfinger, measuring the dimensions of rooms which he was to modernize, answering the telephone, and drawing Greek columns, I overheard Goldfinger saying, "To be an architect, one must devote one's life solely to architecture." I then left him, for, as I explained, there were other things that interested me, music and painting for instance.

'Five years later, when Schönberg asked me whether I would devote my life to music, I said, "Of course." After I had been studying with him for two years, Schönberg said, "In order to write music, you must have a feeling for harmony." I explained to him that I had no feeling for harmony. He then said that I would always encounter an obstacle, that it would be as though I came to a wall through which I could not pass. I said, "In that case I will devote my life to beating my head against that wall."' John Cage

■ 'One of Mies van der Rohe's pupils, a girl, came to him and said, "I have difficulty studying with you. You don't leave any room for self-expression." He asked her whether she had a pen with her. She did. He said. "Sign your name." She did. He said, "That's what I call self-expression."' John Cage

■ 'Artists talk a lot about freedom. So, recalling the expression "free as a bird", Morton Feldman went to a park one day and spent some time watching our feathered friends. When he came back, he said: "You know? They're not free: they're fighting over bits of food."' John Cage

■ 'Schönberg always complained that his American pupils didn't do enough work. There was one girl in the class in particular who, it is true, did almost no work at all. He asked her one day why she didn't accomplish more. She said, "I don't have any time." He said: "How many hours are there in the day?" She said: "Twenty-four." He said: "Nonsense: there are as many hours in the day as you put into it."' John Cage

■ 'One day when I was studying with Schönberg, he pointed out the eraser on his pencil and said, "This end is more important than the other." After twenty years I learned to write directly in ink. Recently, when David Tudor returned from Europe, he brought me a German pencil of modern make. It can carry any size of lead. Pressure on a shaft at the end of the holder frees the lead so that it can be retracted or extended or removed and another put in its place. A sharpener came with the pencil. This sharpener offers not one but several possibilities. That is, one may choose the kind of point he wishes. There is no eraser.' John Cage

■ The world-famous conductor Otto Klemperer was feared far and wide for his unconventional, often shocking behaviour; a good many five-star hotels refused to have him because of his impossible habits.
Music for him was the only thing that counted, and so his capacity for criticism knew no bounds. It was in fact never good enough, something the musicians he conducted were well aware of; they were all too often getting the rough edge of his tongue. But it was the audience he cared for the least, with a contempt that welled literally from the depths of his soul. On one occasion, a celebrated pianist had just completed a brilliant cadenza and just before Klemperer was to bring the orchestra back in, he turned to him and pronounced, loud enough for the audience to hear: 'Far too ravishing for this lot.'

■ Peter van Anrooy was a composer well-known in this country when I was young (one piece of his that is still played on occasion is his Piet Hein Rhapsody). He also conducted, at, amongst other things, the low-priced concerts for the young, specially intended to give schoolchildren some idea of what classical music was about. Such concerts began with a spoken introduction telling something about the works on the programme and their composers. Van Anrooy was most adept in explaining fairly intricate matters clearly and concisely so that those totally unacquainted with the subject could understand. Once he compared Mozart and Beethoven as follows: 'Let's take Beethoven's music, boys and girls. You can just hear the struggle he's having, what an effort it is for him to scrape his way into heaven by the skin of his teeth. But then listen to Mozart, and it's as if he's just come from there!'

■ 'Architectural design operates with innumerable elements that internally stand in opposition to each other. They are social, human, economic, and technical demands that unite to become psychological problems with an effect on both each individual and each group, their rhythm and the effect they have on each other. The large number of different demands and sub-problems form an obstacle that is difficult for the architectural concept to break through. In such cases I work – sometimes totally on instinct – in the following manner. For a moment I forget the maze of the problems. After I have developed a feel for the program and its innumerable demands have been engraved in my subconscious, I begin to draw in a manner rather like that of abstract art. Led only by my instincts I draw, not architectural syntheses, but sometimes even childish compositions, and via this route I eventually arrive at an abstract basis to the main concept, a kind of universal substance with whose help the numerous quarrelling sub-problems can be brought into harmony.' Alvar Aalto

■ 'The poet has his dealings with things, things have their dealings with him.' Bert Schierbeek

■ 'There are painters who turn the sun into a patch of yellow, but there are also those who through their art and intelligence turn a patch of yellow into the sun.' Pablo Picasso

■ 'What we photographers don't capture immediately, is lost for ever.' Henri Cartier-Bresson

■ Le Corbusier was in the habit of having his often world-famous perspectives set up by one of his assistants, who immersed himself in the master's handwriting. At the end he took over from the draughtsman, who then served as a model to be included in the drawing in the master's hand together with the suggestion of a cloud, some green and perhaps a bird. Tense and controlled in equal measure as always, he completed the piece with his own signature. Sferre Fehn, at that time working at Le Corbusier's studio, on one such occasion heard him mutter half under his breath: 'There, the footprint of the lion.'

■ Aldo van Eyck was less an impossible person than a person of impossibilities. He had a passion for these and went to great lengths so as to best accommodate the impossible. After a harsh expedition through Romania, impenetrable as it was in those days, and arriving at Brancusi's Column which was so much more impressive and taller than one could imagine (it was literally measureless right there in front of you) he could only talk of one thing: of then wanting to see the upper surface. He would also travel to the furthermost reaches of the earth to take into his keeping stones gathered there and later leave them at Cape Horn (to confuse archaeologists, he said). Bring literally everything into what you do; 'the world in your head'. And know that you must persevere when faced with the inevitability of the road you have taken. He was quick to say of others that 'they tried hard, but not hard enough'.

■ 'Don't ask for a rainbow, fetch it!' Aldo van Eyck

■ It is crucial that first-year students have the right approach. What applies to everyone applies to them even more; you should not be showing students just how difficult it all is but how exciting and also how easy, providing they go about it the right way. Whet their appetites for knowledge instead of feeding them information. This is why the best task to start with is to design a large city, with no restrictions and no prior information, preferably in groups and in collaboration, and with a deadline of, say, two weeks. Teachers usually think in terms of increasing complexity and regard such an assignment as more suited to the final year than to the beginning. They tend to forget that during their training students have admittedly heard about all the complications and problems but that these are insoluble even for so-called expert urban designers. In any case, who said they had to be solved? Why does everything always have to be resolved forthwith? A fortnight spent by first-year students on the task of designing a city once elicited, in the eighties at the Ecole d'Architecture in Geneva, a great many of the basic concepts on hand throughout the history of urbanism, as a kind of ontogenesis of types. For the students this was the most normal thing. Open-minded as they are, they had expected nothing less, having enrolled at university with the intention of tackling serious matters such as these. The student about to leave university knows better. Relieved there of so many habits, what, exactly, has he been given in return?

625

■ The porter's lodge in the reception area of Alvar Aalto's sanatorium in Paimio once drew attention through its sleek detailing, its pliant form resembling before anything else an inordinately magnified version of one of Aalto's magnificent vases. Such sinuous lines, which the rest of the designing world tends to splash about at any and every opportunity, always have a most definite purpose with Aalto. Thus, his vases are eminently suited to variation in use in that each curve or billow invites filling in individually, so that what you really have is a number of vases in one. Just as the vases holds flowers, so too the porter's lodge receives its visitors where the shape curves inwards. This elementary condition could not have been designed more precisely, certainly not in the way it coincides with the drum rooflight set at the very place you would expect it. One would be hard put to conceive of anything of greater beauty and logic.

Looking at the floor plan as it appears in every publication, this porter's lodge is nowhere to be seen. Originally it must have been an open reception area which was later closed in, no doubt for practical reasons. Did Aalto make this exquisite modification himself or is it the work of others? If that last-named is the case, then I for one would willingly allow my buildings to be adapted with such sensitivity.

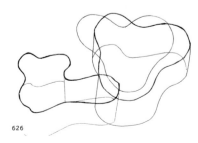

626

■ 'I was invited one day to dinner at the Corbusiers' apartment – they were living at the time in an old building in the Rue Jacob – and I expected to find an ultra-modern apartment with huge expanses of window and bare, bright lit walls, an apartment similar to the one he had designed for the millionaire Charles de Beistégui, the painter Ozenfant, the sculptor Lipchitz, and many others.

'Imagine my surprise when I entered a fairly messy apartment crammed with odd pieces of furniture and a weird collection of bric-à-brac. Even the huge drawing table the architect used was so loaded with objects, books and files that he was left only with a tiny cleared area where he could draw or write. I even wondered whether the old apartment had a bathroom. However, Madame Le Corbusier adored the apartment, which was in the heart of Saint-Germain-des-Prés, and they had been living there since 1917. She loved the rustic shutters that opened onto a tiny tree-filled garden in which the birds began chirping at dawn. '"Can you imagine, Brassaï," Yvonne said to me one day with tears in her eyes, "we have to leave the apartment in Rue Jacob. Corbu has finally has enough of all the sarcastic remarks people make about it; he wants to live in a Le Corbusier building. He's putting up an apartment house near the swimming pool out at Molitor, in the Rue Nungesser-et-Coli, and he's set aside a duplex on the eighth and ninth floor for us, with a roof garden. I've been to see it. You can't imagine what it's like! A hospital, a dissecting lab! I'll never get used to it. And way out in Auteuil, far from everything, far from Saint-Germain-des-Prés, where we've been living for sixteen years."

'They moved in 1933. And although it took Yvonne years to get used to her duplex, the architect was delighted with it. He especially liked the vast wall of his eighth-floor studio, made of raw stone, which became his "daily companion".' Brassaï

■ 'I was labelled a revolutionary, whereas my greatest teacher was the Past. My so-called revolutionary ideas are straight out of the history of architecture itself!' Le Corbusier

■ 'The artist doesn't make what others regard as beautiful, but only what he considers necessary.' Arnold Schönberg

■ 'It is easier to pulverize atoms than prejudices.' Albert Einstein

■ You are never too old to learn, it is unlearning that gets more and more difficult.

■ 'His works, which appear almost to have been improvised, were frequently very slow in getting started and underwent many changes. He often took one or two years to finish a canvas, and he would sometimes return to it years later. There is a story of how he once took advantage of a guard's absence from a room in the Musée du Luxembourg to dash over to alter a detail that had bothered him in one of his pictures with some paints and brushes he had concealed in his pockets.' Brassaï on Pierre Bonnard

■ **TAKE HOME ASSIGNMENT**
Part of the curriculum of the Faculty of Architecture at Delft consists of so-called 'take-home tasks': written assignments that students come and collect. These are to be completed and handed in fourteen days later, after which there is a discussion involving the teacher who set the task and those who took it on.

The essence of the task is that you can only resolve it properly through a combination of perspicacity, empathy and enthusiasm. It entails a written rather than a drawn situation; much like the physics problems you get at secondary school. It is a situation familiar to everyone, as intriguing as a puzzle you feel obliged to solve if only to keep up with the others.

These assignments never involve problems, they are challenging more than anything else. They call not for diligent draughtsmanship but for an idea, a brainwave-in-miniature, and are expressly aimed at bringing out the assignee's own ideas, interpretation and choice of site. Thinking up a problem is possibly just as mentally taxing as thinking up a solution. As a teacher you have to extricate yourself from all the stuff that constitutes ninety per cent of the architect's practice and that you are all too readily inclined to immerse your students in, to show them just what a difficult business it all is. Instead you should be looking for the exciting, challenging and, most importantly, the fun sides to architecture that will arouse interest and hopefully curiosity too. Looking through the results of the take-home exams (example see pp. 282-283), a coherent image has taken shape through the years. There are always a few who get totally stumped and a large group of boring, decent, reasonable students clearly divided into those who went out of their way to resolve the task and those who ploughed through it with an often remarkable dexterity. But there is also a select band whose responses are frequently surprising and at times even astonishing.

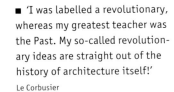

627

■ TAKE-HOME EXAM

9 September 1997
Professor Herman Hertzberger BI
Module A4, History and Design

GENERAL In many designs too much emphasis is unconsciously given to the walls (the construction). In these terms the spaces can be regarded as in-between space, residual areas left by the placing of walls. The present task proceeds from a situation in which there is no need to place walls to make spaces, but instead where spaces can be scooped out.

GIVEN A sheer cliff forms a right angle with both the horizontal top face and the sea into which it plunges. At ebb tide, the plateau is 12 metres above sea level and the water 2 metres deep at that point. The cliff face runs north-south with the sea to the west. The climate is subtropical and almost always sunny. The difference between the tides is half a metre. The rock of which the cliff face is made is easy to work with, to hollow out, and at the same time of a enduring quality, that is, in principle no finish is required. On the plateau there is a road set not too far from the edge.

TASK Make the water accessible from the upper plateau and devise one or more added social spaces. Suggestions: restaurant, café, sauna, chapel, dentist's surgery, gallery for exhibiting archaeological or geological finds, and so forth. It is possible to build onto or suspend from the wall a lightweight structure, but keep in mind that it must consist of easily transportable materials and that transporting it there would be more expensive than quarrying the stone on site.

JUDGING CRITERIA There must be a meaningful, appropriate response to the programme in view of the exceptional situation. The project will also be judged on the use it makes of the above-mentioned mode of 'building' suggested by that situation.

628

629

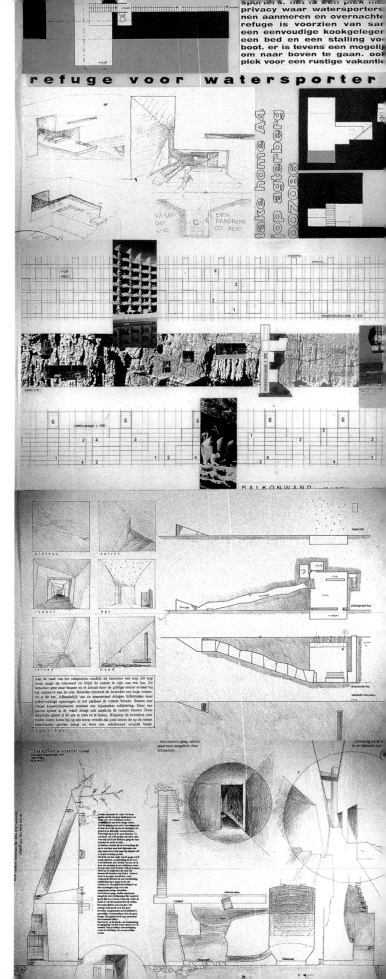

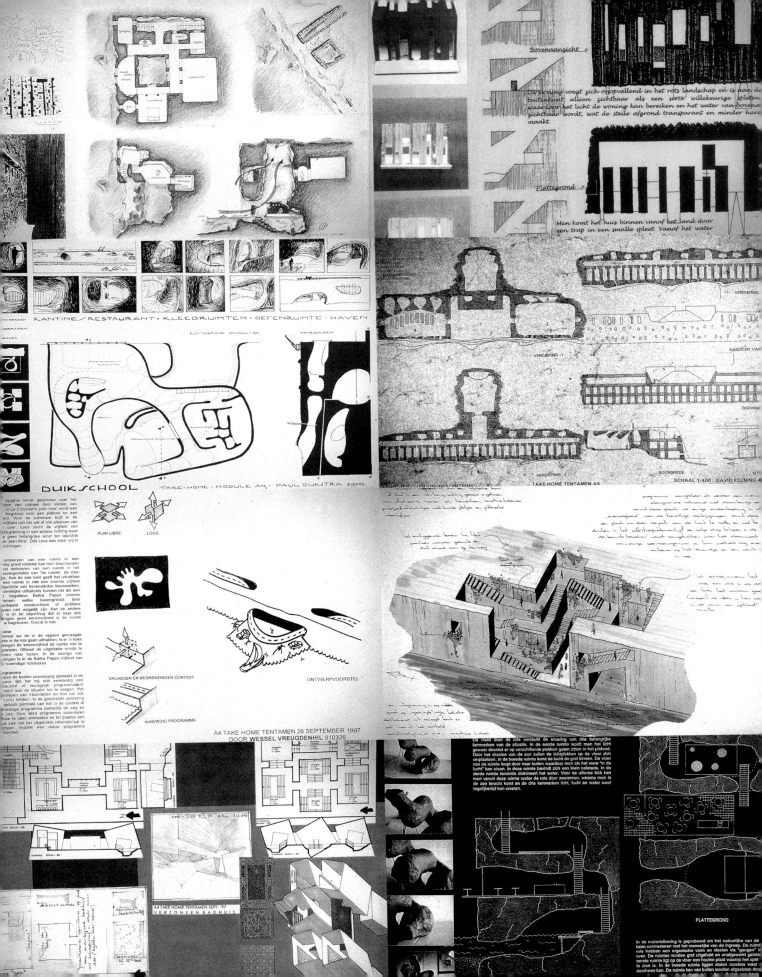

■ The climate at the university is overly determined by fear. Fear on the part of the professors that students will not get a thorough training, and the students' fear of failing to satisfy the expectations of the professors. And yet the two parties agree on one count: it has to do with being able to think about your subject of study, the rest is a question of looking things up. And because you are only able to think when you get pleasure from thinking, it is 'the pleasure of thinking' that should colour every task you are set. The best tasks I know of in this respect are the following:

1 Comparative analysis (introduced by Kenneth Frampton at the Berlage Institute) of buildings. This involves carefully choosing a number of objects that have to be of one type per analysis (i.e. railway stations, residential areas, schools) and expressly suitable for comparison. Groups of students (this can only be done in groups) try to assess, on the basis of what are initially self-imposed criteria, the extent to which the different objects satisfy those criteria and which score the most points. They therefore have to think about how a building fits together, why this is so, and whether this really is the case. The basic conditions that projects have to satisfy are exposed together with whatever unexpected and exceptional spatial discoveries they may prove to elicit.

2 Once again by dint of comparison, a number of preferably large buildings or structures, whose construction was of decisive influence on the underlying concept, are examined to ascertain the degree of influence the form had on the construction or indeed the construction's influence on the form. The exercise gains added depth by the inclusion of examples from the past as well as the present, such as the Hagia Sofia,

the Gothic cathedral and the Sagrada Familia, thus presenting quite differently grounded relationships of form, material and ways of spanning.

Without referring to history as such, various eras and their specific possibilities can then be compared, thereby laying low the unspoken but generally prevailing prejudice that there is no place for the past in the maelstrom of the present.

■ 'Art is the highest expression of an inner, unconscious mathematics.' Gottfried Wilhelm Leibniz

■ 'Let's forget the things and only pay attention to the relations between them.' Georges Braque

■ 'We all know that art isn't truth. Art is a lie that makes us realize truth, at least the truth that is given us to understand.'
Pablo Picasso

■ 'You must aspire the simplest solution, but no simpler than that.' Albert Einstein

■ 'The only way to find something is not to look for it.'
Jorge Luis Borges

■ INDESEM is a two-yearly International Design Seminar. A short-lived school of architecture held at the Faculty of Architecture in Delft, it is an explosion of learning without education. This time it is the students that decide which teachers they want to hear and what the subjects are to be. Students themselves are one hundred per cent responsible for everything and it is they who see to it that the technical and academic staff warm to the idea of breaking plenty of rules for a week. And you should see what happens when you do! Work continues into the early hours and the building is turned inside out to get at its hidden qualities. The daily routine is disrupted and the cleaners are made aware of their importance.

Spectacular though the week of the seminar undoubtedly is, it is merely the tip of the iceberg of preparations attendant on each new INDESEM when twenty or so individuals are kept busy for at least nine months. Each time a group of students comes together to perform the Herculean task of getting this event off the ground, their own regular studies largely left to one side for the duration. It is only much later that they realize just what they have received

in return when, their studies over, it transpires that designing and realizing a building demands an identical attitude where it is again all down to anticipating, deliberating, seeking out conditions, making (and keeping) appointments.

The task is enacted in the city. It is not primarily about building itself but about what building in the city does to space.

Those taking part come from all over the world, perhaps initially attracted by names and by the Netherlands, but also for the thrill of actually being able to meet and talk with so many others in the same boat. The task is no more than a pretext and catalyst for coming into contact with others and having something to discuss with them.

No-one really believes that a week is long enough to do more than make a start on a barely underpinned plan, nor is that the prime reason for INDESEM. The idea of results is chiefly to drive the process. The performance that needs generating is to get a group of complete strangers, almost all of whom are obliged to try to express themselves in a language other than their own, to formulate and present an idea and go on to defend it against all others.

630

631

■ In 1963 Le Corbusier was awarded the Sikkens Prize in the Stedelijk Museum in Amsterdam. Everyone was there at the reception after the official ceremony and speeches to witness his brief presence in Holland. In the throng I suddenly found myself no more than two metres away from the man for whom I, at age 31, had such admiration. Chance had it that at that very moment there was no-one conversing with him and he had been left at the mercy of all those people whose language he could not understand. This, then, was the perfect moment to approach him, touch him, maybe even shake his hand. A moment I knew would never come again. But, what important things did I have to say to him or enquire of him out of the blue like that? 'I think you're wonderful', 'You're my hero' or 'Thank you very much'. And in decent French too. Then someone caught his attention and the crowd closed on him. The moment had passed.

Two days later a representative of one or other building material came to the office and insisted on speaking to me personally and showing me something that was bound to interest me. My curiosity aroused, I agreed, and before he could begin eulogizing his most excellent product he had to get off his chest the fact that he had shaken the hand of none other than Le Corbusier at a reception. Proudly he showed me his card which he had craftily got Le Corbusier to sign and which gained him such rapid access to his clients.

632

■ 'When a job is handed to me I tuck it away in my memory, not allowing myself to make any sketches for months on end. That's the way the human head is made: it has a certain independence. It is a box into which you can toss the elements of a problem any way, and then leave it to "float", to "simmer", to "ferment".Then one fine day there comes a spontaneous movement from within, a catch is sprung: you take a pencil, a charcoal, some coloured crayons … and you give birth on the sheet of paper. The idea comes out... it is born.' Le Corbusier

■ Long after the Schröder house was in place Rietveld kept on making modifications, various small practical additions requested by Madame Schröder, say to make her bathroom more comfortable.

When visiting the house, I discovered in a corner above the bath two unprepossessing undulating slivers of glass built into the wall on which to place the soap. Rietveld could have made them slanting but that would have been foreign to his vocabulary. How, then, did he arrive at this rippling Aaltoesque form? It was my ex-Delft colleague Gerrit Oorthuys who solved the problem. He told me that during World War Two an ammunition truck exploded near the house, shattering the windows. Assessing the damage, Rietveld and Truus Schröder were struck by the fanciful shapes of the broken glass, keeping the most attractive pieces and later using them. The solution to this riddle once again drives home the fact that the artist finds before he conceives.

NOTES

CHAPTER 1

1 Herman Hertzberger, *Lessons for Students in Architecture*, 010 Publishers, Rotterdam 1991, pp. 219-220.
2 Albert Einstein, Foreword to Max Jamme, *Concepts of Space. The History of Theories of Space in Physics*, Harvard University Press, Cambridge (Mass.) 1954: 'two concepts of space may be contrasted as follows: (a) space as positional quality of the world of material objects; (b) space as container of all material objects. In case (a), space without a material object is inconceivable. In case (b), a material object can only be conceived as existing in space; space then appears as a reality which in a certain sense is superior to the material world. Both space concepts are free creations of the human imagination, means devised for easier comprehension of our sense experience.'
3 Martin Buber, *Reden über Erziehung*, Verlag Lambert Schneider, Heidelberg 1956.
4 Georges Perec, *Espèces d'espaces*, Editions Galilée 1974. 'Notre regard parcourt l'espace et nous donne l'illusion du relief et de la distance. C'est ainsi que nous construisons l'espace : avec un haut et un bas, une gauche et une droite, un devant et un derrière, un près et un loin. Lorsque rien n'arrête notre regard, notre regard porte très loin. Mais s'il ne rencontre rien, il ne voit rien ; il ne voit que ce qu'il rencontre : l'espace, c'est ce qui arrête le regard, ce sur quoi la vue butte : l'obstacle : des briques, un angle, un point de fuite : l'espace, c'est quand ça fait un angle, quand ça s'arrête, quand il faut tourner pour que ça reparte. Ça n'a rien d'ectoplasmique, l'espace ; ça a des bords, ça ne part pas dans tous les sens, ça fait tout ce qu'il faut faire pour que les rails de chemins de fer se rencontrent bien avant l'infini.'
5 Maurice Merleau-Ponty, *L'Œil et l'Esprit*, Editions Gallimard 1964, p. 47.
6 Gustave Flaubert, *Madame Bovary*, transl. Alan Russell, Penguin Books, Harmondsworth, UK 1950, p. 57. Original text: 'A la ville, avec le bruit des rues, le bourdonnement des théâtres et les clartés du bal, elles avaient des existences où le cœur se dilate, où les sens s'épanouissent. Mais elle, sa vie était froide comme un grenier dont la lucarne est au nord, et l'ennui araignée silencieuse, filait sa toile dans l'ombre à tous les coins de son cœur.'
7 *Ibid.*, p. 309. Original text: Elle arriva sur la place du Parvis. On sortait des vêpres: la foule s'écoulait par les trois portails, comme un fleuve par les trois arches d'un pont, et, au milieu, plus immobile qu'un roc, se tenait le suisse. Alors elle se rappela ce jour où, tout anxieuse et plein d'espérances, elle était entrée sous cette grande nef qui s'étendait devant elle

moins profonde que son amour; et elle continua de marcher, en pleurant sous son voile, étourdie, chancelante, près de défaillir.'
8 *Ibid.*, p. 251. Original text: 'Le nef se mirait dans les bénitiers pleins, avec le commencement des ogives et quelques portions de vitrail. Mais le reflet des peintures, se brisant au bord du marbre, continuait plus loin, sur les dalles, comme un tapis bariolé. Le grand jour du dehors s'allongeait dans l'église en trois rayons énormes, par les trois portails ouverts. De temps à autre, au fond, un sacristain passait en faisant devant l'autel l'oblique génuflexion des dévots pressés. Les lustres de cristal pendaient immobiles. Dans le chœur, une lampe d'argent brûlait; et, des chapelles latérales, des parties sombres de l'église, il s'échappait quelquefois comme des exhalaisons de soupirs, avec le son d'une grille qui retombait, en répercutant son écho sous les hautes voûtes. Léon, à pas sérieux, marchait auprès des murs. Jamais la vie ne lui avait paru si bonne. Elle allait venir tout à l'heure, charmante, agitée, épiant derrière elle les regards qui sa suivaient, – et avec sa robe à volants, son lorgnon d'or, ses bottines minces, dans tout sorte d'élégances dont il n'avait pas goûté, et dans l'ineffable séduction de la vertu qui succombe. L'église, comme un boudoir gigantesque, se disposait autour d'elle; les voûtes s'inclinaient pour recueillir dans l'ombre la confession de son amour; les vitraux resplendissaient pour illuminer son visage, et les encensoirs allaient brûler pour qu'elle apparût comme un ange, dans la fumée des parfums.'
9 David Cairns (trans./ed.), *A Life of Love and Music. The Memoirs of Hector Berlioz 1803-1865*, The Folio Society, London 1987, p. 134.
10 Theun de Vries, *Het motet voor de kardinaal*, Querido, Amsterdam 1981.
11 Herman Hertzberger, *Johan van der Keuken, Cinéaste en photographe*, Brussels 1983.
12 Michel Foucault, *Les mots et les choses*, Editions Gallimard 1966.
13 *Lessons for Students in Architecture*, pp. 26-27.
14 *Ibid.*, p. 192.
15 *Ibid.*, pp. 190-201.
16 *Ibid.*, p. 28.
17 Mark Strand, 'The Room'. This poem was read at the cremation of Aldo van Eyck by one of his grandchildren, 16 January 1999. *Selected Poems*, Alfred A. Knopf, New York 1998.

THE ROOM

I stand at the back of a room / and you have just entered. / I feel the dust / fall from the air / onto my cheeks. / I feel the ice / of sunlight on the walls. / The trees outside / remind me of something / you are not yet aware of. / You have just

entered. / There is something like sorrow / in the room. / I believe you think / it has wings / and will change me. / The room is so large / I wonder what you are thinking / or why you have come. / I ask you, / What are you doing? / You have just entered / and cannot hear me. / Where did you buy / the black coat you are wearing? / You told me once. / I cannot remember / what happened between us. / I am here. Can you see me? / I shall lay my words on the table / as if they were gloves, / as if nothing had happened. / I hear the wind / and I wonder what are / the blessings / born of enclosure. / The need to go away? / The desire to arrive? / I am so far away / I seem to be in the room's past / and so much here / the room is beginning / to vanish around me. / It will be yours soon. / You have just entered. / I feel myself drifting, / beginning to be / somewhere else. / Houses are rising / out of my past, / people are walking / under the trees. / You do not see them. / You have just entered. / The room is long. / There is a table in the middle. / You will walk / towards the table, / towards the flowers, / towards the presence of sorrow / which has begun to move / among objects, / its wings beating / to the sound of your heart. / You shall come closer and I shall begin to turn away. / The black coat you are wearing, / where did you get it? / You told me once / and I cannot remember. / I stand at the back / of the room and I know / if you close your eyes / you will know why / you are here; / that to stand in a space / is to forget time, / that to forget time / is to forget death. / Soon you will take off your coat. / Soon the room's whiteness / will be a skin for your body. / I feel the turning of breath / around what we are going to say. / I know by the way / you raise your hand / you have noticed the flowers / on the table. / They will lie / in the wake of our motions / and the room's map / will lie before us / like a simple rug. / You have just entered. / There is nothing to be done. / I stand at the back of the room / and I believe you see me. / The light consumes the chair, / absorbing its vacancy, / and will swallow itself / and release the darkness / that will fill the chair again. / I shall be gone. / You will say you are here. / I can hear you say it. / I can almost hear you say it. / Soon you will take off your black coat / and the room's whiteness / will close around you / and you will move / to the back of the room. / Your name will no longer be known, / nor will mine. / I stand at the back / and you have just entered. / The beginning is about to occur. / The end is in sight.

CHAPTER 2

1 Yves Arman, *Marcel Duchamp plays and wins/joue et gagne*, Marval, galerie Yves

Arman/galerie Beaubourg/galerie Bonnier, Paris 1984.
2 *Lessons for Students in Architecture*, p. 169.
3 Edward T. Hall, *The Hidden Dimension*, Doubleday & Co., Inc., New York 1966.
4 Claude Lévi-Strauss, *La pensée sauvage*, Librairie Plon, 1962.
5 Howard F. Stein and William G. Niederland (eds.), *Maps from the Mind: Readings in Psychogeography*, 1989.
6 According to the survey in Willy Boesiger (ed.), *Le Corbusier*, Thames & Hudson, London 1972. This abridged edition gives the most information, naturally together with the indispensable 'œuvre complet'.
7 Herman Hertzberger, 'De Schetsboeken van Le Corbusier', *Wonen-TABK*, no. 21, 1982. Written in conjunction with the publication of the collected sketchbooks as *Le Corbusier, Sketchbooks, 1914-1948*, MIT Press, Cambridge (Mass.) 1981.
8 Herman Hertzberger, 'Homework for more hospitable form', *Forum*, no. 3, 1973.
9 Dick Hillenius, *De hersens een eierzeef*, open lectures at the University of Groningen, November 1986, Martinus Nijhoff, The Hague 1986.
10 Yi-Fu Tuan, *Space and Place*, University of Minnesota, 1977.
'Experience is the overcoming of perils. The word "experience" shares a common root (*per*) with "experiment", "expert", and "perilous." To experience in the active sense requires that one venture forth into the unfamiliar and experiment with the elusive and the uncertain. To become an expert one must dare to confront the perils of the new.'

CHAPTER 3

1 Frits Bless, *Rietveld 1888-1964*, Bert Bakker, Amsterdam 1982.
2 Michel Foucault, *Surveiller et Punir; naissance de la prison*, Schoenhoff's Foreign Books inc., 1975.
3 *Lessons for Students in Architecture*, pp. 246-248.
4 *Ibid.*, pp. 28-30, 62, 153-155, 193.
5 *Ibid.*, pp. 31, 142-144, 183-184, 213-215, 242.
6 Ivan Illich, *Deschooling Society*, Harper & Row, New York 1971.
7 *Lessons*, pp. 246-248.
8 *Ibid.*, p. 33.
9 Nelson (1895-1979) was best known for this design. He otherwise distinguished himself with specialist solutions in hospital building.
10 *Lessons*, p. 65.
11 When asked whether he could have done with a bit more green Le Corbusier retorted testily: 'A few stalks, if that'.
12 TH *documentatie bouwtechniek*, Delft Architecture Faculty, September 1971.
13 *De wording van een wondere werkplek*, VPRO, Hilversum 1997.

CHAPTER 4

1 Cf. Brancusi: 'La simplicité n'est pas un but dans l'art, mais on arrive à la simplicité malgré soi en s'approchant du sens réel des choses.' Carola Giedion-Welcker, *Constantin Brancusi*, Editions du Griffon, Neuchâtel-Suisse 1958.
2 Herman Hertzberger, 'Introductory Statement', in *The Berlage Cahiers 1, Studio '90/'92*, 010 Publishers, Rotterdam 1992.
3 Jean Nouvel, lecture at the Berlage Institute, 1996.
4 David Cairns (trans./ed.), *A Life of Love and Music. The Memoirs of Hector Berlioz 1803-1865*, The Folio Society, London 1987, p. 13.
'My father would not let me take up the piano; otherwise I should no doubt have turned into a formidable pianist in company with forty thousand others. He had no intention of making me an artist, and he probably feared that the piano would take too strong a hold of me and that I would become more deeply involved in music than he wished. I have often felt the lack of this ability. On many occasions I would have found it useful. But when I think of the appalling quantity of platitudes for which the piano is daily responsible – flagrant platitudes which in most cases would never be written if their authors had only pen and paper to rely on and could not resort to their magic box – I can only offer up my gratitude to chance which taught me perforce to compose freely and in silence and thus saved me from the tyranny of keyboard habits, so dangerous to thought, and from the lure of conventional sonorities, to which all composers are to a greater or lesser extent prone. It is true that the numerous people who fancy such things are always lamenting their absence in me; but I cannot say it worries me.'
5 *Ibid.*, p. 13.
6 Herman Hertzberger, 'Designing as Research' in *The Berlage Cahiers 3, Studio '93/'94, The new private realm*, 010 Publishers, Rotterdam 1995.
7 From Herman Hertzberger, 'Do architects have any idea of what they draw?', in *The Berlage Cahiers 1, Studio '90/'92*, 010 Publishers, Rotterdam 1992.
8 See note 7.

CHAPTER 5

1 *Lessons for Students in Architecture*, pp. 48-60.
2 *Ibid.*, p. 103.
3 *Ibid.*, pp. 64-65.
4 Manuel de Sola Morales. 'Collective space is neither public nor private but far more and far less than public space.'
5 *Lessons*, p. 68.

6 *Ibid.*, pp. 82, 226-227.
7 Harry Hosman, interview with Johan van der Keuken, VPRO *Gids*, 12 October 1996.
8 *Lessons*, p. 86.
9 *Ibid.*, pp. 138-142.
10 *Ibid.*, p. 26.
11 *Ibid.*, pp. 213-215.
12 Leon Battista Alberti, book I, chapter 9 of *Ten Books on Architecture*, MIT Press, Cambridge (Mass.) 1988, original title: *De Re Aedificatoria*.
Original Italian text: 'E se è vero il detto del filosofi, che la città è come una grande casa, e la casa a sua volta una piccola città, non si avrà torto sostenendo che le membra di una casa sono esse stesse piccole abitazioni: come ad esempio l'atrio, il cortile, la sala da pranzo, il portico, etc.: il tralasciare per noncuranza o tracuratezza uno solo di questi elementi danneggia il decoro e il merito dell'opera.'
13 *Ibid.*, book 5, chapter 2. Original Italian text: 'Nella casa l'atrio, la sala e gli ambienti consimili devono essere fatti allo stesso modo che in una città il fòro e i grandi viali non già, cioè, in posizione marginale, recondita a angusta, ma in luogo ben cationis ratio suadeat, non ita distinguemus, ut commoda ab ipsis necessariis segregemus.'

CHAPTER 6

1 For my theory of structuralism in architecture see part B of *Lessons for Students in Architecture*.
2 *Lessons*, pp. 94-95.
3 *Ibid.*, pp. 122-125.
4 *Ibid.*, p. 125.
5 In both the Students' House (*Lessons*, p. 55) and De Drie Hoven home for the elderly (*ibid.*, pp. 130-132) the floor plans could be drastically altered and adapted to meet today's housing norms. This was thanks to the concrete skeleton. Many buildings of that time (boasting the solid concrete partition walls then deemed so efficient) were unable to withstand such changes and so were demolished.
6 'Das Unerwartete überdacht/Accommodating the unexpected', in *Herman Hertzberger. Projekte/Projects, 1990-1995*, 010 Publishers, Rotterdam 1995, p. 6.
7 *Lessons*, p. 170.
8 'Das Unerwartete überdacht/Accommodating the unexpected', in *Herman Hertzberger. Projekte/Projects, 1990-1995*, p. 8.
9 *Lessons*, pp. 244-245.
10 Klaus Herdeg, *Formal Structure in Indian Architecture*, Ithaca 1967.
11 Claudia Dias, graduation project from the Berlage Institute
12 *Lessons*, pp. 97-98.
13 Herman Hertzberger in Francis

Strauven, *Aldo van Eyck's Orphanage. A Modern Monument*, NAI Publishers, Rotterdam 1996.
14 See the text (1975) accompanying the design 'Martinuskerk Groningen... Universiteitsbibliotheek?'
'By being included in the urban centre the University is required to open itself up more, and in that sense accessibility is the urbanistic equivalent of a less exclusive, more democratic attitude. The library, by coming across less as the University's memory and more as its consciousness, could act as a 'gateway' to the city and to society. Libraries should not merely make food available to those hungry for knowledge but also whet the appetite even of those who are showing no interest. A library is not only for the motivated but should itself motivate! In that respect it should be more like a modern bookshop where you can enter without premeditation and discover all sorts of things by browsing. Formerly libraries were not averse to space as they are today, most of which fail to rise above the level of storerooms filled with so many square metres of racks: the projection of a cerebral dimension of efficiency but none too efficient for the larger space of human consciousness. If architectural space is the outward projection of our mental space, then libraries are by rights entitled to another spatial characteristic; one that is less like memory (that which we control but which also controls us) and much more like consciousness and that which we experience.'

CHAPTER 7

1 Leo Vroman, part of a poem from *Details*, Amsterdam 1999.
BETWEEN
We contain the wildest places / of a most foreign land. // In the spaces between / my fingers / lives another hand. // There lives between / two words of every text // there lives between / this moment and the next // rarely heard / and barely seen / a most essential third. // Through it, all is passed, / it modifies and selects / what must last / what dies / wafts a heady smell / of heaven through our heavy hell, / creates the flow of still / un-ended reality at will, / is of dead oaks, green sky, /red flies, purple weeds / and the unintended / survival of our deeds.
2 *Lessons for Students in Architecture*, pp. 176-189.
3 See *Forum* no. 3, 1973.
4 We used this term at the time in *Forum*, 1959-1964.
5 *Forum* 8, 1959, p. 277
6 *Forum* 8, 1960-61, pp. 272-273
7 This computer model was made with much enthusiasm by Christian Janssen of Delft.

8 *Lessons*, p. 254.
9 *Ibid.*, pp. 258-261.
10 Le Corbusier, *La Ville Radieuse*, Paris 1964, p. 55. Original text: 'Parce qu'une échelle humaine juste (celle qui est à la vraie dimension de nos gestes) à conditionné chaque chose. Il n'y a plus de vieux ni de moderne. Il y a ce qui est permanent: la juste mesure.'
11 *Lessons*, p. 262.
12 *Ibid.*, pp. 102-103.
13 *Ibid.*, pp. 108-110.
14 *Ibid.*, pp. 56-57.
15 Gilles Deleuze and Felix Guattari, *Mille Plateaux*, les Editions de Minuit, 1980.
16 Herman Hertzberger, 'The Permeable Surface of the City', in *World Architecture I*, Studio Books, London 1964.
17 Collective name for the many peoples inhabiting the country before the Spanish conquest.
18 Bernhard Rudofsky, *Architecture without Architects*, The Museum of Modern Arts, New York 1965.
19 Leonardo Benevolo, *Storia della Città*, Laterza, Rome 1975.
20 *Lessons*, pp. 213-215, pp.142-144.
21 *Ibid.*, pp. 238-241.
22 *Ibid.*, pp. 106-107.

1932 Born in Amsterdam
1958 Graduates from the TU Delft (then Delft Polytechnic)
Since 1958 Own practice
1959-63 Editor of *Forum* with Aldo van Eyck, Bakema and others
1965-69 Teaches at the Academy of Architecture, Amsterdam
1970-99 Professor at the TU Delft
Since 1975 Honorary member of the Académie Royale de Belgique
1966-93 Visiting professor at several American and Canadian universities
1982-86 Visiting professor at the Université de Genève (Switzerland)
Since 1983 Honorary member of the Bund Deutscher Architekten
1986-93 'Extraordinary professor' at the Université de Genève
1990-95 Chairman of the Berlage Institute, Amsterdam
1991 Ridder in de Orde van Oranje Nassau (Royal Dutch Knighthood)
Since 1991 Honorary member of the Royal Institute of British Architects
Since 1993 Honorary member of the Akademie der Künste, Berlin
Since 1995 Honorary member of the Accademia delle Arti del Disegno (Florence)
Since 1996 Honorary member of the Royal Incorporation of Architects in Scotland
Since 1997 Honorary member of the Académie d'Architecture de France
1999 Ridder in de Orde van de Nederlandse Leeuw (Royal Dutch Knighthood)
Since 1999 Teaches at the Berlage Institute, Amsterdam
Since 2000 Honorary citizen (notable de classe exceptionelle) of Ngouenjitapon (Cameroon)

AWARDS

1968 City of Amsterdam Award for Architecture for the Students' House, Amsterdam
1974 Eternitprijs for Centraal Beheer office building, Apeldoorn
1974 Fritz-Schumacherprijs for the entire œuvre
1980 A.J. van Eckprijs for Vredenburg Music Centre, Utrecht
1980 Eternitprijs (special mention) for Vredenburg Music Centre, Utrecht
1985 Merkelbachprijs, City of Amsterdam Award for Architecture, for the Apollo Schools, Amsterdam
1988 Merkelbachprijs, City of Amsterdam Award for Architecture, for De Evenaar primary school, Amsterdam
1989 Richard Neutra Award for Professional Excellence
1989 Berliner Architekturpreis, City of West Berlin Award for the Lindenstrasse/

Markgrafenstrasse housing project, Berlin
1991 Premio Europa Architettura, Fondazione Tetraktis award for the entire œuvre
1991 Berlage Flag (Dutch architecture award) for the Ministry of Social Welfare and Employment, The Hague
1991 BNA Cube (Royal Institute of Dutch Architects' award) for the entire œuvre
1991 Betonprijs (award for concrete) for the Ministry of Social Welfare and Employment, The Hague
1993 Prix Rhénan 1993, European architecture award for school-building, for Schoolvereniging Aerdenhout Bentveld, Aerdenhout
1998 City of Breda Award for Architecture for the Library and De Nieuwe Veste Centre for Art and Music (Music and Dance department), Breda
1998 Premios Vitruvio 98 Trayectoria Internacional for the entire œuvre

BUILDINGS AND PROJECTS

Realized works
1962-64 Extension to Linmij, Amsterdam (demolished 1995)
1959-66 Students' House, Weesperstraat, Amsterdam
1960-66 Montessori primary school, Delft
1967 House conversion, Laren
1967-70 8 experimental houses (Diagoon type), Delft
1968-70 Extension to Montessori School, Delft
1968-72 Centraal Beheer office building (with Lucas & Niemeijer), Apeldoorn
1964-74 De Drie Hoven nursing home, Amsterdam
1972-74 De Schalm community centre, Deventer-Borgele
1973-78 Vredenburg Music Centre, Utrecht
1978-80 Residential neighbourhood (40 houses) in Westbroek
1977-81 Second extension to Montessori School, Delft
1980-82 Pavilions, bus stops and market facilities for square (Vredenburgplein), Utrecht
1978-82 Haarlemmer Houttuinen urban regeneration programme, Amsterdam
1979-82 Kassel-Dönche housing project, Kassel (D)
1980-83 Apollo primary schools, Amsterdam: Amsterdam Montessori School and Willems Park School
1980-84 De Overloop nursing home, Almere-Haven
1982-86 LiMa housing, Berlin (D)
1984-86 De Evenaar primary school, Amsterdam
1986-89 Het Gein housing project (406 one-family houses and 52 apartments), Amersfoort
1988-89 8-classroom extension to pri-

mary school (Schoolvereniging Aerdenhout Bentveld), Aerdenhout
1989-90 Studio 2000, 16 live-work units in Muziekwijk neighbourhood, Almere
1979-90 Ministry of Social Welfare and Employment, The Hague
1990-92 De Polygoon, 16-classroom primary school, Almere
1990-92 11 semi-detached houses, Almere
1990-93 Benelux Patent Office, The Hague
1991-93 Extension to Willems Park School, Amsterdam
1986-93 Theatre centre on Spui, The Hague, complex consisting of apartments and retail premises; theatre and film facilities (Theater aan het Spui, Cinematheek Haags Filmhuis, Stichting Kijkhuis); World Wide Video Centre; and Stroom, The Hague Centre for the Arts
1991-93 Library and De Nieuwe Vest Centre for Art and Music (Music and Dance department), Breda
1993-94 Anne Frank primary school, Papendrecht
1990-95 Extension to Centraal Beheer, Apeldoorn
1993-95 De Bombardon, 20-classroom remedial school, Almere
1992-95 Chassé Theatre, Breda
1993-96 Housing on Vrijheer van Eslaan, Papendrecht
1994-96 Extension to Library, Breda
1993-96 Markant Theatre, Uden
1993-96 Rotterdamer Strasse housing project, 136 units, Düren (D)
1994-96 First phase of Bijlmer Monument (with Georges Descombes), Amsterdam
1988-96 Amsterdamse Buurt housing project, 43 units, Haarlem
1995-97 De Koperwiek primary school, Venlo
1993-97 Extension to Vanderveen department store, Assen
1993-97 Stralauer Halbinsel housing project – Block 7+8, Berlin (D)
1991-97 YKK Dormitory/guesthouse, Kurobe City (Toyama District) (J)
1996-98 Second (final) phase of Bijlmer Monument (with Georges Descombes), Amsterdam
1989-99 'Kijck over den Dijck' housing project, Merwestein Noord, Dordrecht
1995-99 Housing project, Prooyenspark, Middelburg
1996-99 Schirmeister House on Borneo-eiland, Amsterdam
1993-99 Montessori College Oost, secondary school for approx. 1650 pupils, Amsterdam

Projects in preparation/under construction
Housing project (new-build, renovation), Noordendijk, Dordrecht
Study of extension (incl. third auditorium) to Vredenburg Music Centre, Utrecht
Media Park office complex with studios and housing, Cologne (D)

Urban design/masterplan for Stralauer Halbinsel, Berlin (D)
Urban design for Clemensänger area in Freising, near Munich (D)
Housing project for Stralauer Halbinsel (Block 12), Berlin (D)
Supervisor of urban design for Veerse Poort development plan, Middelburg
De Eilanden Montessori primary school, Amsterdam
Urban design for community centre, Dallgow (D)
Paradijssel housing project, Capelle aan den IJssel
Urban design for Tel Aviv Peninsula (IL)
Extension to De Overloop nursing home, Almere-Haven
Theatre, Helsingør (DK)
Residential building, courtyard H at Veerse Poort residential area, Middelburg
Urban growth units for Veerse Poort development plan, Middelburg
Housing, offices, swimming pool and parking facility for Paleis quarter, 's-Hertogenbosch
Spuikom (33 houses), Vlissingen
Urban design for former Bombardon area, Almere-Haven
Conversion and extension of RDW office building, Veendam
Primary school and 32 houses, Oegstgeest
Water-houses for Veerse Poort development plan, Middelburg
Office building, Céramique site, Maastricht
188 houses, Ypenburg
14 experimental houses, Ypenburg
Museum, library and municipal archives, Apeldoorn
Extension/renovation of Orpheus Theatre, Apeldoorn
Atlas College, secondary school, Hoorn
DWR office building, Amsterdam
Study for complex of buildings (sports/leisure, church, nursing home etc), Leidscheveen

Studies/unrealized projects
1968 Monogoon housing
1971-72 Objectives report on Groningen city centre (with De Boer, Lambooij, Goudappel et al.)
1969-73 Urban plan for city extension and structure plan, Deventer
1974 City centre plan, Eindhoven (with Van den Broek & Bakema)
1975 Housing, shops and parking near Musis Sacrum (Theatre) and renovation of Musis Sacrum, Arnhem
1975 Planning consultant for University of Groningen
1975 Proposal for university library incorporating 19th-century church, Groningen
1976 Institute for Ecological Research, Heteren
1977 Urban plan for Schouwburgplein (theatre square), Rotterdam
1978 Library, Loenen aan de Vecht

1979 Extension to Linmij, Amsterdam-Sloterdijk

1980 Proposal to develop Forum district, The Hague

1980 Housing project, West Berlin/Spandau (D)

1984 Extension to St Joost Academy of the Arts, Breda

1986-91 Esplanade Film Centre (academy, museum, library etc), Berlin (D)

1986 Experimental housing project for Zuidpolder (floating 'water-houses'), Haarlem

1988 Koningscarré residential project, Haarlem

1989 Urban study (residental area) for Jeker quarter, Maastricht

1989-91 Urban study for Maagjesbolwerk (part of the old centre), Zwolle

1992 Amsterdam Music Centre for chamber music, Amsterdam

1993 Study for a design for an academy (art, music, architecture etc), Rotterdam

1997 Urban study for a shopping centre, Monheim (D)

1999 Two office buildings, Roosendael

Competition projects/invited competitions (= first prize)*

1964 Church, Driebergen

1966 Municipal Hall, Valkenswaard

1967 City Hall, Amsterdam

1970 Urban design for Nieuwmarkt, Amsterdam

1980 Urban design for Römerberg, Frankfurt am Main (D)

1982 Crèche, West Berlin (D)

1983 Urban design for Cologne/Mülheim-Nord (D)

1983 Office building for Friedrich Ebert Stiftung, Bonn (D)

1983 Office buidling for Grüner & Jahr, Hamburg (D)

1985 Office building for Public Works, Frankfurt am Main (D)

1985* Film centre (academy, museum, library etc), West Berlin (D)

1985 Extension to town hall, Saint-Denis (F)

1986 Urban design for Bicocca-Pirelli, Milan (I)

1986 Gemäldegalerie (museum for paintings), West Berlin (D)

1988 Housing project for Staarstraat, Maastricht

1988 Office building for Schering, West Berlin (D)

1989 Bibliothèque de France (national library building), Paris (F)

1989 Cultural centre and concert hall 'Kulturzentrum am See', Lucerne (CH)

1989 Street furniture for riverside walk, Rotterdam

1990 Branch of Nederlandsche Bank, Wassenaar

1990 Urban design for a suburb of Grenoble (F)

1991* Benelux Patent Office, The Hague

1990-91* Components of Media Park competition, Cologne (D)

1991 Office building in Richeti-Areal, Zurich-Wallissen (CH)

1991* City Theatre, Delft

1991 School for Collège Anatole France, Drancy (F)

1992 Office complex for Sony, Potsdamer Platz, Berlin (D)

1992-93* Berlin Olympia 2000/urban design study for part of Rummelsburger Bucht, Berlin (D)

1993 Housing project for Witteneiland, Amsterdam

1993* Housing project, Düren (D)

1993* Urban design (offices for Clemensänger area), Freising (D)

1993-94 Auditorium, Rome (I)

1994 Government office building for Céramique site, Maastricht

1995 Extension to Fire Department School, Schaarsbergen

1995 Extension to Van Gogh Museum, Amsterdam

1995 Office building for Landtag Brandenburg, Potsdam (D)

1995 Musicon concert hall, Bremen (D)

1995-96 Luxor Theatre, Rotterdam

1995-96 Urban design for the Tiburtina railway zone and Ruscolana area and for the Tiburtina-Colombo axis, Rome (I)

1996 Crèche, Berlin (D)

1996 Lothar Gunther Buchheim Museum, Feldafing (D)

1996* Urban design for community centre), Dallgow (D)

1996 Academy of Arts and Design, Kolding (DK)

1996* Urban design, Tel Aviv – Peninsula (IL)

1996 New-build for Ichthus Hogeschool, Rotterdam

1996 Urban design for Axel Springer Multi Media, Berlin (D)

1996 Urban design for Theresienhöhe, Munich (D)

1997* Theatre, Elsinore (DK)

1997 Urban design for university complex, Malmö (S)

1997 Urban design, Berlin Pankow (D)

1998* Urban design of Paleis quarter (housing, offices, parking), 's-Hertogenbosch

1998* Alterations and extensions to governmental RDW office building, Veendam

1998* Primary school and 32 houses, Kasteel Unicum, Oegstgeest

1998-99 Urban design for 'Alte Hafenreviere', Bremen (D)

1999* Museum, library and municipal archives, Apeldoorn

1999 Conversion and extension of law courts, Zwolle

1999 Urban design for Site 5 of Theresienhöhe, Munich (D)

2000* DWR office building, Amsterdam

Group and one-man shows

1967 Biennale des Jeunes, Paris (F) [Students' House]

1968 Stedelijk Museum, Amsterdam [following award of City of Amsterdam Award for Architecture]

1971 Historical Museum, Amsterdam [show of plans for Nieuwmarkt quarter, Amsterdam]

1976 Venice Biennale (I)

1976 Stichting Wonen, Amsterdam

1980 Kunsthaus, Hamburg (D)

1985 Berlin (D)/Geneva (CH)/Vienna (A)/Zagreb (YU)/Split (YU)/Brauschweig (D)/Cologne (D) and further ['Six architectures photographiées par Johan van der Keuken', travelling exhibition featuring built work (Student House, De Drie Hoven, Centraal Beheer, Vredenburg Music Centre, Apollo Schools), three recent competition projects added in 1986 from Zagreb onwards (Filmhaus Esplanade, Bicocca-Pirelli, Gemäldegalerie)]

1985 Stichting Wonen, Amsterdam [exh. 'Architectuur 84'; De Overloop]

1985 Frans Hals Museum, Haarlem [exh. 'Le Corbusier in Nederland'; Student House]

1986 Fondation Cartier, Jouy-et-Josas (F) [Student House]

1986 Centre Pompidou, Paris (F) [exh. 'Lieux de Travail; Centraal Beheer]

1986 Milan Triennale (I) [exh. 'Il Luogo del Lavoro'; Centraal Beheer, Biccoca-Pirelli]

1986 Stichting Wonen, Amsterdam/Montreal (CDN)/Toronto (CDN)/Los Angeles (USA)/Raleigh (USA)/Blacksburg (USA)/Philadelphia (USA)/Tokyo (J)/London (GB)/Edinburgh (GB)/Florence (I)/Rome (I) and further [exh. 'Herman Hertzberger'; various competition and other projects since 1979]

1987 MIT, Cambridge (USA)/various other universities in the USA [Filmhaus Esplanade, Bicocca-Pirelli, Gemäldegalerie]

1987 Stichting Wonen, Amsterdam [exh. 'Architectuur 86'; De Evenaar]

1988 New York State Council of the Arts, New York (USA) [Haarlemmer Houttuinen, Kassel-Dönche, Lindenstrasse]

1989 Global Architecture International, Tokyo (J) [Filmhaus Esplanade]

1989 Institut Français d'Architecture, Paris (F) [exh. 20 entrants to the competition for the Bibliothèque de France]

1991 Global Architecture International, Tokyo (J) [Ministry of Social Welfare]

1991 Tetraktis, travelling exhibition of projects and travel sketches by Herman Hertzberger, L'Aquila (I)

1992 World Architecture Triennale, Nara (J) [Ministry of Social Welfare, Media Park Cologne]

1993 De Beyerd, Breda [exh. 'Herman Hertzberger', several projects]

1995 Architekturgalerie, Munich

(D)/Centraal Beheer, Apeldoorn/De Pronkkamer, Uden; travelling exhibition ['das Unerwartete überdacht'/'Accommodating the Unexpected', projects 1990-1995]

1995 De Beyerd, Breda [Chassé Theatre]

1996 Deutsches Architektur Museum, Frankfurt am Main (D) [projects for Stralauer Halbinsel, Berlin]

1998 Deutsches Architektur Zentrum, Berlin (D)/Museo Nacional de Bellas Artes, Buenos Aires (RA)/Bouwbeurs, Utrecht/Netherlands Architecture Institute, Rotterdam/Technische Universität, Munich (D); travelling exhibition 'Herman Hertzberger Articulations', compiled by the Netherlands Architecture Institute, Rotterdam

Publications

'Concours d'Emulation 1955 van de studenten', *Bouwkundig Weekblad* 1955, p. 403

'Inleiding', *Forum* 1960, no. 1

'Weten en geweten', *Forum* 1960/61, no. 2, pp. 46-49

'Verschraalde helderheid', *Forum* 1960/61, no. 4, pp. 143, 144

'Three better possibilities', *Forum* 1960/61, no. 5, p. 193

'Naar een verticale woonbuurt', *Forum* 1960/61, no. 8, pp. 264-273

'Zorg voor zorg over architectuur', *Stedebouw en volkshuisvesting* 1961, pp. 216-218

'Flexibility and Polyvalency', *Ekistics* 1963, April, pp. 238, 239

'The Permeable Surface of the City', *World Architecture* 1964, no. 1

'Gedachten bij de dood van Le Corbusier', *Bouwkundig Weekblad* 1965, no. 20, p. 336

'Aldo van Eyck 1966', *Goed Wonen* 1966, no. 8, pp. 10-13

'Form and program are reciprocally evocative' (written 1963) and 'Identity' (written 1966), *Forum* 1967, no. 7

'Some notes on two works by Schindler', *Domus* 1967, no. 545, pp. 2-7

'Place, Choice and Identity', *World Architecture* 1967, pp. 73, 74

'Form und Programm rufen sich gegenseitig auf', *Werk* 1968, no. 3, pp. 200, 201

'Montessori Primary School in Delft', *Harvard Educational Review* 1969, no. 4. pp. 58-67

'Schoonheidscommissies', *Forum* 1970, July, pp. 13-15

'Looking for the beach under the pavement', *RIBA Journal* 1971, no. 2, pp. 328-333

'Homework for more hospitable form', *Forum* 1973, no. 3

'De te hoog gegrepen doelstelling', *Wonen/TABK* 1974, no. 14, pp. 7-9

'Presentation', *Building Ideas* 1976, no. 2, pp. 2-14 (first published in *Forum* 1973, no. 3)

'Strukturalismus-Ideologie', *Bauen + Wohnen* 1976, no. 1, pp. 21-24

'Architecture for People', *A+U* 1977, no. 75, pp. 124-146

'El deber para hoy: hacer formas más hos-pitalarias', *Summarios* (Argentina) 1978, no. 18, pp. 3-32 (about De Drie Hoven and Centraal Beheer)
'Shaping the Environment', in B. Mikkelides (ed.), *Architecture for People*, Studio Vista, London 1980, pp. 38-40
'Architektur für Menschen', in G.R. Blomeyer and B. Tietze, *In Opposition zur Moderne*, Vieweg & Sohn, 1980, pp. 142-148
'Motivering van de minderheidsstandpunt', *Wonen/TABK* 1980, no. 4, pp. 2, 3
'Un insegnamento de San Pietro', *Spazio e Società* 1980, no. 11, pp. 76-83
'Ruimte maken – Ruimte laten', in *Wonen tussen utopie en werkelijkheid*, Callebach, Nijkerk 1980, pp. 28-37
'De traditie van het Nieuwe Bouwen en de nieuwe mooiigheid', *Intermediaire* 8- 8-1980
'The tradition behind the "Heroic Period" of modern architecture in the Netherlands', *Spazio e Società* 1981, no. 13, pp. 78-85 (first published in *Intermediaire* 8-8-1980)
'De traditie van het nieuwe bouwen en de nieuwe mooiigheid', in Hilde de Haan and Ids Haagsma, *Wie is bang voor nieuwbouw?*, Intermediaire Bibliotheek, Amsterdam 1981, pp. 141-154
'The 20ste-eeuwse mechanisme en de architectuur van Aldo van Eyck', *Wonen/TABK* 1982, no. 2, pp. 10-19
'De schetsboeken van Le Corbusier', *Wonen/TABK* 1982, no. 21, pp. 24-27
'Einladende Architektur', *Stadt* 1982, no. 6, pp. 40-43
Het openbare rijk, lecture notes A, Delft Polytechnic (now TU Delft), 1982 (reprinted March 1984)
'Montessori en ruimte', *Montessori Mededelingen* 1983, no. 2, pp. 16-21
'Une rue habitation à Amsterdam', *L'Architecture d'Aujourd'hui* 1983, no. 225, pp. 56-63
'Une strada da vivere. Houses and streets make each other', *Spazio e Società* 1983, no. 23, pp. 20-33
'Aldo van Eyck', *Spazio e Società* 1983, no. 24, pp. 80-97
Ruimte maken, ruimte laten, lecture notes B, Delft Polytechnic (now TU Delft), 1984
'Over bouwkunde, als uitdrukkingen van denkbeelden', *De Gids* 1984, no. 7/8/9, pp. 810-814
'Building Order', *Via 7*, MIT Press, Boston, 1984
'L'Espace de la Maison de Verre', *L'Architec-ture d'Aujourd'hui* 1984, no. 236, pp. 86-90
'Architectuur en constructieve vrijheid' (discussion between the three winners of the Van Eckprijs: Herman Hertzberger, Jan Benthem and Mels Crouwel), *Architec-tuur/Bouwen* 1985, no. 9, pp. 33-37
'Montessori en ruimte' in *De Architectuur van de Montessorischool*, Montessori Uitgeverij, Amsterdam 1985, pp. 47-55
'Stadtsverwandlungen', in Helga Fass-binder and Eduard Führ, *Materialien 1985*, no. 2, pp. 40-51
'Right Size or Right Size', in *Indesem*, TU Delft 1985, pp. 46-57
'Espace Montessori', *Techniques & Architecture* 1985/86, no. 363, pp. 78-82, 93
Stairs (first-year seminar notes), TU Delft, 1987
Arnulf Lüchinger, *Herman Hertzberger, 1959-86, Bauten und Projekte/Buildings and Projects/Bâtiments et Projets*, Arch-Edition, The Hague 1987
'Shell and crystal', in Francis Strauven, *Aldo van Eyck's Orphanage. A Modern Monument*, NAI Publishers, Rotterdam 1996, p. 3 (originally published as *Het Burgerweeshuis van Aldo van Eyck. Een modern monument*, Stichting Wonen, Amsterdam 1987)
'Henri Labrouste, la réalisation de l'art', *Techniques & Architecture* 1987/88, no. 375, p. 33
Uitnodigende Vorm, lecture notes C, TU Delft, 1988
'The space mechanism of the twentieth century or formal order and daily life: front sides and back sides', in *Modernity and Popular Culture*, Building Books, Helsinki 1988, pp. 37-46
'Das Schröderhaus in Utrecht', *Archithese* 1988, no. 5, pp. 76-78
'Het St. Pietersplein in Rome. Het plein als bouwwerk', *Bouw* 1989, no. 12, pp. 20, 21
Hoe modern is de Nederlandse architectuur?, 010 Publishers, Rotterdam 1990, pp. 61-64
'Voorwoord', in Jan Molema, *ir. J. Duiker*, 010 Publishers, Rotterdam 1990, pp. 6, 7
'The Public Realm', *A+U* 1991, pp. 12-44
'Mag het 'n beetje scherper alstublieft?', in *Joop Hardy: Anarchist*, Delft 1991, pp. 143, 144
'Introductory Statement' and 'Do architects have any idea of what they draw?', in *The Berlage Cahiers 1, Studio '90-'92*, Berlage Institute, Amsterdam/010 Publishers, Rotterdam 1992, pp. 13-20
Herman Hertzberger, *Lessons for Students in Architecture*, 010 Publishers, Rotterdam 1991 (first edition), 1993 (second revised edition), 1998 (third revised edition). Elaborated versions of the lecture notes previously published as 'Het openbare rijk', 'Ruimte maken, ruimte laten' and 'Uitnodigende vorm'. German and Japanese editions followed in 1995, Italian, Portuguese and Dutch in 1996, and Chinese in 1997.
'Een bioscoop met visie', *Skrien* 1994, no. 197. pp. 58-61
'Klaslokalen aan een centrale leerstraat', in *Ruimte op school*, Almere 1994, pp. 16, 17
Herman Hertzberger Projekte/Projects/1990-1995, 010 Publishers, Rotterdam 1995
Herman Hertzberger, *Vom Bauen, Vorle-sungen über Architektur*, Aries Verlag, Munich 1995 (translation of *Lessons for Students in Architecture*)
'Designing as research', in *The Berlage Cahiers 3, Studio '93-'94, The New Private Realm*, Berlage Institute, Amsterdam/010 Publishers, Rotterdam 1995, pp. 8-10
Herman Hertzberger, *Chassé Theatre Breda*, 010 Publishers, Rotterdam 1995
'Learning without teaching', in *The Berlage Cahiers 4, Studio '94-'95, Reflexivity*, Berlage Institute, Amsterdam/010 Publishers, Rotterdam 1996, pp. 6-8
Herman Hertzberger, *Ruimte maken, ruimte laten. Lessen in architectuur*, 010 Publishers, Rotterdam 1996 (Dutch edition of *Lessons for Students in Architecture*)
'P.S.: Vulnerable nudity!' in Wiel Arets, *Strange Bodies, Fremdkörper*, Birkhäuser, Basle 1996, pp. 65-67
'A Culture of Space', *Dialogue, architecture + design + culture* (Taiwan) 1997, no. 2, pp. 14, 15
Herman van Bergeijk, *Herman Hertzberger*, Birkhäuser, Basle 1997
'Le Corbusier et la Hollande', in *Le Corbusier, voyages, rayonnement international*, Fondation Le Corbusier, Paris 1997
'Anne Frank Basisschool, Papendrecht – LOM-Basisschool "De Bombardon", Almere', *Zodiac* 1997/98, no. 18, pp. 152-161
'Lecture by Herman Hertzberger', in *Tech-nology, Place & Architecture*, Rizzoli, New York 1998, pp. 250-253

CREDITS

© 2000 Herman Hertzberger / 010 Publishers, Rotterdam (www.010publishers.nl)
Originally published in Dutch in 1999 as 'De ruimte van de architect. Lessen in architectuur 2'

Compilation by
Jop Voorn
Translated from the Dutch by
John Kirkpatrick
Book design by
Piet Gerards, Heerlen
Printed by
Veenman Drukkers, Ede

ISBN 90 6450 380 X